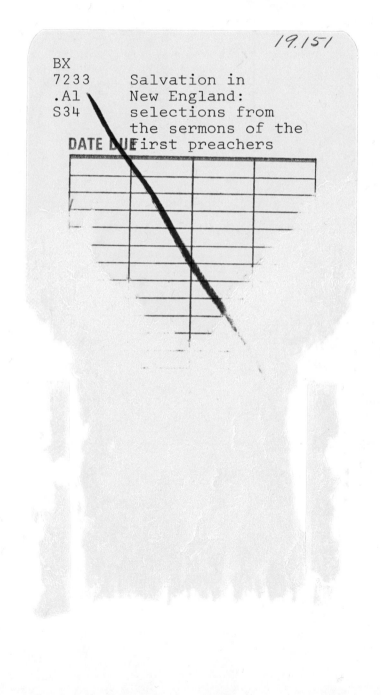

Salvation in New England

Salvation in New England

Selections from the Sermons

of the First Preachers

Edited by Phyllis M. Jones and

Nicholas R. Jones

University of Texas Press, Austin & London

Library of Congress Cataloging in Publication Data

Main entry under title:
Salvation in New England.
    Bibliography: p.
    1. Congregational churches—Sermons. 2. Sermons, American.
3. Preaching—History—New England. I. Jones, Phyllis M., 1945–.
II. Jones, Nicholas R., 1946–.
BX7233.AIS34   252'.05'874   76-46554
ISBN 0-292-77532-6

FRONTISPIECE

*John Davenport in the year of his death, 1670. This oil painting shows the
preacher in his seventy-fourth year, ten years after the preaching of* The
Saint's Anchor-Hold. *Two other portraits, of preachers identified as John
Wheelwright and John Cotton, are tentatively attributed to the same
painter, thought to be John Foster of Dorchester (1648–1681). See Louisa
Dresser and Alan Burroughs,* XVII th *Century Painting in New England
(Worcester, Mass.: Trustees of the Worcester Art Museum, 1935), and
Oskar Hagen,* The Birth of the American Tradition in Art *(New York:
Charles Scribner's Sons, 1940). By permission of the Yale University Art
Gallery.*

for our parents

Mary Belle Johnson and Fred J. Johnson

Marian Ginn Jones and William Powell Jones

Contents

Illustrations

Preface

This volume emerged from our sense of the significance of the sermon in American literature. It is a genre that makes itself felt in such diverse forms as the sermon-in-the-novel, as in *Moby-Dick* and *The Sound and the Fury*, and the prophetic style of nineteenth-century romances like *The Scarlet Letter*. *Salvation in New England* took shape specifically from what we believed to be the origin of this tradition: the importance of sermons in the lives of the first colonists of New England. Since most of the immigrants regularly attended the preaching of the word in the meeting house and since voluminous numbers of published sermons were available for study at home, this main type of spiritual communication became a prominent literary form in early New England. As we studied the sermons of the first preachers —delivered between 1620 and 1670—we saw the form of the doctrinal matter to be a narrative, mythic in its repetition and heroics, about the salvation of the soul. Working with this central emphasis on the soul's salvation, we saw there was a need for its representation and explication as a major imaginative and doctrinal legacy of the first New England preachers.

In fact, there has been a need for editions representing the preaching of the first New England ministers, for these sermons have as a rule been available only in rare-book libraries. A few reprints can be found in scattered periodicals or in facsimile monographs, and excerpts from some of the important titles have appeared in anthologies of colonial literature. A nineteenth-century edition—an inaccurate reprinting of randomly selected early editions, *The Works of Thomas Shepard*, ed. John A. Albro—has recently been reissued by AMS Press and G. Olms. Only lately has there appeared a substantial modern edition of the sermons—the very early ones—of a major founding preacher of New England: *Thomas Hooker: Writings in England and Holland, 1626–1633*, ed. George H. Williams, Norman Pettit, Winfried Herget, and Sargent Bush, Jr. The predecessors, English contemporaries, and American successors of those preachers who founded New England have fared better in their availability in modern editions. For example, in 1970 *The Work of William Perkins*, ed. Ian Breward, was published. A significant number of the predecessors and contemporaries of these preachers can be studied in their own words in *English Puritanism from John Hooper to John Milton*, ed. Everett

H. Emerson. Similarly, full sermons of the American successors of the first New England ministers are available in *The Wall and the Garden: Selected Massachusetts Election Sermons, 1670–1775*, ed. A. W. Plumstead. But there has remained a need for an edition containing substantial selections representative of the literary and spiritual breadth of the sermons of the first preachers.

Our grouping of John Cotton, Thomas Hooker, Thomas Shepard, Peter Bulkeley, and John Davenport—preachers who began their ministries in England and established the first churches in New England—acknowledges the traditional assessment of their unique history and distinctive sermonic message. The first major biographer and historian of these figures, Cotton Mather, separated the "first generation" from its successors as he commemorated the founders' ecclesiastical leadership and power in the pulpit (*Magnalia Christi Americana*, 1702). Since Mather, historians—notably Perry Miller—have corroborated the historical logic of this grouping. For example, David D. Hall, in *The Faithful Shepherd: A History of the New England Ministry in the Seventeenth Century*, recently demonstrated how the first generation was bound together by such common undertakings as the radical decision to emigrate and the intense struggle to establish the Congregational system.

From Perry Miller's *The New England Mind: From Colony to Province* (Cambridge, Mass.: Harvard University Press, 1953) to Plumstead's *The Wall and the Garden* (1968) and Emory Elliott's *Power and the Pulpit in Puritan New England* (1975), scholars have separated sermons published after the middle of the seventeenth century from those of the founders. Miller labeled the predominant theme and form of preaching in the latter half of the seventeenth century as a "jeremiad," a public sermon lamenting communal sins that evoked God's judgment and punishment. Plumstead has found that in addition to the jeremiad, the "theme of denouncement," there is a lyrical celebration of a new civilization in the Massachusetts election sermons published after 1670. In the most thorough study of the sermons of 1660 to 1700, Elliott argued that the metaphors and myths of doom and decay of the 1665 to 1675 decade shift to a new message of assurance, to a language of exuberance, by the 1680s and 1690s. Our own reading of the pulpit literature of the seventeenth century confirms that the saga of the soul's salvation is the distinctive material of the first-generation preachers of New England. But in citing the distinctions we must recognize historical and thematic continuities as well. The introduction to this volume points out how the first ministers of New England resemble English Puritans in the form and matter of their preaching. Furthermore, the jeremiad finds initial utterance in the preaching of the first generation, a development fully traced by Sacvan Bercovitch in "Horologicals to Chronometricals: The Rhetoric of the Jeremiad," in *Literary Monographs*, ed. Eric Rothstein.

Of the eighty or so clerics emigrating to America in the 1630s, only about ten were published preachers. We have selected sermonic materials from five, those whose preaching seemed powerful to their contemporaries and to us and whose ecclesiastical and civil leadership was significant. To represent this group accurately we have emphasized the sermonizing of Cotton, Hooker, and Shepard, the three most important and substantially published of the entire first generation. We have chosen sermons delivered over a thirty-five-year period: about 1625 to 1660. Although a few of the sermons in this volume were preached in England, all were published after the important migrations and circulated broadly to an American readership. Because of the extraordinary output by these five preachers of similarly focused sermons—about eighteen individual sermons and forty sermon-series —we found it possible to meet simultaneously these aims: to illustrate the literary vitality and imaginative authority of the preaching of the period, to present substantial and representative selections from major sermonic works, and to demonstrate the narrative and doctrinal stages of the salvation of the soul. We hope that our historical, doctrinal, and literary interpretations will aid twentieth-century readers, especially those unfamiliar with this period. The vitality and importance of the selections themselves make us confident that this volume will prove useful and enduring for all readers, colonialists and general students alike.

We would like to thank those who assisted us at various stages in preparing the manuscript: Gwynne B. Evans, Alan Heimert, Thomas M. Davis, Dewey Ganzel, Robert Pierce, Lawrence Buell, Clyde A. Holbrook, Barbara Marshall, Harriet Griesinger, David Griesinger, and Margaret Johnson. A few portions of the introduction were published in *Early American Literature* and appear here with the permission of its editor. Our research was greatly expedited by the courtesy and efficiency of the staff of the Houghton Library and the generous support of the National Endowment for the Humanities.

Salvation in New England

Introduction

i. The Role and History of Preaching
in Early New England

It would be difficult to find in American literature any genre that has had ascribed to it more affective power than the sermon as crafted by the first New England preachers. They proclaimed that God's principal means of converting sinners into saints—the most important event in the life of a Puritan—was the sermonic explication and development of a biblical passage. As Thomas Hooker, revered first preacher of Hartford, explained, the "Lord hath ordained and set apart the preaching of the word, he hath sanctified it, and set it apart to call the soul" (see selection IV). Through the means of the preacher and his sermon, the Spirit of God could bring grace to the humbled and contrite listener. Such a prominent role derived ultimately from the authority of the Bible: "God hath ordained, that when he would come to repair decayed nature, by the same means by which he made the world, by the same will he repair it, and therefore in his name must the word be spoken, and by the breath [Holy Spirit] of the Lord, a Congregation is gathered together, and Christians established in grace."[1] The early New Englanders, finding in that word the unfolding drama of God's plan for redemption, held that preaching based on the Bible—especially the Gospel—was an even more efficacious tool of salvation than a sacrament like the Lord's Supper.[2] They believed that the sermon was the ordinary means of conversion, the regular channel of the Spirit.[3]

Finding sermons to be a principal means of redemption, Puritans had few alternatives other than to center their worship on the pulpit, although that choice ultimately forced many English Puritans to cross the Atlantic and settle a wilderness. Even though by 1630 their ministers were unable to preach in the particular ways they wanted, in the Old World the preaching and publishing of sermons was no small enterprise. The most direct origin for the popularity of preaching was the Reformation. The Thirty-nine Articles, defining the doctrine of the Protestant church in England, held to the argument of great reformers like Luther and Calvin "that preaching was one of the marks of the true church."[4] Preaching also met commercial, political, and social needs as well as religious ones. In the age we remember as Shakespeare and Marlowe's, the *Short Title Catalogue* shows that the publication of sermons was a big business.[5] Christopher Hill states: "Until 1640 the publication of home news was prohibited . . . in the absence of other media of communication, sermons were for the majority of Englishmen their main source of political information and political ideas."[6] By the middle of the seventeenth century in England, during the Puritan Revolution and some fifteen years after the settlement of Massachusetts, preaching is said to have played a more significant part "in political and social life" than at any other time "in the world's history."[7]

As English Protestants of Puritan persuasion grew increasingly discontent with the national church, they improvised within the established order to specialize the profession of preaching. Drawing especially on Calvin's vision of church order, the Puritans urged that there should be different types of preachers: a "pastor" to comfort and exhort a congregation and a "teacher" to emphasize doctrinal issues. Such reformed notions of church governance would lead to the proliferation of sermons in early New England.[8] Furthermore, the Puritans, from the time of the return of the Marian exiles, encouraged "lecturers" to free-lance outside authorized parish pulpits; thus, a town or wealthy individual paid a lecturer to provide the emphasis on preaching that the service of the Church of England denied.[9]

Given this tradition, it is not surprising that during one of the major crossings to America there were three sermons delivered daily: John Cotton, later teacher of the Boston congregation, preached in the morning; Thomas Hooker in the afternoon; and Samuel Stone, later colleague of Hooker's in Connecticut, in the evening.[10] Once settled in Massachusetts, Cotton added a weekday lecture to his Sunday sermon, a practice he had established in England.[11] Attending weekday lectures came to be so popular throughout the colony that civil authorities in 1634 restricted mid-week preaching to two days, so that the business of the week would not be disrupted.[12] Yet the governing officers, firmly committed to encouraging preaching, were unwilling to risk the central role of sermons in the lives of the colonists to popular demand alone. The governors also took measures to insure that the sermons would be heard. For example, in 1635 the General Court of Massachusetts ruled that no dwelling could be erected more than half a mile from the meeting house and that magistrates could censure nonattendance at church.[13] Similarly, although only professed believers could be church members, the governors of the colonies of Massachusetts, New Haven, and Connecticut, to guarantee the conversion of the wayward and thereby fulfill the evangelical responsibility of the church, passed laws in the 1640s requiring every resident of a town to attend the preaching of the word.[14]

And that preaching flourished. If we imagine the Victorians eagerly snatching up the newest installment of a novel by Dickens, we might well envision the early New Englanders avidly listening to sermons, discussing them at home, and buying them in published form. Puritan emphasis on the word meant that frequently a scriptural passage, or several related texts, provided the common focus for an extensive sequence of thematically related sermons—known as a sermon-series. Typically, a minister preached twice on Sunday and once during the week on the lecture day. Special events like artillery elections, civil elections, and days proclaimed for public thanksgiving and humiliation created an occasional demand for additional sermons. An impressive number of these sermons found their way into print, accounting for the extensive body of sermon literature from the American colonial period.[15] From just the five preachers represented in this volume came about forty sermon-series and eighteen published sermons, a small fraction of their total preached sermons.

The preachers in this anthology were among eighty or more who emigrated to Massachusetts Bay during the 1630s.[16] They are John Cotton of Boston, Thomas Shepard of Cambridge, and Thomas Hooker of Hartford, the three foremost "lights of the western churches," and two eminent colleagues, Peter Bulkeley of Concord and John Davenport, first of New Haven and later of Boston.[17] Their colleagues who were also published include Charles Chauncy, second president of Harvard College, Richard Mather of Dorchester, John Norton of Ipswich and Boston, and John Wilson of Boston. When these preachers arrived in New England, they had considerable expertise in the pulpit. Rhetorical excellence had been a primary concern for them during their years of study at the British universities, as it was for any student. But far beyond an emphasis on oratory, the special benefit of study at Emmanuel College of Cambridge, which Cotton, Hooker, and Shepard attended, was a grounding in Puritan homiletics and theology.[18] The training of the first New England ministers for the pulpit derived not only from the university but also from the brotherhood, the informal community of like-minded Puritan ministers who strove to educate and place preachers throughout the country.[19] As a result, the first New England preachers brought to America an extensive understanding of the form and content of preaching. They were prepared for the pulpit by the writing, teaching, and preaching of many, notably the Continental reformers John Calvin and Martin Bucer; the English explicator of Calvin and psychologist of the process of salvation, William Perkins; the British articulator of Puritan belief and practice, William Ames; and such respected preachers of the brotherhood as Richard Sibbes, Laurence Chaderton, Arthur Hildersam, John Dod, and John Preston.[20]

The emphasis on preaching that the brotherhood demanded became increasingly difficult to implement in England. Although Cotton practiced his ministry with relative freedom in Boston, Lincolnshire

(1612–1632), Hooker and Shepard found that leaving the university in the 1620s for parishes of the Church of England meant conformity to disagreeable customs—kneeling, bowing, wearing the surplice—that subjected the pulpit to ceremony. Like many other Puritan ministers, they took positions as lecturers or chaplains in wealthy households. But even these pulpits began to vanish in 1629, when the high churchman William Laud sought measures from the king to prevent such preaching.[21] Hence the ministers fled to Holland or America, or both, to congregate believers in a way suitable for preaching the word of God.

ii. The Structure of the Sermons

The word of God initiates and controls early New England sermons. Beginning with a specific biblical text, they progress from an explication of that "text" and a derivation of a "doctrine" from it to an enumeration and development of "reasons" for and "uses" of that doctrine. This structure could serve equally well a pastor in his Sunday exhortations or a teacher in a mid-week lecture or a cleric selected to preach at a general election. In Puritan England, this four-part structure had come to be the accepted form of the sermon: not only did the first New England ministers have the opportunity to learn this method of preaching from its practice by the brotherhood, but they could also consult manuals on preaching published especially for English preachers of Puritan leanings. The most important were *The Art of Prophesying* (1592) by William Perkins, the chapter "Of Ordinary Ministers, and the Office in Preaching" in *The Marrow of Sacred Divinity* (1623) by William Ames, and *The Faithful Shepherd* (1607 and 1621) by Richard Bernard. To understand the theory that guided the preachers in structuring a sermon, it is most efficient to consider these handbooks. But first it is necessary to understand that the writers of these manuals constantly acknowledged that the method of preaching had two important determinants: human psychology and biblical precedent.

At every point, theorizing about the organization of sermons is governed by faculty psychology, a version of human behavior subdividing the soul into the faculties of reason, conscience, imagination, memory, will, and affections.[22] Leaving "to the philosophers" all "curious discussion respecting the faculties," Calvin had simplified this system for "the comprehension of all," dividing the soul into "the understanding" and "the will."[23] Similarly, these Puritan preachers, concerned with effecting inward holiness and outward piety, simplified human nature by dividing it into reflective and active halves. In general, pious behavior was said to originate in the active side of persons (the heart or will) only after the reasoning half (the understanding) had been educated. It was common belief that regenerate souls, converted sinners, must guide their actions by their understanding: "See that the heart, which is the seat of practical knowledge be fitted to order the conversation and practice, by sound principles, in the mind, and right conclusions, in the understanding" (see selection IX). It was also common belief that the heart, for all its unsteadiness, was the wellspring of the spiritual life. In *The Way of Life*, Cotton offers this reason for his exhortation to the Christian to "keep his heart": "if the will be good, then is the understanding good; . . . then is the conscience good, the affections and speeches good; the works of our hands, and the words of our mouths, come all from a well-kept heart, that is a good will" (see selection VII).[24]

Just as individuals had first to understand the salvation offered in Jesus Christ before their hearts opened to accept this grace, so likewise the sermon—the means of conversion—had first to instruct the mind before it could stir the will. Dividing the sermon into the text, doctrine, reasons, and uses, the preacher was adapting his message to the hearers' faculties. For example, Hooker explains that the application of the uses has an "uncontrollable power" to move the will only if it follows the dictates of the understanding. The uses, then, must first be "bottomed" *"on the blessed Word of the Lord rightly apprehended, and opened plainly by undeniable Evidence."*[25] And because inciting the heart to action was his ultimate aim, the preacher generally expended the bulk of his energy and words on these uses.[26]

In addition to accommodating his message to human nature, the early New England preacher, in using the text-through-uses method, perceived himself to be following an authoritative precedent. This manner of preaching had been practiced in medieval and Renaissance times and, even more important, was upheld by Puritan authorities on homiletics as the biblical way of sermonizing.[27] The prophets, apostles, and even Jesus Christ are said to have used each of these four main parts in their preaching. For example, Bernard argues that the sermon should begin with the "Canonical Scripture" because the prophets drew upon "the word of the Lord; our Savior uttered only the word of his Father . . . S. *Paul* taught nothing but Scripture."[28]

As the manuals directed, the preacher followed the example of such venerable authorities. He began his sermon by reading "the text distinctly out of the canonical scriptures" and presenting it in "translation to vulgar people."[29] He then proceeded to "open" the text by explaining the author, occasion, and "coherence with that which goes before or follows after."[30] Because it is often difficult to discover the "scope or principal intendment of the holy Ghost," the preacher, according to the three major authorities, needed the tools of logic. He should, according to Bernard, investigate the person, thing, time, place, and means and uncover "the method how the arguments are laid down, which method is often cryptic, and not natural." Such thoroughness in "dividing" the text would make the sermon understandable "to the capacity of the simplest hearer."[31]

Once the text had been explained, the preacher drew from it a doctrine, a "Theological Axiom, either consisting in the express words of Scripture, or flowing from them by immediate consequence."[32] Doctrines, "propositions drawn from the Scripture," may be either clearly expressed in the biblical context or obscured by such rhetorical devices as allegory.[33] When doctrines are not openly stated in the Bible, all the manuals direct the preacher to the logical exercise of gathering, a bringing together of points in inference or conclusion.[34] The minister next turned to the third main part and gave reasons for the doctrine. Such substantiation was to take a similarly analytic form in proving the doctrine against other scriptural texts and illustrating it by such logical means as "dissentaneous, and comparate arguments," that is, by dissimilar and similar examples.[35]

The doctrines were to be gathered and proved "only for informing of the judgment"; "to effect and do is another part of the Sermon." That part, directed to the will, is commonly called the uses. Bernard breaks this fourth part down into three units—"uses" of the doctrine, "application" of the uses to the hearer, and "prevention of objections." He cites four main uses: redargution, the confutation of "an error or heresy"; instruction, "when the doctrine is used to bring us to the exercise of Christian duties to God and man"; correction; and consolation.[36] He sees the use of a doctrine as "plainly distinct" from its application, which he defines as "a nearer bringing of the use delivered, after a more general sort, in the third person, as spoken to persons absent; to the time, place, and persons then present: and uttered in the second person, or in the first, when the Minister, as often the Apostle doth, will include himself with them." Here, in this "home-speaking," in this "nearer bringing" of the use in application, the preacher will "pierce into the minds of such, as are present, with a moving of godly affection."[37] Both Bernard and Ames advise that "use and application in Preaching may be conjoined in one speech" because of their similarity.[38] The preachers often took this advice, with the result that the last major section of a sermon is usually designated by only one of these terms but tends to include both. Since "men are no sooner spoken unto, but if they dislike anything they will speak against it," then the preacher must immediately counter their objections. After this "prevention of objections" and after placing "upon the people the Lord's blessing," the minister should draw the sermon to a close.[39]

A significant advantage of the method was its predictability. Listeners were expected to recapitulate the sermon at home with their families or in private meditation. An auditor, knowing how the text would be opened and applied, was aided in taking notes or recording the sermons by a form of shorthand.[40] The method, however, was not mechanically predictable; it was adaptable to each circumstance of delivery. During one session of preaching, the minister might employ the text-through-uses structure more than once or spread it out over several sessions.[41] For example, Hooker worked with only one doctrine and its reasons and uses in the entire last half of *The Soul's Vocation*; over 100,000 words in length, this one sequence clearly took many separate occasions of delivery. It was possible, too, for a large unit of preaching to deviate from the standard four-part presentation or for the parts to be mingled.[42] Important as these four main sections of the sermon were, they were not to be emphasized to the point that they subverted belletristic unity. Bernard clarifies: "my meaning is not, that in Preaching, a Minister, after he be entered upon his text, should ever say: This is the doctrine, this is the proof, this the use: now to the reasons, now we will make application . . . it interrupts the course of the speech, and it is too disjointed, and less pathetical . . . the Preacher, which will follow this course, may in speaking knit them altogether in a continued speech after the manner of an oration."[43]

iii. The Style of the Sermons

Despite instructions that the method of preaching could and should accommodate to artistic effects, its systematic four-part progression and its didactic intent have led some critics to characterize Puritan preaching as "mechanical" and to maintain that it lacks "literary grace."[44] Contemporary theory and practice in the seventeenth century, however, acknowledged that certain kinds of ornamentation could assist the Spirit in moving the auditor. Concern for that auditor was the single greatest determinant of the plain style, the accepted label for the Puritan practice of sermonic expression. Suggesting distrust of rhetorical embellishment, it likewise encouraged the assumption that the preachers were inartistic; their contemporaries disparaged the plain style just as modern critics have. Robert Cushman, in his preface to the first published American sermon (1622), offered this defense against those who termed Puritan discourse "rude and unlearned": "to paint out the Gospel in plain and flat English, amongst a company of plain Englishmen (as we are), is the best and most profitable teaching."[45] Successful instruction of "plain" listeners— the adjective "plain" describes the auditors more appropriately than the style—was viewed as a preacher's greatest strength and the main requirement of the plain style. Increase Mather, for example, found reasons to praise the preaching of his father, Richard, because of its "plainness":

> His way of Preaching was plain, aiming to shoot his Arrows not over his people's heads, but into their Hearts and Consciences. Whence he studiously avoided obscure phrases, Exotic words, or an unnecessary citation of Latin Sentences, which some men addict themselves to the use of. Mr. *Dod* was wont to say, That *so much Latin was so much flesh in a Sermon*:[46] So did this humble man look upon the affectation of such things in a *Popular Auditory* to savor of Carnal wisdom. The Lord gave him an excellent faculty in making abstruse things plain, that in handling the deepest Mysteries he would accommodate himself to Vulgar Capacities, that even the meanest might learn something.[47]

In other words, the plain style is seen as a means to an end: "The sum is, that nothing is to be admitted which doth not make for the spiritual edification of the people, neither any thing to be omitted whereby we may in a sure way attain to that end."[48] If today we tend to describe the plain style by what the preachers "omitted" rather than by what they "admitted," we merely follow their way of defining it. A main source for their theory of plain expression was their opposition to the witty and often obscure style of preaching of the ministers of the established church. For the first New England preachers, the manner of preaching, as well as the liturgical practice and the ecclesiastical polity of the established church, needed purification. Hence the preachers omitted, as a rule, allusions to classical or scholarly authorities; words and phrases in Latin, Greek, or Hebrew; and complex rhetorical figures and patterns like conceits. These were, in general, deemed educationally suspect and spiritually dangerous.[49]

Although the first preachers of New England disapproved of many of the rhetorical patterns of ministers loyal to the Church of England, they did advocate and practice ornamentation. Because of years of academic training in the rhetoric of figurative language and an understanding of the symbolic nature of Christianity, the preachers were led to value certain modes of nonliteral expression. Whereas Puritans rejected certain symbols, such as relics, idols, and some sacraments, they fully accepted the symbolic ordinances of baptism and the Lord's Supper. Perceiving the incarnation to be a visible symbol of God's mysterious redemption, they admitted that the word of God as it proclaimed this miracle also had figurative qualities. "And where," asks first-generation preacher Charles Chauncy, "are there such high strains of all sorts of *Rhetorical Tropes, & figures*, to be found in any Author, as there are in the writings of the *Prophets & Apostles*?"[50]

Hence, the preachers in opening the text helped the auditors recognize any figures of speech that the Spirit employed.[51] Furthermore, they relied on the biblical existence of *"Rhetorical Tropes, & figures"* to authorize their own ornamentation. Ministers, advises Perkins, may in their preaching use allegories, though "sparingly and soberly," since "Paul in his teaching useth them often."[52]

A broad term in the preachers' usage, allegory denotes many of the rhetorical devices that they found suitable for a popular audience: homely comparisons, parablelike illustrations, dialogs of the simple listener and the wise pastor, and stories about the honorable saint and the despicable hypocrite. The sermons display many examples of such tropes as metonymy, synecdoche, and metaphor and of figures that Bernard had recommended to stir the affections: exclamation, interrogation, compellation, observation, optation, prosopopeia, apostrophe, and dialogism.[53] But some of the liveliest and most imaginative passages result from what the ministers termed a similitude: a comparison or analogy, generally concrete, drawn from one kind of experience that makes clear a concept or idea of a totally dissimilar experience.

As early as the sixteenth century, Luther had urged preachers to clarify their preaching with similitudes; and about two hundred years later Cotton Mather, in his rhetorical handbook for third-generation preachers, advises them to "find out *Similitudes*, wherewith you may clothe your Ideas, and make them sensible to the lowest and meanest Capacities, yea, to all *Flesh*."[54] Not surprisingly, a principal authority for using similitudes is the Spirit. When Puritans determined that the Spirit was communicating cryptically in the word, they frequently concluded that it was employing a similitude: when the Spirit "doth allegorize," Bernard explains, it actually uses "an argument drawn from a similitude, when the words are expounded mystically, otherwise than the literal sense doth afford."[55] In unraveling the Spirit's allegorizing, Davenport teaches that the valley and dry bones of Ezekiel 37:2 are the elements of a similitude, the valley representing "the low estate of the Church" and "the many dry bones," "the discouraging apprehensions the people of God have."[56] The prophet, then, used the similitude to clarify the experience of the Spirit with the more familiar experience of the landscape of the desert.

Although in the sermons introductory words like "so," "as," "like," and "thus" were generally given to make explicit the use of figurative language, such words by no means mark the beginning of every similitude in these sermons. Similitude, then, designates more than a simile; for example, Cotton defines a metaphor as a "short similitude."[57] Today most readers are fascinated less by the form of the similitudes than by the content—what present critical vocabulary terms the imagery. The body of imagery ranges over an excitingly wide area: family and love relationships, medicine and bodily functioning, the home and related activities, the cultivation of plants and crops, journeying, war, occupations, merchandising, and natural matter, particularly water.[58]

Despite their study and conscious practice of an extensive aesthetic theory for the structure and style of their sermons, the preachers ultimately attributed the rhetorical effectiveness of their sermons to the power of the Spirit in both text and preacher. Calvin had passed on to the English Puritans a belief that the power of Scripture was independent of rhetoric: "Now, since that uncultivated and almost rude simplicity procures itself more reverence than all the graces of rhetoric, what opinion can we form, but that the force of truth in the sacred Scripture is too powerful to need the assistance of verbal art?"[59] The Puritans applied that same notion to any "graces of rhetoric" found in their sermons: they believed that powerful preaching derived ultimately from the same conveyor of truth, the Spirit. If the sermon were to be the means of conversion, then the Spirit must speak through it. Hence the first requirement for admission to the preaching ministry was evidence of the Spirit's presence in the candidate's state of grace.[60] The sermons of Paul, for example, were seen by an early New England preacher as "the effects of that Savior-like disposition, wherewith the Lord Jesus still inspires the Instrumental Saviors of Mount *Sion*."[61] Calling the minister a "Spiritual Artificer," Hooker acknowledges his craft but emphasizes that if he is to "be Powerful, an inward spiritual heat of heart, and holy affection is required." In effect, "He that mourns in speaking of sin, makes another mourn for sin committed. An Exhortation that proceeds from the heart, carries a kind of Authority and Commission with it."[62] Thus, only if the Spirit stirs within the preacher can the preacher move the auditor.

iv. The Subject Matter of the Sermons

For the early New England preachers the "main business" of life, the "daily task and study," was the "labor to get faith."[63] Consequently, the intricacies of the way the soul acquires this faith—how it comes to be saved—constitute the principal content of their sermons. The sermons became a means of instruction about every minute detail related to that all-important event of conversion. Over and over again this pulpit literature tells the story of the soul's spiritual stages, its successes and crises. The preachers collectively shaped a narrative about the life of faith, mythlike in both its countless recitations and its wide applicability. A glance at the titles of the sermon-series of the first preachers demonstrates this absorption with the redemption of the soul. For example, book after book by Hooker discusses phases in the regenerative process: *The Soul's Preparation for Christ, The Soul's*

Humiliation, The Soul's Implantation, The Soul's Exaltation. Hooker's *The Faithful Covenanter* and *The Poor Doubting Christian* and Shepard's *The Sincere Convert* and *The Sound Believer* characterize in their titles the soul working for saintliness. And sermons on the covenant of grace—Cotton, Hooker, and Bulkeley all titled works on the new covenant or gospel-covenant—disclose God's great plot for humanity's redemption, the framework of the stages of salvation.

Not all the sermons treat salvation in the same manner: the Sunday sermons and those of the pastor tend to be more exhortative, whereas the weekday lectures and those of the teacher are more polemical. Occasional sermons, preached at a funeral or a Harvard commencement, dwell primarily on contemporary concerns. Some begin the laments over the inadequacy of the next generation that the sermons of the 1660s and 1670s will expand. But frequently topical sermons, especially those preached at public events like an election, contribute to the common focus on redemption. For example, Davenport's *God's Call to His People to Turn unto Him*, preached in 1669 on "two public fasting-days appointed by Authority," speaks about the backsliding of the community in terms of the framework of individual salvation.[64] In American pulpit literature this intensive and imaginative investigation of the soul's progress through the stages of salvation is a feature unique to the sermons of the first New England preachers. The preachers of the second generation are distinguished for their jeremiads; they excelled in anatomizing the sins of the community rather than the heroics of the saint.[65]

The subject matter of the sermons has its immediate origins in the doctrine of salvation as it was refined and particularized by the brotherhood in England, especially by William Perkins. He passed on to the preachers who went to New England a complex conceptualization of the life of faith, a sense that it involved many steps. In their sermons, the ministers describe three general stages in the redemptive process: preparation—the readying of the sinner for conversion; vocation—the conversion of the elected soul; and regeneration—the growth of the saint in holiness. During preparation, the elected soul discovers its sin to be loathsome and experiences contrition and humiliation. Generally, the preachers emphasize the Law—the obligations prescribed at Sinai—to facilitate this conviction of total unworthiness: the Law is a *"School-master"* to bring people to Christ.[66] In the second stage, during God's vocation of his elect, the sinner is converted into a saint—joined to Jesus Christ. Conversion might be sudden and dramatic for some, but for many it will be protracted and apprehensible only by a variety of signs and events. During the third stage, regeneration, the soul experiences justification, pardoning of sins; reconciliation, "peace with God"; adoption, becoming a child of God; and sanctification, restoration of the image of God.[67] The saints' growth in holiness demands many years; their essential humanity occasions setbacks and frustrates their sanctification. Godlike purity requires a lifetime of effort before the soul is readied for glorification, for full union with God after bodily death, when at last it is "fit to be made a vessel . . . of glory hereafter."[68]

Breaking down salvation into stages came to imply, among other things, that conversion would probably occur gradually rather than suddenly. But if a soul could not expect one clear and dramatic signal of redemption, how could it know that it had been called? Unable to determine when their conversion occurred, some of the preachers' auditors apparently doubted whether their regeneration had ever begun. It is likely that such anxiety led the preachers to redouble their efforts in detailing the process of salvation; the sermons imply that with a broad understanding of the stages and signs of salvation the anxious listeners might eventually assure themselves that they had received grace.[69] Particular historical events, as well as widespread needs for assurance, also encouraged detailed sermons on the stages of redemption. In early New England, Congregational churches demanded evidence of salvation before a candidate was granted full membership. Having to declare whether their conversion had occurred, the candidates needed extensive preaching on the stages of salvation so that they had a normative pattern for appraising their own spiritual state. In practice, the stages of salvation had varying uses. With their help, hopeful aspirants to the life of faith verified their redemptive progress, early New Englanders framed the narratives of conversion they related to gain church membership, and spiritual autobiographers and biographers traced the soul's spiritual pattern.[70]

It is the progress of the soul through these stages of salvation that the order of the selections in this volume traces. The common theological interpretation that explicates the process of God's redemption, the covenant of grace, is treated in the selections from Bulkeley's *The Gospel-Covenant* and Cotton's *A Treatise of the Covenant of Grace*. The soul prepares for conversion in Shepard's *The Sound Believer* and experiences vocation, its indeterminate occurrence and immediate benefits, in the selections from Hooker's *The Soul's Vocation* and its sequel, *The Soul's Exaltation*. The joys and uncertainties of the sinner turned saint are detailed in the selections describing regeneration, the last stage of salvation: Cotton's *The Way of Life*, Shepard's *The Parable of the Ten Virgins*, and Davenport's *The Saint's Anchor-Hold*. The selections demonstrate that the soul negotiates the stages of salvation in various ways, determined by individual application, each preacher's theology, and historical circumstance.

How sharply these three factors could conflict became apparent during the Antinomian controversy (1636–1638), at root a theological dispute over the nature of salvation and its principal stages.[71] Anne

Hutchinson, a member of Cotton's congregation in Boston, correlating his preaching on conversion with her experience of vocation, charged that the other ministers—notably Shepard, Hooker, and Bulkeley[72]— were preaching works, not grace. That is, she found that ministers were encouraging people to consider themselves saved if they behaved like saints: sanctification was used to argue justification. Such a connection between human actions and God's regeneration amounted in her view to a covenant of works, a heretical doctrine to any Protestant. The ministers soundly repudiated this interpretation and even more vigorously denounced Hutchinson's belief that a saint experienced assurance of conversion only through an immediate awareness of the Spirit. In a related point of contention, Hutchinson forced the two sides into preparationist and antipreparationist positions. She criticized her opponents' notion that the soul could prepare for salvation; the first stage in the process of salvation—preparation—denied, in her view, the all-important notion that grace came as a free gift of God, not as an earned reward for the soul's efforts.

Hutchinson had taken to a logical extreme genuine differences between Cotton's view of the redemptive process and that of the others.[73] More radically than Calvin, Cotton taught humanity's utter depravity and inability to respond to an offer of grace until God dramatically seized the elected sinner: the soul could do little to prepare for conversion.[74] Furthermore, he assumed that conversion brought assurance of redemption, whereas the other preachers argued that only lengthy self-examination could determine the presence of effectual vocation. For Shepard, particularly, the only certainty of salvation was its uncertainty. Paradoxically, the less assured believers felt about their state of grace, the more assured they could be about it.[75] Although Cotton held that the doctrine of free grace did not exempt men and women from the Law—indeed it brought conviction of conscience and fear of divine punishment—Hutchinson and her followers argued a radical disjunction between grace and duties.[76]

Cotton modified his views during the synod held in 1637 to resolve the issues raised by the Antinomians, as Hutchinson and her followers were called by their opponents. Consequently, Hutchinson was excommunicated; and the principal stages of salvation, particularly the preparatory phase, were upheld. Furthermore, belief in the soul's active involvement in each phase of salvation, which Shepard and Hooker had stressed throughout their preaching careers, was confirmed as orthodox doctrine. Before conversion, sinners could prepare by such activities as going to church, meditating on their sins, and expressing contrition; after vocation, believers might assure themselves of justification if they behaved industriously in their earthly calling or profession, loved their neighbors, obeyed their magistrates, and honored their ministers.

By definition, then, faith was more than a mere consequence of conversion.[77] It is presented in the sermons of the first preachers of New England as a total "way of life," an active commitment of the soul during each stage of salvation. Read collectively, these sermons convince us that the way of faith demands from the soul deeds and commitments that in public life would be called heroic.

The Texts of the Sermons

Because of the customs of seventeenth-century preaching, it is likely that few of the texts of the sermons printed here existed in full copies before their delivery.[1] The use of manuscript in the pulpit was strongly discouraged by both Puritan and courtly audiences; therefore, a preacher who had written out his sermon in full was faced with the task of memorizing a discourse of an hour's length.[2] Such a formal degree of preparation—writing an exact copy and memorizing it for delivery—was in general reserved for infrequent and important state occasions like Massachusetts election sermons or for the public outdoor sermons at Paul's Cross in London, when the preacher's message would be considered in detail for its political and controversial implications and when immediate publication was likely.[3] Ordinarily, the preacher memorized not a fully written copy of his sermon but a much briefer outline of its major arguments, topics, and texts, which he called notes.[4] One of the most respected preachers of the century, the Anglican John Donne, seems to have used this combination of memorized and extemporaneous delivery: "he did not read his sermons, but carefully prepared the heads of his discourse beforehand, making voluminous notes, and trusting his meditations to his memory."[5]

Puritan preachers, too, apparently availed themselves of this compromise between spontaneity and thoughtful preparation: "we are told of John Dod (who died in 1645) that, having found the disadvantage of 'binding himself to words and phrases,' which resulted in his being 'at a *Non-plus*' in a University sermon—'he resolved afterwards never to pen his sermon *verbatim*, but his usual manner was to write only the *Analysis* of his Text, the proofs of Scripture for the Doctrines, with the Reasons and Uses, and so leaving the rest to meditation, in which course he never found defect.' "[6] Dod's notes may have resembled Thomas Shepard's sermon notes, preserved at Harvard, and those of John Davenport at Yale: small pages (about five by seven inches), densely covered on both sides with very small handwriting; the divisions of the sermon clearly marked (doctrines, reasons, and uses); texts of Scripture cited and often copied in full; and the contents of each division swiftly detailed in a few complete sentences. By comparison with the general nature of printed sermons by Shepard and Davenport, it is obvious that the use of such notes left to the preacher's "meditation" most of the transitions, the narrative and descriptive parts of the similitudes, the explanatory part of the arguments, and most of the figures of impassioned rhetoric—the interjections, the pleadings, the bulk of the colloquies and soliloquies of the soul.

If after delivery of a sermon or sermon-series, the preacher decided to publish his sermons in printed form, he needed an accurate, fair copy to present to the printer. If in fact he had no copy of his sermons, he turned to his notes and began to expand them; how closely he adhered to the original preached version would depend on the time and events intervening between delivery and transcription.[7] In the case of Davenport's fairly brief sermon-series, *The Saint's Anchor-Hold*, printed under his direction shortly after delivery, the transcription can be assumed to represent with relative exactness the original delivery.

Divergence of the printed sermon from the spoken one becomes more apparent in Bulkeley's *The Gospel-Covenant*, a considerably longer work. In the process of transcribing the notes of his sermons, Bulkeley must have significantly exceeded the length of the preached versions, for at the time of publication of the incomplete first edition he expressed surprise at the growing bulk of the sermons. It seems to have taken him five more years to complete the transcription for the second edition. Such expansion of notes under Bulkeley's hand so amplified the work that it became known as a treatise, implying composition for readers rather than listeners.[8]

Although Shepard in his autobiography is far from clear about the exact history of the forms of *The Sound Believer* (subtitled *A Treatise of Evangelical Conversion*), some sequence like the following is probable: the original notes were composed in England, but the sermons were not delivered until years later in New England. They were then (rather reluctantly) transcribed at length by Shepard and sent to a friend in England to be printed.[9] An even greater variety of stages between inception and publication is found in the history of the other volume of Shepard's represented in this anthology: the long sermon-series *The Parable of the Ten Virgins*, preached by him from notes, was transcribed over a period of twenty years by several different people, including Shepard himself, who died before completing the transcription.

Such authorized and carefully supervised publications, issued with the knowledge and consent of the preacher, perhaps transcribed by him or at any rate by his friends or students, and printed under the supervision of a responsible editor, should be distinguished from the other major form of sermon publication. Many sermons were, in essence, pirated—recorded during delivery and published with little or no direct involvement of the preacher. Seventeenth-century auditors were accomplished listeners, trained to fix the sermon in mind by memorizing its outline and by taking it down word for word during delivery.[10] Notetakers, many of them proficient in shorthand, were a common sight in churches, especially among Puritan congregations.[11] Given the importance of sermons in Puritan spiritual life, and given the probable number of recorded versions of the sermons of the most popular preachers, it is not surprising that many of them found their way into print without the consent of the preacher.

The publication of unauthorized versions caused a great deal of concern on the part of those preachers who valued accuracy of style and content in the printed evidence of their preaching. A letter of Shepard's, for example, expresses dismay at the careless recording of the companion sermon-series to *The Sound Believer*: "That which is called *The Sincere Convert*, I have not the book, I once saw it; it was a Collection of such Notes in a dark Town in England, which one procuring of me, published them without my will or privity; I scarce know what it contains, nor do I like to see it, considering the many [typographical errors], most absurd, and the confession of him that published it, that [it] comes out gelded and altered from what was first written."[12] The loss of editorial control caused by shorthand reporters and unscrupulous borrowers of notes plagued John Cotton as well: the journal of John Winthrop, recording the publication of one of Cotton's works, notes that "Mr. Humfrey had gotten the notes from some who had took them by characters [shorthand], and printed them in London, he had 300 copies for it [in payment?], which was a great wrong to Mr. Cotton, and he was much grieved at it, for it had been fit he should have perused and corrected the copy before it had been printed."[13]

Inevitably, a sermon recorded during delivery and published without supervision would seem rough and inaccurate to the preacher: he would notice mistakes in the note taking (incorrect biblical citations, misunderstood syntax, or even omissions of important sections) as well as unthinking transcription of rhetorical devices that he might consider appropriate to the pulpit but not to the printed page.[14] But without such a method of transmission, given the arduous labor of transcribing one's own pulpit notes for the reading public, many sermons of the first-generation New England preachers would have been lost. The literary fame of John Cotton, for example, is thus described by his grandson, noting "his printed works, whereof there are many, that praise him in the gates, though few of them were printed with his own knowledge or consent."[15] One of Cotton's volumes anthologized here, *The Way of Life*, illustrates publication from a recorded version. The sermons were preached in England, recorded during delivery, and printed much later without Cotton's permission or supervision, after he had left the country for New England. The same is true of Hooker's volumes represented in this anthology—preached and recorded in Chelmsford, England, and published in London with-

out the consent of the far-distant preacher. Indeed, of Hooker's twenty-two books, only four "seem definitely to have been prepared for the press" by the preacher himself. Nearly all were delivered as sermons and published from recorded versions without his knowledge.[16]

The sermons of these popular preachers, then, like the plays and poems of other writers of the early seventeenth century, were subject to pirating. The statements of the preachers and their friends, however, disowning or disparaging such unauthorized editions—statements found in later revised editions, in letters, and in other publications—should not be completely or literally trusted. The repudiation of an earlier work may well be a device of the publisher to draw customers to the work presently in print.[17] Furthermore, the myth of the pirated version is fairly common in seventeenth-century letters as a method of distancing the author from a work not quite as elegant or polished as the preacher thinks it should be.[18] Moreover, it is clear that the preacher was in some cases willing to work with a recorded version of his preaching, to revise and polish it, and to acknowledge it as his: such is apparently the case with Cotton's *A Treatise of the Covenant of Grace*, the two very different early editions of which seem to be derived from two separate recorded versions, each perhaps reviewed and edited by Cotton himself.

Ideally, the preacher took pains to balance the demands of a hungry press and an eager readership, on the one hand, with the standards of accuracy and orthodoxy on the other. A letter of 1650 from Davenport in New Haven to Cotton in Boston illustrates the constraints on the preacher's control. The letter replies to a letter of Cotton's from which Davenport had learned that a certain Mark Pierce had delivered to Cotton the recorded transcript and the preacher's notes of a sermon-series preached by Davenport. "The forenamed brother [Pierce] diligently wrote, as his manner was, but finding that his head and pen could not carry away some material expressions, he earnestly desired me to let him have my notes, to perfect his own by them." Because of the fear of complete loss of control over his own sermons, Davenport was particularly concerned to comply with Pierce's request. Having first charged Pierce "that, when he had transcribed them, he would return my copy again, by a safe land-messenger, not by sea," he added a further condition: "My second charge was, that when he had transcribed them, he would show them unto you [Cotton], and make no other use of them than privately for himself, but by your advice. This I added, because I feared that he had a purpose for the press, from some words that I observed now and then to fall from him." Davenport requested Cotton, then, to be a de facto editor of these sermons: "keep them, till you have sifted them thoroughly. . . . If you meet with anything . . . that you do not approve, *deleatur* [take it out]. I thought it better to let him have mine own notes, to rectify his, by them, than to let him print great mistakes for want of that help."

Modernized: . . . they cried out (1 Samuel 12:19), *We have added . . .*

There are some citations, however, that seem to indicate more than parenthetic reference and have been given stronger emphasis. Some apparently indicate that in delivery a quotation was given a more extended introduction than actually appears in the printed text; these have been set off by more emphatic punctuation:

Original: . . . the Lord gives it no peace: *Ier.* 8. 6. Why doth the horse goe on in the battel . . .

Modernized: . . . the Lord gives it no peace. Jeremiah 8:6: Why doth the horse go on in the battle . . .

Other citations show that quotations that do not appear in the printed text were read or recited by the preacher; these have been followed by semicolons or periods.

The next three examples are from selection IV.

Original: . . . it is but counterfeit coine: so it is here. 1 *Cor.* 1. 21. Let a man study . . .

Modernized: . . . it is but counterfeit coin: so it is here. 1 Corinthians 1:21. Let a man study . . .

Original: . . . hee himselfe would be a miracle; *Gal.* 3. 2. for there goes a spirituall power . . .

Modernized: . . . he himself would be a miracle; Galatians 3:2; for there goes a spiritual power . . .

A clue to the intention of the text at such points is found where the preacher takes time to read two texts, one after the other:

Original: . . . as it was with the Israelites, 1 *Sam.* 8. 19. compared with 1 *Sam.* 12. 18. What is the reason they do so at the one, and not at the other . . .

Modernized: . . . as it was with the Israelites; 1 Samuel 8:19 compared with 1 Samuel 12:18. What is the reason they do so at the one, and not at the other . . .

The words "do so" in the preacher's comment are obscure unless the texts have been consulted at the time of citation.

When emendations of the copytext other than those mentioned above have been made, they are listed in the notes. These include emendations of punctuation as well as additions, omissions, and significant changes of words. If in modernizing spelling, a choice between two homonyms has been made, the original spelling is noted. All differences in wording between the copytext and other editions of the text are recorded in the notes. Unless of major significance, differences of punctuation, spelling, capitalization, and italics have been ignored in the notes, as have such changes in word form as "further/farther."

In each case, the copytext is the latest edition that demonstrates any authorial influence—the first edition except for Bulkeley's *The Gospel-Covenant* (second edition). Alterations of the copytext have been sparingly introduced, whether from later editions or by our judgment, and then only in situations where the sense is drastically hindered in the copytext. The annotations are designed to identify unfamiliar and ambiguous words and constructions, to direct the reader where appropriate to unidentified biblical references or quotations, to indicate briefly some of the contexts of the selections, and to reproduce the marginalia of the copytexts.

SELECTION I

The Gospel-Covenant

Peter Bulkeley

A portrait presumed to represent Peter Bulkeley as rector of Odell, Bedfordshire, England. Nothing is known of the origin of this oil painting, now in the possession of a descendant of Bulkeley. He succeeded his father, Edward Bulkeley, in the rectorship of Odell in 1620, at the age of thirty-seven, and held it until his emigration to Massachusetts in 1635. Courtesy of Mr. Peter Bulkeley Brainard, West Hartford, Connecticut.

THE SERMONS COMPRISING *The Gospel-Covenant* must have been among the first preached in the town of Concord, Massachusetts. In the epistle prefacing the first edition (1646), Bulkeley implies that the sermons first took form in 1638 or 1639.[1] Their occasion was one of controversy, for it was, in his words, "a time then full of trouble in these American Churches." His treatment of the covenant of grace directly and vehemently opposed the heresies of the Antinomian faction. Even at the time of publishing the first edition, he saw fit to remind his readers of "the inordinate activeness, and impetuous violence of some busy spirits . . . deeming all others (except themselves) to be wholly ignorant of the Covenant of grace, and to be shut up under a Covenant of works." He could still parody the Antinomian position: "All the Preachers in the land were legal Preachers, the Christians, legal Christians, as having only the letter of the Gospel, but not understanding the mystery or spiritual meaning of it, as it was revealed unto themselves by the spirit."[2] According to Bulkeley, it was upon the urging of many of his listeners that he polished his rough drafts and published the first edition. That work, however, was incomplete, "partly because I saw the Treatise to exceed in bulk what I expected in the beginning."[3] Five years later, therefore, he published a new edition, the title page of which claimed it to be "much enlarged, and corrected by the Author."[4] In the prefatory letter to the reader of this edition, he explains that he has clarified his discussion of the similarities between the "old Covenant" and "the New," demonstrated that "the Law [is] to be still of use, as a rule of life," and shown how "the New-Covenant . . . comprehends the children of believing Parents."[5]

The title page of the 1651 edition also announces the organization and subject matter of the work: (1) the differences between the covenants of grace and of works; (2) the differences in the "administration" of the covenant of grace before and after the coming of Jesus Christ—in "substance," Paul taught the same covenant as did Moses; (3) the benefits and blessings of the covenant of grace, namely, the presence of God, forgiveness, regeneration, and constancy; (4) the condition of the covenant of grace—faith (the selection is taken from this part); and (5) the properties of the covenant of grace—it is "free," "sure," "everlasting," and "holy." Thomas Shepard, in a prefatory letter to the work, heartily praised "the holy, judicious, and learned labors of this aged, experienced, and precious servant of Christ Jesus; who hath taken much pains to discover . . . the great mystery of godliness wrapped up in the Covenant."[6] Shepard's unqualified thanksgiving for the "blessed covenant" typifies the preachers' general belief in the covenant of grace as the principal divine structure for redemption: "God conveys his salvation by way of covenant."[7] Several sermon-series on the covenant of grace are found in this literature, but no work explicates federal theology—as the doctrine of the covenants was often termed—as fully as the five-part *Gospel-Covenant*.

In the covenant of grace, as the preachers explained it, God offers temporal blessings and eternal salvation to the elect, if through faith they accept his grace offered in Jesus Christ. God's covenanting with human beings, as the ministers interpreted Scripture, started with human life; he had promised Adam to be his God if Adam obeyed him. In failing to follow God's injunction, Adam abrogated the covenant of works for all humanity. Hence, out of his love and his bounteous generosity God formed a new covenant. In this covenant of grace women and men had merely to believe in Jesus Christ's mediation, in his assumption of their guilt and justification of their manifold sins. Bulkeley explains the major difference between the two covenants: "Look what place works had for our justification to life in the Covenant of works, the same place hath faith in the Covenant of Grace . . . the Covenant of grace is not broken asunder by many transgressions, so long as we follow God in a way of faith and repentance." [8] The doctrine of the covenant also explains God's special relationship with his chosen followers, be they organized in a church community or a public state. If those individuals placed faith in God, then he would be their protector and benefactor. Thus, part of the breadth and excitement of *The Gospel-Covenant* is its continual expansion from the individual in covenant with God to the church and state in league with him: "And for ourselves here, the people of *New England*, we should in a special manner labor to shine forth in holiness above other people . . . because we profess ourselves to be a people in Covenant with God." [9]

The selection typifies how carefully throughout *The Gospel-Covenant* Bulkeley defines the ways God and humans together enter into a covenant. In his understanding of how "God prepares his own way for entering into Covenant with us," we see a principal advantage of this concept: it enables individuals to understand more fully God's workings in salvation. Functioning principally as a teaching device, the covenant led the preachers to predict God's actions far more than their predecessor Calvin, awed by God's inexplicable majesty, had dared.[10] Bulkeley, for example, precisely specifies three ways God woos humans and enumerates two particular gifts of the covenant—the mercy of pardon and the government of his rule. Bulkeley, clearly aware of the dangers of diminishing God's omnipotence, notes throughout *The Gospel-Covenant* that God can act otherwise if he chooses. He further cautions that God offers the covenant only to a few: "Out of the whole mass of sinful men, the Lord picks out a few base, poor, despised ones, things of no account." [11]

In the selection, Bulkeley's principal strategy for stressing the inequality of the parties in the covenant is to qualify how women and men perform their part of the agreement. Because "the confederacy is mutual," they must meet their "condition": "The condition then of the Covenant of Grace is faith."[12] Faith is defined both as an active quality of the believer and as a gift of the Spirit. At points, the selection leads the reader to think that the elect can do many things to fulfill the covenant—indeed, Bulkeley enumerates six ways that they "lay hold of the Covenant." At first glance, the soul's action seems to meet the definition of faith that Bulkeley offers just prior to this selection: "faith is the hand of the soul, and the putting of it forth is the act by which we receive Christ offered." [13] But the former moderator of the Cambridge synod, which convened in 1637 to resolve the issues Anne Hutchinson had raised, protects himself constantly from the charge that the soul works its own salvation. Hence, in the selection, he also defines the human response to God's offer of a covenant as relatively passive: "Now the work of Faith in respect of this offer of grace is only to accept the grace offered." Further, humans are energized "to accept" by "a touch of [God's] Spirit upon the heart," not by any capability of their own. Similarly, Bulkeley's constant personification of faith makes it seem a force independent of the soul.[14]

The selection itself demonstrates that like Shepard and Hooker, Bulkeley was a preparationist in his view of the salvation process: the soul meets the "condition" before it "enters into a Covenant" (that is, undergoes conversion). After preparation and conversion, after the covenant has been accepted by the soul's acknowledging God's rule, the soul *then*, Bulkeley emphasizes throughout, acts according to the Law of God out of love for God, not out of an effort to earn salvation. Indeed, love as the very essence of the covenant relationship occasions much of the intensity of the selection. Without elaborate imagery, such as Shepard's adaptation of the bride and bridegroom in *The Parable of the Ten Virgins*, Bulkeley depicts God as courting the soul. The imagery, such as the personification of desire, is much more ingeniously worked out by Hooker (see selection V). The same can be said for the soliloquies of the soul: Hooker's and Shepard's outshine Bulkeley's. Much more imaginative strength resides in Bulkeley's rigorous exegesis of the biblical theme of the covenant than in his figurative language. He stirs his auditors not by abundant imagery but rather by biblical analogy. Salvation for each soul compares to the experience of scriptural heroes. "I am separated from the Lord, an Alien from his people" suggests the people of Israel, God's chosen, to whom the ministers often likened the New England settlers. An even more audacious analogy is this passage: "he will have his way hereto prepared in the Desert; not in the throng of a City, but in a solitary Desert place, he will allure us, and draw us into the wilderness, from the company of men." The passage equates the preparation of the soul for salvation with the preparation for Jesus Christ, the source of salvation.

Genesis 17:1,7: *The Lord said unto Abraham, I am God all-sufficient, walk before me and be thou upright; And I will make my Covenant between me and thee, and thy seed after thee in their generations, for an everlasting Covenant, to be a God unto thee, and to thy seed after thee.*[15]

CHAPTER IIII.[16] *Showing what be the acts of faith in closing with the Covenant: in both the parts of it; scilicet* 1. *that God will be a God of blessing to us to bless us.* 2. *That he will be a God over us, to rule us.*

Question.[17] But what is that act or acts of faith, by which we perform the condition of the Covenant?

Answer. 1. First, there is an act of faith, by which we do (as it were) first close with the Covenant revealed and offered unto us.

2. There is also another act of it, by which we are carried on to an answerable[18] walking before God, according to the Covenant made with him.

1.[19] For the former before we give a direct answer, we must lay down these two grounds.[20]

First,[21] That in the making up of the Covenant betwixt God and us, God is first with us, he is the first mover, he begins with us before we begin with him; we should never seek to be in Covenant with him, if he did not allure us, and draw us unto him. Thus in Ezekiel 20:37: *I will bring them* (saith the Lord) *into the bond of the Covenant*; It is the Lord which brings them; they do not first offer themselves.

And first God prepares his own way for entering into Covenant with us, and then he finisheth the work; and in this preparation he doth these three things.

1. He breaks us off from our covenant with Hell and Death, makes us sensible of our undone[22] estate, makes us see that we are without God, without Christ, without hope (Ephesians 2), that we are not under mercy, that we are not of his people (1 Peter 2).

2. He opens unto us his mind and will, showing himself willing to receive us to grace, and to enter into a new Covenant with us, yet again to take us to be his people, and he to be our God; he goes into the streets and open places, as it is in Proverbs 1:20,21, and there makes public proclamation, *Ho, ho, everyone that will, Come ye unto me, and I will make an everlasting Covenant with you* (Isaiah 55:3, Isaiah 65:1), yea more, he comes and beseeches us to be reconciled unto him (2 Corinthians 5:20), and speaks to us as pitying us (Jeremiah 3:12); and lamenting over us (Ezekiel 33:11), thereby to persuade us to come into a covenant with him.

3. By the hearing of these promises and offers of grace, the Lord usually scattereth some little seeds of faith in the hearts of those that he will bring unto himself; which seed being sown, doth sometimes

quickly put forth, and acts towards the Covenant propounded, and lays hold of it, as we see in *Lydia*, the Jailer, Zacchaeus,[23] and others; but sometimes (and that most usually) before that[24] faith hath done any great thing in seeking after God, to make a Covenant with him, the Lord doth again withdraw himself, and goes away (as Hosea 5: end):[25] hiding himself, as if he would regard us and look after us no more; so that now if we will get into Covenant with him, we must seek after him, as he before sought after us, and must sue unto him for grace, to take us into Covenant with himself; and herein faith begins to show itself, beginning to work and move towards the Covenant which the Lord offereth to make with us.

For though the Lord hath withdrawn himself, yet he hath left such a touch of his Spirit upon the heart as makes the soul affectionate towards him, so as now it cannot rest, but feeling its own woe, being without God, and without Covenant, and having heard of the Lord's willingness to enter into Covenant[26] with us, it now begins to seek after the Lord, to be in Covenant with him; This is the first ground, that God is first, he begins with us.

Secondly,[27] The second is, that whatsover faith doth in seeking to enter into Covenant with God, it doth it always in that way, and according to that order in which the Lord hath gone before us in the offer of his Covenant unto us; Faith doth always follow the Word, and doth nothing but as it hath a word of Faith to guide its way, it goes step by step as it hath the light of the word directing and going before; Faith doth not prescribe unto God, it will not presume to appoint the conditions of the Covenant, only it answers and applies itself to God's offer, taking conditions of peace, but giving none. It doth not seek to wind about the promise of grace to our own mind and will. It doth not say I will have it thus, thus it shall be, or else I will admit of no conditions of peace; but the soul now finding that the everlasting estate of it for weal or woe, life or death, stands at the mere good pleasure and mercy of God; and knowing that either it must submit to that way of the Covenant, and to those conditions, which the Lord is pleased to set down, or it must perish forever; it gladly comes in humbly accepting the offer of Grace, in the same way, as it is tendered and offered unto us of God.

Here then (that we may see how faith closeth with the Covenant propounded) we must see first how God offers himself in his Covenant unto us. Now in that main promise of the Covenant (which is indeed the sum of all) *I will be thy God*, God offers himself unto us two ways (as hath been before showed in the opening of that promise); First,[28] he offers himself unto us as a God of mercy to pardon us; as a God of blessing to bless us with all sufficient blessings. Secondly, As a God over us, and above us, to order us and to rule us in all our ways, to govern us according to his own will, that he may be glorified in us; Thus God offers himself unto us in his Covenant, etc.

Now[29] the answer is ready to the question propounded, how faith doth act in closing with the Covenant; the work of faith herein, is to carry the soul towards the Covenant in the same order and way as it is propounded; First accepting the grace offered, resting upon God for all the mercy which he hath promised. Secondly, Taking God to be God[30] over us, submitting[31] to his government and authority, to command us and to rule us in all things according to his own will; these two things faith doth, and so takes hold of the Covenant in the same way and order as God offers it.

1.[32] God makes himself known to us as a God of mercy, gracious, long-suffering, pardoning iniquity, transgression and sin, he offers himself to be reconciled unto us, though we have rebelled against him, promising to be a Father unto us, and to accept of us as his sons and daughters in his beloved.

Now the work of Faith in respect of this offer of grace is only to accept the grace offered, to lay hold on it and take it unto ourselves being so freely offered; Faith brings nothing to God of our own, it offers nothing to stand in exchange for the mercy offered; it receives a gift, but giveth no price. The Lord holds out, and offers the free grace of the Covenant; faith receives it, and makes it our own. Hence is that expression used by the Prophet in Isaiah 56,[33] where we are said to lay hold of the Covenant; God holds it forth, and we take hold of it, the hand of grace offers it, and the hand of faith receives it and makes it our own, and this it doth by such steps and degrees as these that follow, wherein though I would not limit the Lord's dealing with all his, yet I will show what I conceive is the most usual and ordinary course of God's dispensation towards those whom he brings into Covenant with himself: Here then faith closeth with the Covenant in this manner.

1. By hearing the great things proposed in the Covenant, it stirs up in the heart a deep and serious consideration of the blessed condition of those people that are in Covenant with God; Oh what a blessed estate it is (thinks such a one), to be in favor with God, to be one of his Covenanted people! It[34] makes him say with *Moses, Blessed art thou O Israel, a people saved by the Lord* (Deuteronomy 33). It saith with *David, No people O Lord, is like thy people Israel, whom thou hast redeemed unto thyself* (2 Samuel 7:23). Time was when we counted the proud blessed, and placed our felicity in other things, as in riches, preferments, favor and credit with men, etc. but now these are become vile and things of no value; faith makes us change our voice, and to speak with a new tongue, and to say, not, Blessed are the people that be so, but, *Blessed are the people whose God is the Lord* (Psalm 144:ult.).[35]

This high esteem of grace being accompanied with a sense of the want of it, makes us seem[36] unto ourselves as undone men, lost, wretched, miserable. The poor soul thinks with itself, no sin like my sin, no misery like my misery: I am separated from the Lord, an Alien from his people; Oh blessed are they that are at peace, and in Covenant with him: this[37] is now the only *pearl of price*; the *rich treasure in the field*,[38] for which such a one is content to give all the substance of his house. In the prodigal when he began to think of returning to his Father,[39] these two things were found in him.

First, a deep sense of his own misery (*I die for hunger*).

Secondly, a consideration of the welfare of those that were in his Father's house (*they have bread enough*). So it is with those poor souls in which faith begins to work, to draw them back into Covenant with God; sensible are they of their own woe, highly also do they prize the excellency of grace, if by any means they might attain to have a part in it.

2. This high esteem of grace, and being in Covenant with God, begets a longing desire of it; good being believed, cannot but be desired, and longed for, and therefore faith now believing the benefit of being in favor and Covenant with God, it cannot but work desires after it; desire naturally springeth from the apprehension of any good made known. Faith is both in the understanding and in the will; as it is in the understanding, it opens the eye to see, and clearly to discern the blessing of the Covenant, and then stirs up the will to pursue and desire the attaining of the grace revealed: Never did *David* more long for the waters of the well of *Bethlehem*,[40] than such a soul touched with the sense of sin, doth desire to be at peace with God and in covenant with him, and therefore it is that they are said, to *thirst after the Lord* (Psalm 42:2), *to pant after him* (Psalm 42:1), to gasp after him (Psalm 119), longing for communion and peace with him. Thus in Isaiah 26:9: *With their souls they desire him in the night, and with their spirit in the morning*; the desire of their soul is set upon him, and cannot be satisfied by anything without him; peace with him is their life; and to be separated from him, is unto them as the shadow of death.

3. Faith being yet weak, and but as in the bud, or in the seed, and being yet unacquainted with the Lord's dealing with his people, not knowing how he useth by terrors of death to bring them to life and peace; hence it comes to pass that the soul being pressed with sense of sin, therefore though its *desires be strong, yet hope* of obtaining *is but feeble* and weak, we seeming to ourselves utterly unworthy (as indeed we are) and uncapable (which we are not) of so high a privilege as this is, to be in favor and Covenant with the most high God. Here therefore faith is taken up with many thoughts, thereby to support and keep up the heart in hope, carrying the eye of the soul towards God, though as beholding him afar off; fain would the poor soul be *joined with*[41] the Lord (Isaiah 56:6),[42] but being as yet dismayed with the sense of sin, he stands like the poor *Publican afar off*,[43] as one afraid to come near into the presence of the holy God; as yet faith

can scarce speak a word to God, it cannot come near to call upon him, only it can with *Jonah look towards his holy Temple*,[44] as being like the poor weak Babe which lies in the Cradle, being both sick, and weak, and speechless, and can only look towards the Mother for help, the cast of the eye (after a sort) expressing and signifying what it would say: Thus doth faith being yet weak, it would speak unto God but cannot, only it hath its eye towards heaven, looking for grace and mercy according to *Jehoshaphat's* speech, *Our eyes are towards thee* (2 Chronicles 20). It hungers and thirsts after grace, but fears it shall never be satisfied; it feels a need and fain would have; but sense of unworthiness, consciousness of manifold sins, the sentence of the Law like the thundering and lightning at Mount *Sinai*, all of them being sharpened by Satan's working in them and with them, do strike such a fear into the heart (as was in *Israel* then), that though desires be stirring and working, yet hope is very feeble, causing us to do as *Israel* did there, who though they heard the Lord say, I am the Lord your God, yet the terror of the thunder made them to stand afar off;[45] and so we, we hear the Lord offering to be our God in Covenant with us, but such are the discouragements that we dare not come near to seek after the grace which is revealed; Hitherto therefore the mind of the poor sinner desiring to be in Covenant with God, is unquiet within itself, hurried to and fro finding no rest; it hears of peace with God, but feels it not; but instead of peace finds trouble, fear, doubtings, discouragements to keep it off from the way of peace; Faith being yet young and faint, hath much ado to sustain the heart in any hope that it sink not down in discouragement. But yet though it be weak, it will be doing what it is able; setting the mind to consider the promises, and encouragements which God hath given us in his Word; how he invites all to come unto him, even every one that thirsts (Isaiah 55), telling us, That *whosoever comes unto him he will not cast away* (John 6:37).

And hence, while the mind is possessed with these things, because so great a business as making a Covenant of peace with the high God, and about so great an[46] affair as the life and salvation of our soul, cannot be transacted in a tumult, Therefore

4. In the Fourth place, Faith takes the soul aside, and carries it into some solitary place; that there it may be alone with itself, and with God, with whom it hath to do. This business, and multitude of other occasions, cannot be done together, and therefore the soul must be alone, that it may the more fully commune with itself, and utter itself fully before the Lord; Thus the poor Church in the time of her affliction when the Lord seemed to hide himself from her, she sat alone, as she speaks (Lamentations 3:28,29, and Jeremiah 15:17), *I sat alone, because of thy plague: The way of the Lord is prepared in the Desert* (Isaiah 40:3), when the Lord will come to the soul, and draw it into communion with himself; he will have his way hereto

prepared in the Desert; not in the throng of a City, but in a solitary Desert place, he will allure us, and draw us into the wilderness, from the company of men, when he will speak to our heart, and when he prepares our heart to speak unto him (Hosea 2). Not that such a one doth despise or neglect the fellowship of God's people, but he now sees and knows full well, that his help is not in man, and therefore waits not upon the sons of *Adam* (Micah 5:7). He is glad to hear of any hope, and how others have been succored and pulled out of the like distress, etc. but though he hath an ear open unto these and the like helps, yet the soul cannot rest in them, but must retire itself, and get alone, where it may think its full, and satisfy itself in thoughts of its own estate, and of the offers and promises of grace, which God hath made to such lost sinners: And whiles the soul is thus alone, with itself and with God, sometimes thinking of its own misery and sin, sometimes of the Lord's mercy now presented in such and such promises; sometimes calling to mind how others have found favor with God, notwithstanding their sins, sometimes thinking what should move the Lord thus to invite us, and call us unto him, and to give us these desires after him; why (thinks the soul) should the Lord do thus, if there were no hope that he would receive me? whiles I say, the soul being alone, is thus exercised in these thoughts, at length the fire kindles, so as the soul can now rest no longer, but a spirit of Faith being within, like fire in the bones, the heart hitherto having been as a wine-vessel, which hath had no vent, yet now the spirit within, compels him to open his lips, and to utter [47] before the Lord the meditations of his heart; And therefore

5. In the fifth place, the soul resolves now to go to the throne of Grace, suing for grace, proving whether the Lord will be gracious and merciful, to accept of a reconciliation; faith speaks within, as they did in Jonah 3:9, *Who can tell whether the Lord will return, etc.* and as Amos 5:15, *It may be the Lord may yet be merciful*; such an one *cannot* yet *say that he will*, yet knows not *but he may be gracious*, and therefore doth as those Lepers in 2 Kings 7:3, who knowing that they were sure to perish if they sat still, resolved to try what might befall them in going into the Camp of the *Aramites*; and as *Esther* who would try whether the King would hold out his golden Scepter towards her, yea or no;[48] so the poor sinner, knowing how it is with him, and thinking he must perish if he thus continue, and hearing also such gracious invitations, etc. thereupon resolves to go and seek the Lord begging grace and acceptance before him. Doth the Lord say, *Seek ye my face?* the heart answers[49] within, *Lord I will seek thy face*; Doth the Lord say, *Come*[50] *unto me?* the heart answereth, *Behold we come unto thee for thou art the Lord our God* (Jeremiah 3:22), and now the soul betakes itself unto God, sending up complaints against itself, with lamentations for its own sinful rebellions, accompanied with strong cries to heaven, with sighs and groans of Spirit which cannot

be expressed; it confesseth with grief and bitter mourning, all former iniquities, smites upon the thigh with repenting *Ephraim*,[51] lies down at God's footstool, putting its mouth in the dust,[52] acknowledging God's righteousness if he should condemn and cast off forever, and yet withal pleads for grace, that it may be accepted as one of his; It says unto God, *Lord, I have nothing to plead why thou mayst not condemn me; but if thou wilt receive me, thy mercy shall appear in me, thou*[53] *mayst show forth all thy goodness; take away therefore all mine iniquities, and receive me graciously* (Hosea 14:2).[54] It pleads God's promise, Lord, thou hast said thou wilt be gracious; Lord make good this word to the soul of thy servant, be my God, my merciful God, and make me thy servant; thus the soul lies at the throne of Grace and pleads for Grace.

6. As faith is thus earnest in suing to God for Grace and acceptance with him, so it is no less vigilant, and watchful in observing and taking notice what answer comes from the Lord, how he answers the desires we have presented before him. As the Prisoner at the Bar, not only cries for mercy, but marks every word which falls from the Judge's mouth, if anything may give him hope, and as *Benhadad's* servants lay at catch with the King of *Israel*, to see if they could take occasion by anything which fell from him, to plead for the life of *Benhadad*;[55] so doth the poor soul that is now pleading for life and grace, it watcheth narrowly to see if anything may come from God, any intimation of favor, any word of comfort that may tend to peace; thence it is that the Saints have so often called upon God for answer of their prayers; they thought it not enough to pray, but they would see how the Lord answered them (Psalm 102:1,2). Thus Psalm 51:8: *O let me hear joy and gladness,* etc. *David* did not only pray for mercy, but desires to hear from heaven a word spoken to his conscience, by which he might know he was accepted; though *David* was not in the beginning of that work we now speak of, yet the case is alike, he was now in his own sense as if he had been to begin anew, and thus in Psalm 85:8, *I will hear what the Lord will say, for he will speak peace unto his people,* etc.

7. As faith doth thus wait for an answer from God, so likewise according as the Lord doth either answer or not answer, so doth faith demean itself.

First, Sometimes he answers not, to our sense (I mean) and discerning; as we see in *David's* case; he felt himself as one forsaken, he[56] prayed unto God, but found no audience (Psalm 22). What doth faith in this case? it follows God still, and cries after him with more strength and earnestness, as resolving never to give over, till the Lord either save or destroy; if the Lord will destroy, yet the soul chooseth to die at God's foot, as *Joab* did at the horns of the Altar, when he was bidden to come forth from thence, to take his death in another place; Nay (saith *Joab*) but *I will die here*;[57] Here the humbled soul doth as that woman did in Matthew 15, she sues to Christ, but Christ seems to have no regard of her, gives her not one word, but she seeks still; still she cries after him, and though still repulsed, yet she comes a third time, and cries, *Lord help me*; and though still the Lord gives her another repulse, yet still she hangs upon him, and follows him for mercy, and would never give over till she had[58] gotten even what she desired. Even as Christ in his agony, when he saw deliverance came not, he prayed more earnestly (Luke 22:41), so doth the poor sinner in the time of his agony, when he is striving, as for life, and death; if help come not at first call, he prays again, and that more earnestly; faith will be urgent with God, with an humble importunity; and *the more slack* the Lord seems to be in answering, the *more instant* is faith in plying God with prayer. It will be wrastling with God, as *Jacob* did with the Angel;[59] it will not rest without a blessing, it will take no denial, but will crave still, as he did, *Bless me, even me also, send me not away without a blessing*; it resolves to wait, and look up, *until the Lord show mercy* (Psalm 123:2, Lamentations 3:49,50).

Secondly, Sometimes again the Lord doth answer, but yet he speaks but as out of the dark cloud, giving some little ease, but not speaking full peace; much like as he spake to the woman (John 8:11), *Go thy way and sin no more*, saith[60] Christ; he doth not say, go in peace, thy sin is forgiven thee (that had been a word of full comfort) but *go thy way and sin no more*; a middle kind of expression, neither assuring her that her sin was pardoned, nor yet putting her out of hope, but it might be forgiven. And hereby faith gets a little strength, and looks after the Lord with more hope, and begins to plead with God, as *Moses* did,[61] Lord *thou hast begun* to show grace unto thy servant; go on Lord to manifest in me all thy goodness; here faith takes a little hold on the Covenant, though with a feeble hand, as yet shaking and trembling for want of strength, and yet now it begins to follow the Lord with more encouragement, as finding that its former seeking hath not been wholly in vain.

Thirdly, Sometimes again the Lord speaks more fully and satisfactorily to the souls of his people; applying some promise of Grace to the conscience by his own spirit, letting the soul feel and taste the comfort of such a promise, more effectually than ever it could before; it hath often heard and thought on such a promise, but could never feel any peace in it, because it could never apply it to its own particular; but now being applied by the help of the Spirit, it finds and feels peace.

Here then the Lord doth not any longer hold the soul in suspense and doubting, by propounding unto it such *promises of hope* (as I may so call them). *It may be* ye shall be hid in the day of wrath (Zephaniah 2:3), but he speaks full peace; as Isaiah 41:10: *Fear not, for I am thy God; I will subdue your iniquities, and cast all your sins behind my back, and I will remember them against you no more; I have received a reconciliation* (Job 33), *Go in peace.* Here faith waxeth bold, and with a glad heart entertaineth the promise thus brought home unto it; the Apostle expresseth this with a word very significant, calling it *an embracing of the promise* (Hebrews 11:13), *embracing,* implies an affectionate receiving, with both arms opened, to show an heart enlarged to those that come unto us; and now the soul having thus embraced the promise, and the Lord Jesus Christ in the promise, and having him (like *Simeon*) in our arms, it lays him in the bosom, and having before gone forth to meet him, he being now come, it brings him into the chamber of the heart, there to rest, and abide forever; now the soul possesseth him as her own, rests in him, and is satisfied with him, lays itself down in a holy rest, after all its former troubles, praising God for his mercy as *Simeon* did when he had Christ in his arms,[62] and committing itself forever to that mercy and goodness which hath been thus revealed unto it.

And thus the poor soul which hath been at enmity with God, comes by little and little to touch the top of the golden Scepter, and to enter into a Covenant of peace with the high God; now the hand is given to the Lord; as *Hezekiah* spake (2 Chronicles 30). As God reacheth out to us the hand of Grace and of saving help; so do we give unto him the hand of faith, yielding up ourselves unto him, committing ourselves unto him to be kept by him unto salvation, according to his Covenant and promise.

And thus is this part of the Covenant made up betwixt God and us, and the soul now says within itself, I that was sometimes an enemy, he hath now reconciled unto himself; I that was in times past without God, without Christ, without promise, without Covenant, without hope, none of God's people, not under mercy; yet now I have God for my God, Christ is my peace, in him I have obtained mercy, and am now become one of God's people; the Covenant of his peace now belongs unto me, the Lord also is become my salvation; and here the soul rests, and is satisfied, as with marrow and fatness; saying as *Jacob, The Lord hath had mercy on me; therefore I have enough, I have all that my heart hath desired* (Genesis 33:11).

Thus we see how faith closeth with the first part of the Covenant, that God will be a God of mercy unto us, to bless us with blessings of peace, etc.

2.[63] Concerning the other part of it; wherein God offers himself unto us to be a God over us, to rule us and govern us in obedience to his will, faith works the soul to a closing with this also.

The converting sinner, having tasted the fruit of his own former ways, and finding how bitter and evil it is that he hath sinned, doth now desire to resign up himself to the Lord's government, being willing to deny his own will, and to take up the Lord's yoke, and to be subject thereunto; he now says no more, who is Lord over me (Psalm 12). He doth no longer look at himself as his own, to live to himself, after his own mind and will; but being weary of his own ways, and finding it sufficient (and too much) that he hath spent the time past in the lusts of the flesh, now he commits himself to the Lord's government, taking him to be a God over him; to rule and order him in all his ways: The Covenant which passeth betwixt God and us, is like that which passeth between a King and his people; the King promiseth to rule and govern in mercy and in righteousness; and they again promise to obey in loyalty and in faithfulness; faith sets up God upon his throne, and says; Let the Lord reign forever and ever, reign thou over me (O Lord), and lead me in the way which leads unto thee. And this doth faith work in us by these or the like means.

1.[64] Faith looks at the manner of God's invitation and call, when he invites us to come and enter into Covenant with him; he doth not offer himself to be a God to us to bless us, without being a God over us, to order and govern us, but links these two both together; *If we will have his blessing, his peace, we must be under his Dominion*: Look as in a Commonwealth or Kingdom, none hath the benefit of the Law, but those that subject themselves to the Law: none have the protection of authority, but those that obey it; so here; God doth not promise to pardon our sins, leaving us still at our own liberty to live as we list, but if he do at all make a Covenant with us, *he will be a God to us, as well to rule us, as to save us;* To say, live as ye will, sin as ye will, and yet you shall be saved, is the Devil's Covenant, not God's; and therefore it is that when the Lord calls us into a Covenant with himself, he bids us come out from among the wicked, separate yourselves, and touch no unclean thing saith the Lord (2 Corinthians 6:17), and in this way he promises to receive us, and to be a God unto us; How vile soever we have been before time, it hinders us not from entering into Covenant with God, but if we will now become his people, we must *henceforth* walk no more as we had wont to do; we must *henceforth* be separate from our uncleanness (Ephesians 4:17). Isaiah 1:verses 16,17,18:[65] *Come let us reason together, let us make an agreement, but withal wash you, make you clean, etc.* This is the Lord's manner of invitation, so that faith sees a necessity of submitting to God's authority, because it may not take hold of one part of the Covenant without the other: If we will have God to be our God to pardon us, and to bless us, we must have him a God over us to govern us after his own will.

2.[66] Faith opens the understanding, convincing us by arguments, how just, how equal and reasonable it is, that God should rule, and we obey; by faith we see the invisible things of God, that is, his eternal power and Godhead, which before we saw not; by faith we see him in his Excellency and Majesty, clothed with glory and honor, riding upon the Heavens, attended upon with thousand thousands of Angels ministering unto him: By faith we see him moderating the whole world by his wisdom and power (Psalm 103). We look at him as King of Kings, as Prince of all the Rulers of the Earth; Neither do we by faith thus see God, as he is in himself only,[67] but as he is to us, as having power in his hand either to save or destroy; so that there is no resisting; we know now that if *we fall upon that stone*,[68] by our rebellion, it will grind us to powder; now there is no more question made, who shall have the dominion, though in times past we had said, *this man shall not reign over us* (Luke 19), yet now it is our chief desire, that his Kingdom may come into us, and bear sway in us; Faith sets before us also the benefits and kindness of God towards us, and so persuades us by those mercies of God to give up ourselves as a sacrifice in humble obedience unto his will (Romans 12:1). Faith reasoneth in the heart, as *David* did, *I will praise thee, O Lord, with my whole heart; yea, I will glorify thy name forever, for great is thy mercy towards me, thou hast delivered my soul from the lowest grave* (Psalm 86:12,13). Faith makes us speak to God as the *Israelites* did to *Gideon*, when he had delivered them out of the hand of the *Midianites, Come* (say they unto him) *and*[69] *reign over us, both thou and thy son, for thou hast delivered us out of the hand of* Midian (Judges 8:22). *Now God is counted worthy of all honor and service* (Apocalypse 4:7 and 5:12,13).[70] Worthy to be exalted and glorified; thus faith urgeth it as a thing most reasonable, that God so glorious in himself, having power over us, to save or destroy, and when he might have destroyed us, yet hath saved us from so great a death, and prepared for us so great salvation, should be glorified by us, we submitting ourselves unto the obedience of his will.

3.[71] Faith makes us look at the Lord's government as a merciful government, bringing peace and blessing unto those that are under it; it looks at this King of *Israel* as a merciful King (1 Kings 20). It counts those subjects happy that are free of this Kingdom, and those servants happy that stand before this King (1 Kings 10). It makes the soul lament its bondage under other Lords; as in Isaiah 26:13: *Lord* (saith the Church there) *other Lords besides thee, have ruled over us*, but in thee is our only hope; having felt the misery of those former slaveries in which it hath been holden, having been in the Iron Furnace of *Egypt*, and sat by the waters of *Babel*, and wept there, having been under such cruel Lords, now they are weary of the yoke of the oppressor; and now they see[72] the blessing of the Lord's government, the Laws of God which were before counted as cords and bands, fitter for bondslaves than for freemen, are now esteemed holy, and just, and good (Romans 7). Faith believes that which the Lord hath said, that he hath given us his Commandments *for our good*, that it may go well with us forever (Deuteronomy 12).

4.[73] Faith reconciles the heart unto God, it doth not only believe that he is reconciled unto us, but also reconciles us unto God, whereas before we hated him, and would none of him, and thrust him away from us, as the *Israelites* did *Moses* (Acts 7:27). Yet now the soul having by faith believed his goodness towards us, is thereby reconciled unto him, it lays down all weapons of defiance, and submits in love. Like as a Traitor having found the gracious favor of his Prince, in pardoning his treacherous practices, his naughty heart which was before so full of treachery, is now overcome with this undeserved favor; so we also, having been in times past rebels against God, haters of him, enemies unto him, having had our minds set upon evil things (Colossians 1), are now overcome by his goodness towards us, our heart is turned to him, our hatred is turned into love, faith working love causing us to love him, for that great love wherewith he hath loved us in Christ (1 John 4). So that now we come to God, as they did to *David* (in 1 Chronicles 12:18), Thine are we, we are wholly thine: And thus faith slays the hatred, and pulls down the partition wall which was betwixt God and [74] us, reconciles the enmity, and makes of two one, working peace and love; so that now the believing soul desires nothing more than to be subject to his government; and grieves when it is hindered, that it cannot do that which he hath commanded: And thus the Covenant is made up in both parts of it; *offered* unto us by God, and *received* of us by faith (1 Kings 20:34).

SELECTION II

A Treatise of the Covenant of Grace

John Cotton

*A disputed portrait of John Cotton, later repainted. X-ray and infrared studies of this painting reveal considerable early repainting of the collar, hands, head, and inscriptions. It may well be a portrait of Cotton in 1649, at the age of about sixty-five, reworked in the 1680s to resemble his son-in-law Increase Mather (1639–1723) at a younger age. At the foot of the right-hand page of the Bible may be read, "He that hath an ear let him hear what the Spirit saith unto the Churches" (Rev. 3:22), a text that matches Cotton's interest in Revelations. The scroll reads, "Non est Mortale: quod Opto" ("I choose that which is not mortal"). See Louisa Dresser and Alan Burroughs, XVII*th *Century Painting in New England (Worcester, Mass.: Trustees of the Worcester Art Museum, 1935). Courtesy of the Connecticut Historical Society, Hartford, Connecticut.*

JOHN COTTON'S SERMON-SERIES *A Treatise of the Covenant of Grace*, apparently preached in the mid-1630s in Boston, remained unprinted for two decades. The history of its printed forms attests to the prevalence of note taking at sermons and to Cotton's desire to see his works accurately reported. When the series was first published in London (as *The Covenant of Grace*), three years after Cotton's death in 1652, its editor, Thomas Allen, was eager to assure the reader "that these are neither spurious Copies, nor surreptitiously put forth." According to Allen, his text consisted of notes taken during delivery of the sermons and later given to Cotton for "perusal and emendation." The notes, with "the interlinings of [Cotton's] own hand," were brought to London by "a Gentleman (one of the Church in *Boston* there)," who left them in Allen's care for publication.[1] In 1659, a second edition appeared under the title *A Treatise of the Covenant of Grace*; it differs from the 1655 edition in significantly but sporadically changing the phrasing and in adding new contents, which continue the argument to almost double its original printed length. The publisher's preface ascribes this change not to the hand of any other writer but to "the diversity of the Amanuenses, who did take the Notes of his Sermons, some writing the same more largely and exactly than others."[2] The 1655 edition, lacking so much of the announced material, most likely represents the preached sermons as noted by a transcriber; the notes were probably corrected by Cotton but through some accident, perhaps his death, were truncated near the middle and printed in that form. The 1659 edition, from which this selection is taken, probably collated the earlier edition with the notes—perhaps also reviewed by Cotton—of another transcriber.[3]

The sermons that comprise *A Treatise of the Covenant of Grace* date from the early years of Cotton's American ministry, quite possibly from 1635 and 1636.[4] Thomas Allen's preface to the 1655 edition certainly implies American delivery of the sermons, as do several passages in Cotton's text.[5] The sermons may well have figured in the evangelical success of Cotton's early ministry in America (1633), when through his preaching "Divers profane and notorious evil persons came and confessed their sins, and were comfortably received into the bosom of the church."[6] The more likely context, however, is slightly later, in the early stages of the Antinomian controversy of 1636 to 1638, when Cotton's colleagues began to raise questions of his orthodoxy (see above, Introduction, pt. iv). In these sermons, Cotton treats the points of controversy as unpleasant but necessary topics, neither avoiding nor exacerbating them. For example, on the question of the use of sanctification as evidence of conversion, he treads deliberately but delicately: "I would not speak, but that I might through the good hand of God, the better clear things, that we may not stumble in our expressions, nor in any office of brotherly love, in conference about the Covenant of Grace and Works."[7]

The biblical text of Cotton's sermon-series, like the series itself, considers the covenant of grace from a historical standpoint: "And [God] gave [Abraham] the covenant of circumcision" (Acts 7:8, Stephen's sermon to the council). In the Old Testament covenant to which this New Testament text refers, God offered a conditional agreement, of which Abraham willingly fulfilled the requirement—the external mark of circumcision. In the New Testament covenant, with which the text and the sermons are primarily concerned, God's gift of himself through Jesus Christ replaces human fulfillment of any condition: God's gift of salvation is absolute and he requires no such action in return.

In using the covenant with Abraham as the recurrent motif of his sermon on the new covenant, Cotton is employing a favorite practice of Puritan thought—typology. The need to see the Bible as one consistent record of God's word, combined with the equally strong need to emphasize the New Testament message of salvation, led theologians to view Old Testament events and persons as similitudes (types) of the realities of the Gospel (antitypes).[8] Like the biblical preacher Stephen, Cotton considers the Old Testament covenant typologically as the prophetic image of the new covenant, not fully equivalent but similar enough to illuminate the spiritual condition of the present-day Christian.[9] The ease with which Cotton passes between these two parallel sets of imagery—Old Testament and Gospel—accounts for much of the richness of his treatment of covenant theology.

Cotton's version of the covenant, while it shares much with other Puritan versions, is by no means identical. The theory of the new covenant, as Peter Bulkeley preached it, involved even modern followers of the Gospel in the fulfillment of a condition, albeit an internal, spiritual condition—as Bulkeley wrote, "The condition then of the Covenant of Grace is faith."[10] For Bulkeley, as for Thomas Hooker and Thomas Shepard, the promises of salvation inherent in the covenant were more likely to be accomplished if the elect first showed themselves ready for the grace of God. In Cotton's preaching, however, emphasis upon the illimitable power of God outweighed any need or inclination to preach the doctrine of preparation. Although he left his listeners free to anticipate, passively, the divine action of redemption, he asserts that God in fact fulfills both his own part and humanity's part of the covenant agreement. Cotton insisted upon the doctrine of God's free grace: that is, his theory of the covenant assumed that individual action in preparation is wholly unnecessary and that all action in the covenant—initiation, accomplishment, and preservation—comes from God.[11]

Cotton's formal statement of the doctrine of *A Treatise of the Covenant of Grace* particularly stresses by its syntax the unconditional action of God in salvation: "In the Covenant, these three things are implied, *Viz.* 1. That God gave himself to be a God unto *Abraham*, and his seed. 2. That God did receive *Abraham*, and his seed to be his people. 3. That God takes the *Lord Jesus Christ* to be the *Mediator*, and *Surety* of this Covenant." [12] *A Treatise of the Covenant of Grace* takes up these three branches of the doctrine, individually and in order, but gives by far the greatest emphasis to the first.[13] In this first section (comprising seven-eighths of the treatise), Cotton briefly treats the scriptural basis of the doctrine and then applies it in four uses, of which the fourth—a series of ten questions and answers—fills most of the section. It is certain from the length of this use that much of the purpose of this sermon-series must have been to anticipate and respond to opinions of an opposing group. When, for example, his imagined questioner asks "Whether we do receive the Lord Jesus Christ in an absolute or in a conditional Promise," Cotton, consistent with his doctrine of the freedom of God's grace, replies that no condition can bind the action of Christ.[14]

The extent of the question-and-answer method, unusual for a sermon-series, derives from Cotton's attempt to make a central point of doctrine as clear as possible. The free gift of God in the covenant is, he writes, "such an Argument as the strength and wisdom of men and angels cannot unfold: It is a Catechism-point, and by way of Catechism to be opened (as the Lord hath revealed it), I mean, plainly, and familiarly." [15] The final three "catechism" questions deal with the heart of the doctrine: how God in his three persons of Father, Son, and Holy Spirit gives himself "to be *a God* to *Abraham*, and his seed." The selection printed here, on God's gift of Jesus Christ, is the second of these questions.

Particularly in this selection, but throughout the series, Cotton's emphasis on God's active role and on his listeners' passive reception of salvation finds an eloquent expression. We recognize in the prose his excitement with the high subjects of salvation and redemption. His style is joyfully rhetorical, full of repetitions and parallelisms, imagined colloquies, exclamations and apostrophes. A remarkable similitude, for example, heightens his doctrine of the "Inhabitation" of the Spirit: when the Spirit dwells in us, "we are all one mystical body: and I cannot tell how better to compare it, than to a musical Instrument, wherein though there be many pipes, yet one blast of the bellows puts breath into them all; so that all of them at once break forth into a kind of melody, and give a pleasant sound to the ears of those that stand by; all of them do make but one Instrument, and one sound, and yet variety of music. So is this very case: look at all the living members of Christ, they are all compacted together, and set into one stock, and root; by which means it comes to pass, that though they be many thousands, yet they all make a melodious harmony in the ears of the Lord of Hosts." [16]

Although this selection lacks any such extended similitudes, its style, too, is highly figurative, almost matching the rich style of

Hooker. Cotton excitedly amplifies Christ's ransom of women and men "from a state of bondage, into Christian liberty." The imaginative, heightened style of this selection on the role of Jesus Christ in our redemption, preservation, and knowledge of God points to the centrality of the Son in Puritan theology.[17] The Christ of the Gospel underlies all Puritan messages of salvation but is especially central in this selection. For Cotton, the unmatchable sacrifice of Christ on the cross most clearly demonstrated the unilateral, unconditional action of God in the covenant. Indeed, one of the central concerns in his opposition to the preparationist preachers—Bulkeley, Hooker, and Shepard—was that their concentration on people's actions in the search for assurance skirted the central issue of Christian life—"the true object of faith, which is Christ."[18]

Acts 7:8: *And he gave him the Covenant of Circumcision.*[19]

[*Question 9.*] We now proceed unto the ninth Question, which is, How doth God the *Son* give himself unto *Abraham*, and to his seed, in an everlasting Covenant and union that shall never be dissolved?

[*Answer.*] In three acts or works about *Abraham* and his seed.

1. First, in giving Christ, God doth give himself; and therefore here is the *Son's* work, to come, and *take our nature upon him*: For the *Father* gave him for that end, and the *Son* came to fulfill the will of the Father; and that is the Son's work, even the true distinct work of Christ. It properly belongeth unto the *Son*, to be our actual Redeemer from all sin and misery.

2. As the Father draws us to the Son, and reveals the Son unto the soul; so doth the *Son* reveal the *Father* also: John 1:18, Matthew 11:27.

3. As the Father doth accept us in his Son, as justified by his righteousness, so the Son doth preserve us in this estate, even to his heavenly Kingdom. These therefore are the three works of the *Son* in the Covenant of Grace.

He *takes our nature* upon him for our redemption.

He *reveals* the Father to us.

He *preserveth* us *in the Father* and *in himself*. Let us speak something to each of these in particular.

1. For the first of these, That he *took our nature* upon him; the Apostle saith (Hebrews 2:14,15,[20] etc.), *For as much as the children are partakers of flesh and blood, he also himself took part of the same, that through death he might destroy him who had the power of death, that is the devil, and deliver them who through fear of death, were all their lifetime subject to bondage*, etc. Therefore it was truly

said (Isaiah 9:6), *unto us a Child is born, unto us a Son is given*, etc. He took our nature upon him, lived a miserable life, died a cursed death; this is the proper character, and work of the *Son*; and thus he is made an horn of salvation to us (Luke 1:69), and all this floweth from the everlasting *Covenant*, as also *Zachariah* Prophesied (Luke 1:72, 73), *To perform the mercies promised to our fathers, and to remember his holy covenant, the oath which he sware to our father Abraham: By him we have redemption through his blood* (Ephesians 1:7, Colossians 1:14), *He gave himself for us, that he might redeem us from all iniquity, and purify unto himself a peculiar people, zealous of good works* (Titus 2:14). This then is the first work of the Son, to *Redeem* us: And the very phrase of *Redemption* doth imply a double state of those that are redeemed, without which it cannot be understood, to wit,

The state $\left\{\begin{array}{c} \text{whence} \\ \text{and} \\ \text{whereunto} \end{array}\right\}$ they are redeemed,

Even *from* a state of *bondage, unto* Christian *liberty*; this is found in all redemption properly so called: It findeth us in *bondage*, and setteth us in a state of *liberty*; Hebrews 2:14,15: *He took our nature upon him, that he might deliver them, who through fear of death were all their lifetime made subject to bondage.* And this third thing also is implied (in the word Redemption) with both the former, namely, a certain *price* by which we are redeemed from bondage unto liberty. In a state of Bondage we were under the *Law* and curse of God, but *Christ hath redeemed us from the curse of the law* (Galatians 3:13): and now *sin shall no more have dominion over us, for we are not under the law* (Romans 6:14), that is, not under the *Covenant* of the Law, though we lie under the *Commandment* of it in Christ: we were sometime under the bondage of sin, under the guilt and strength of sin; but by Christ we have redemption, even the forgiveness of our sin: and as the *Law* was the strength of sin; so *sin* was the strength and sting of *death* (1 Corinthians 15:56),[21] but now, O *death where is thy sting! O grave, where is thy victory! the Lord hath delivered us from him that hath the power of death* (Colossians 2:15, Hebrews 2:14), and *from this evil world* (Galatians 1:4): and from *the wrath to*[22] *come* (1 Thessalonians 1:10), so then this was bondage we sometimes lay under, when the Law of God pressed heavily upon us the conscience of sin even unto death: both first, and second death; and both *Law*, and *sin*, and *death* delivered us unto the power of *Satan*, and held us under the wrath of God; the world turned to be our enemy in all the blessings and crosses of it: from all these bondages Christ hath redeemed us; and it is a marvelous work in the eyes of all that enjoy the benefit of it.

If you shall ask, what Ransom the Lord did pay, that we might be redeemed?

The answer is given, in 1 Timothy 2:5,6: *There is one Mediator between God and man, the Man Christ Jesus, who gave himself a ransom for all*, etc., so that he himself is the Ransom. I will not stand disputing whether he gave his *active*, or *passive obedience*, or both; The Text is large,[23] *He gave himself*, from the height of glory to become a mortal man, not sinful, but by imputation; so that from first to last he *gave himself*. Consider him therefore from his first taking our nature upon him, and all is but one ransom; for his very *active* obedience was *passive*, and his *passive* obedience was *active*; if he had not been active in his sufferings, his sufferings had not been satisfactory, therefore he willingly laid down his life; *No man taketh it from him, but he layeth it down of himself* (John 10:17,18), else had not his death been of any sweet smelling savor to the Lord: forced death is no acceptable sacrifice.

Again, on the other side; his *active* obedience was *passive*; he suffered himself to be closed in his Mother's womb, and when he was born he suffered himself to be laid in a manger: and although being God over all, blessed forever, he was subject to no Law, yet now he suffered himself to be obedient unto his Father: now for great Princes to live in other Dominions, to observe their Rules, and be guided by their Laws, it is a suffering. This did the Lord Jesus; for he had a special commandment to observe both *Law*, and *Gospel*; and in this the Divine Nature doth suffer as much, as for the Creator to become a creature, and to take upon him the terms of hardship which become a creature: It is no debasement unto Angels, nor unto Saints, to be obedient; but for the Creator to be obedient unto the Law of God given unto the creature, in this he greatly humbleth himself; when he saith, *Thus it behoveth us to fulfill all righteousness* (Matthew 3:15). And this is such kind of passion as hath all things tending to satisfaction in it. And by all this you may see, that from the first to the last the Lord Jesus is a *Ransom*; take him in his Cradle, and he is a Ransom; take him throughout all the course of his life, and he is *passive*, and in all his sufferings he is *active*: He went up and down doing good, and suffering evil all his life long; and thus he is a Ransom: but above all, whenas he came to wrestle with the wrath of his Father, he did therein exceed all the rest of his sufferings: It was much indeed for the Son of God to make himself a *servant*; but when he that is the Son of the eternal God, and in regard of his Godhead equal with the Father, shall now stand to wrestle with the unsupportable wrath of God, and to cry out, My soul is in an agony unto the very death, and through anguish thereof to sweat drops of blood; and though his heart as it were seems to recoil, so that *if it were possible he desires the cup might pass from him*, yet he is carried before *Pontius Pilate*, and is there condemned, and afterward suffereth the death of the *Cross*: this was the chiefest part of the ransom, which the Lord did intend to pay to the justice of his Father;

wherein he did also undergo the very pangs of *Hell* for our sins, and so gave himself a Ransom for us. And had not all this been, we should never have been redeemed from the terrors of the Law. Thus therefore did the Lord *give himself*, in *taking* our nature upon him, and giving himself unto a state of *bondage*, from a state of liberty, to redeem us unto liberty from a state of bondage under the curse of the *Law* of God, even unto liberty from *sin*, and *death*, and *Satan*, and this *World*, and from the *indignation* of the most High: A wonderful deliverance!

But as it is in all other liberties; so this *Christian liberty* doth stand in two things: First, As in *removing* some *bondage*, and *burdens*: Secondly, So it carrieth with it some such *privilege* and *enfranchisement* as whereby we[24] claim some liberties which others cannot reach unto: and those the Lord Jesus hath dearly paid for, by suffering his Father's wrath, which did so drink up his Spirits, that I believe he died not by the pains of his body, for he died before his time; but the wrath of God did swallow him up principally, though his bodily pains did help it forward. Now by this means we have *access unto the Lord, and into this grace wherein we stand* (Romans 5:2), and that with *boldness*, and *confidence* (Ephesians 3:12),[25] even *to enter with boldness into the holiest by the blood of Jesus* (Hebrews 10:19). Hereby we have *liberty* to call God *Father*, and to come unto him as to a *Father*, and to expect all *blessings* from him for this life, and for a better, both *wisdom*, *righteousness*, *sanctification*, and *redemption* from all miseries and dangers, even from death to life, even life eternal; besides all blessings of the Kingdom of grace here below: All *Church-privileges*, and *Commonwealth-privileges*, hath the Lord purchased for us by his blood: great and large are the liberties which the Lord hath purchased for us, that are recorded everywhere in Scripture. So that *if the Son shall make you free, then are you free indeed.*

2. Now for the *second work* of the *Son* in this everlasting Covenant. Presupposing the Lord God the Father to have drawn the soul unto the Son from all *confidence* in the *world*, and in his own *righteousness*, and in his own *returnings* unto God by believing through his *own power*, from *confidence* in his own *resolutions*, and his own *waiting upon Christ*; and from all *confidence* in *privileges*, and *power* of nature, and grace received; now it may be all this while the poor soul knoweth not who it is, that hath wrought all this work in him, and for him; and[26] it may be he is so far to seek in this, as that he knows not whether it be the Lord God the Father, or the work of some enemy to deceive him: though he all this while seeth his need of Christ, and hath none in heaven but him, none in earth in comparison of him, of the want of whom he is sensible; yet the soul knows not whether all this humiliation, which is wrought in him, come from the wrath or mercy of God, and whether God hath not in

all this, given him only a taste of the very torments of Hell, and the pledge of them, to his everlasting perdition.

Thus may the poor soul be afraid, notwithstanding all this gracious work wrought in him, above all the power of the creature: though the Lord hath not said much of it unto him, yet he hath done it; and[27] happy we that ever the Lord hath owned us so far.

Now here is the special work of the *Son*, he doth *bring us* back again to the *Father*, and *reveals* what the Father hath done unto us, even his rich grace that hath taken all this pains with us; for *as no man knows the Son, but the Father: so neither doth any man know the Father, but the Son, and he to whom the Son will reveal him* (Matthew 11:27). So that the Lord Jesus doth *enlighten* the soul, by the anointing of his blessed Spirit, to see what it is that the Lord hath done for him in mercy; which heretofore he thought was done in wrath: whence the soul begins to see the *Father's love*, even the goodness of a God in what hath passed upon him, far beyond what he could have asked, or thought for; And therefore now begins with some more hope, and liberty to call God *Father*: for from this work of the *Son*, there doth arise the two characters of a Son in the soul, both which are comprised in this one, that is *liberty*: and there is a double liberty wherein a son doth stand: 1. First,[28] He hath *ease* from all his doubtful *fears*, or at least from a great part of the burden of them; some refocilations,[29] some kind of quietness falleth upon the heart of a wearied sinner, whence the heart is eased beyond his thoughts; although as yet his comfort stands rather in expectation, than in actual fruition; as our Savior saith, *Come unto me all you that are weary, and heavy laden, and I will give you rest* (Matthew 11:28,29). He doth not promise *sudden rest*: He will give you *present ease*; but learn of me, for I am meek and lowly, and you *shall* find *rest* unto your souls. The Lord will give rest unto the souls of his people; at the present he gives them ease, and an expectation of much more plentiful fruition of rest and peace, which they have begun to taste of.

And how doth the Lord ease the soul in such a case, so as that they feel the burden a great deal lighter? How doth the *Son* quiet, and still, and refresh the soul? Is it by the sight of his own hungering and thirsting after righteousness?

What saith the Lord in such a case? Or how doth he satisfy the soul? He telleth us plainly where our satisfaction is (John 7:37,38, 39), *If any man thirst, let him come unto me and drink*: So that if a man thirst, how shall he satisfy himself in his thirsting? This is the main question in many a soul; May I not draw consolation out of this, that I do thirst after the Lord Jesus?

You shall find, that the Lord doth not bid me go satisfy myself by seeing my thirst: If a man shall say, I am exceeding thirsty, and I shall tell him that he is a man of a healthful constitution, because a man in a Frenzy[30] is thirsty, and knows it not; this will not satisfy his thirst.

How therefore comes the soul to be freed of his burdens? He thirsteth after Christ, and none of all the creatures can quench his thirst; therefore our Savior proclaims this in the last and great day of the Feast, when most of the Jews were present (for this Feast lasted eight days), *If any man be now athirst*, and not satisfied with all the Ordinances they had now enjoyed: he doth not send them back again, nor doth he bid them satisfy themselves with their own thirstings; neither doth he tell them that their blessedness lieth in that they do thirst (though there be a blessedness in it), but how then shall they be satisfied? *Let him come to me and drink.*

So that this is the *Christian Liberty*, which the Lord brings us unto, when he works in us unquenchable desires after Christ: if you would comfort a soul, and tell him you do thirst after Christ: and that you could not have done if Christ had not wrought it[31] in your soul; you say true, and there may be more in such a soul than he is aware of; yet Christ is not wont to leave the soul to quench his thirst with his thirst: but you will say, Is not hungering and thirsting a sign of health? For a surfeited body doth not hunger: true: yet the Lord doth not direct the soul to content himself with his own act; but, *Come unto me.* But will the Lord Jesus give him drink? He promiseth that he will; *Let him come to me, and drink*: And he saith moreover, *He that believeth on me, out of his belly shall flow rivers of water of life: this he spake of the Spirit, which they that believe on him should receive; for the Holy Ghost was not yet given, because that Jesus was not yet glorified*: so as that which now the *Son* doth, is not the proper characteristical work of the Spirit; but Jesus Christ doth come unto the soul, and comforts[32] it in some measure; and, which is a second degree of liberty, giveth some liberty of *hope*, that the Lord will at length be pleased to fill him with his blessed Spirit, which the Lord did more abundantly pour out upon the Disciples after his Resurrection: And there is yet a more abundant fulfilling of all, when he doth come unto the proper work of the Spirit; and therefore he distinguisheth his own work, from the work of the Spirit (John 14:16,17, 18, and 16:7,13),[33] he saith of himself, that *He will not leave them comfortless*; but he putteth this difference between his own work, and the work of the Spirit (John 16:25), *Hitherto I have spoken unto*[34] *you in parables; but the time comes, when I shall*[35] *show you plainly of the Father*; yet he had spoken much unto them, and told them that *he loved them*, and that *the Father loved them*; but all is but a kind of parable in[36] comparison of what the Lord will further reveal, when he doth more fully send forth his Spirit into their hearts. In the meanwhile himself setteth on[37] some word or other of his grace, whereby he gives the soul such a taste of himself (more than reprobates can have) as makes him thirst after more and more of Christ, until he be satisfied with the riches of the grace of God.

3. Thirdly, When the *Son* hath thus brought us unto the Father, and showed us his fatherly love toward us, as he saith (John 16:26, 27), *I say not, that I will pray the Father for you, for the Father himself loveth you.* Then doth he *keep* us in this estate: And (which is a farther work of the Son) for this purpose, he will *send* us his *holy Spirit*, as He told his Disciples (John 16:7), *It is expedient for you, that I go away: for if I go not away, the Comforter will not come unto you; but if I depart, I will send him unto you.* Thus as the *Father sent* the *Son*: so will the *Son* send the *Spirit*; and in the meanwhile he doth *preserve* us until the Spirit come; and then he preserveth us by his *Spirit*. Now sometimes he makes his people tarry longer, before he send the Spirit in this kind of dispensation (but we leave the times and seasons thereof, unto the free purpose of the grace of God) but I say, meanwhile the *Son* preserveth us; John 6:39: *This is the Father's will, that of all that he hath given me, I should lose nothing.* So John 17:12: *Those that thou gavest me I have kept, and none of them is lost.* He keeps us in a waiting frame of spirit, so that we cannot but thirst after him, and long for him, and mourn for the want of him; and then *a bruised reed shall he not break, and smoking flax shall he not quench, until he bring forth judgment unto victory* (Matthew 12:20). Thus hath the Lord Jesus promised to keep us, and this he doth perform,

1. Partly, by praying for us; Luke 22:31,32: Simon, Simon, *Satan hath desired to have you, that he may sift you as wheat; but I have prayed for thee that thy faith fail not*: so John 17:11,20,21,22,23, etc.: *Holy Father, keep through thy own Name, those whom thou hast given me, that they may be one, as we are*, etc., and this is the eternal efficacy of the *Son*, whereby every believing soul is kept until he do find fullness of accomplishment of his spiritual desires: and though we may be many ways wanting in prayer for ourselves, yet he will give us his Spirit to pray within us with sighs and groans that cannot be expressed.

2. And as he will keep us by his prayer: so secondly, by his *ruling Providence*; for *all power is given unto him, both in heaven, and in earth* (Matthew 28:18), and this power he doth employ to preserve his servants from all the delusions of the sons of men. The Prophet *Ezekiel* complains of some, that thrust away, and shoulder out the people of God (Ezekiel 34:21,22, etc.), but, saith the Lord, *I will set up one shepherd over them, and he shall feed them, even my servant* David; verses 23 and 25: *They shall dwell safely in the wilderness, and sleep in the woods.* None of all the delusions of Antichrist, none of all the power of Tyrants, not all the flattering world, nor all the persecuting world shall be able to shoulder off the Saints of God from

him; 2 Timothy 1:12: *I am persuaded that he is able to keep that which I have committed to him against that day*: and the Lord Jesus engageth both his own power, and his Father's power for this end; John 10:28,29: *I give unto them eternal life, and they shall never perish, neither shall they pluck them out of my hand: my Father, which gave me me, is greater than all, and no man is able to pluck them out of my Father's hand.* Thus have you seen how *Jesus Christ* gives himself unto *Abraham*, and to his seed, to become one with us, to lead a miserable life, and die an accursed death, thereby to redeem us from all our enemies unto a state of *liberty*, by an invaluable price, even by himself. And having thus had the *Father* drawing us unto Christ (though the Father said little unto the soul who had been about him all this while, and so leaves the soul in no small distress), as the *Father's* work is *Power*, so the *Son's* work is *Liberty*, and he revealeth to us our redemption; and reveals it so, that the soul is set in an earnest longing after Christ (in whom there is a way to the Father), and a great mourning after him, hungering for him; so that nothing in heaven nor earth can satisfy him: in which case, the Lord doth give such strength and constancy unto the soul, in looking towards Christ, as encourageth him to expect refreshing in the end; though at present he looks at all that he hath attained as a parable in comparison of what he would further enjoy in communion with Jesus Christ: but it often befalls the servants of God, as it did the Disciples of Christ; they were put unto new demurs, and doubtings: *We thought* (say they) *it had been he that should have restored the Kingdom to Israel* (Luke 24:21; these were *Simon*, and *Cleophas*), if it had not been He, where was the comfort and blessed hope of rest, which they looked for in Jesus Christ; we thought it had been *he*; a sign it was a demur, and dispute in them, whether it was God's grace in them, or Christ that had been with them, yea, or no: whilst they are at this debate in themselves, *Jesus* himself comes unto them, and reproves them for their unbelief, and chargeth them to tarry at *Jerusalem*, and there *to wait for the promise of the Father.* And thus doth the Lord Jesus teach us to *know* the *Father*, and reveals him to us by strengthening us unto all such holy duties as he calleth us unto: and though we be many times afraid to pray, to hear, to come to Christian conference;[38] yet the Lord will not suffer us to refrain, but we must pray, and confer, and hear; and when we have used all, he teacheth us to know, that it is not in all these, as of themselves, to work anything in us; nor doth he suffer us to content ourselves in anything wrought in us, but causeth us to thirst after more of himself in every Ordinance,[39] until the *Spirit* comes in a plentiful measure, according to all the latitude of our desires after Christ Jesus.

[*Use 1.*] Now for the Use of this, in the first place, If so be the work of the *Son* be such a work of redemption, then certainly our

state is a state of *bondage* before we be thus redeemed; yea, it is
such a state of bondage, as wherein we lie bound under God's *Law*,
and under *sin*, under God's *wrath* and *curse*; under the *Devil* and
death, and under the power of this *world*, and all these enemies have
power over us, to carry us captive unto sin and misery: so that great
is the misery we lie under, if we knew our misery; few know it, but
are ready to say, with those (John 8:33), *We were never in bondage
to any*: oh poor hearts! then were you never redeemed to this very
day: if thou never yet knewest thy *bondage*, thou never yet knewest
thy *Redeemer*; the Lord will never so dishonor his own work, as to
pay so great a price to work so great redemption, for those that never
knew what it meant: nay, first he will teach them their *bondage*
(verse 34), *He that committeth sin is the servant of sin; therefore
if the Son make us free, we shall be free indeed*; but otherwise we
cannot be free.

[*Use* 2.] Secondly, It may teach all those that are under bondage,
where your *liberty* and *hope*, and spiritual *redemption* lie: Isaiah
45:22: *Look unto me, and be you saved, all the ends of the earth*:
look unto him.

Objection. But may I not look at such good desires, and hungerings and thirstings, and mournings after Christ, as are in me, to
satisfy myself with them?

Answer. Alas, you may look long, and it may be much ado to
kindle a spark of comfort; it[40] may be you may get out a spark, but
then it is but a sparkling light, neither will the Lord suffer his servants to fasten the satisfaction of their souls there: shall a man that
is hungry look to his hungering and thirsting? will that satisfy him?
It is indeed a sign of health, but it will not satisfy him: so neither
will spiritual hungering and thirsting: therefore he saith, *Come unto
me*, if you mean *to find rest*: it is not a man's weariness that doth
set his bones at rest; but, *Come unto me, all you that are weary and
heavy laden* (Matthew 11:28), there hath he laid up our peace; in
coming to him we shall find ease, even a certain secret refocilation
at least, that will strengthen us to bear temptation; so as that you
may see the Father's love, and you may also see your own hungerings
and thirstings; for unto such the Lord calleth us, and that puts a
great deal of difference between a great deal of common work, and
such as is wrought by God's efficacious drawing of us home to Jesus
Christ. Take you an hypocrite, and if he begin to mourn for Christ,
and the like, he satisfieth himself in these things; but is this the way
of the working of God's almighty power, to bring men unto something that is in themselves? Is it not his effectual calling of us unto
Christ? doth not Christ say, *If any man thirst, let him come to me
and drink*? Otherwise all is but unprofitable work, until you *come*
unto Christ; so far as Christ is there, so far there is life; if we be
drawn unto him, that as he beginneth the work, so he is the end of

it in us; and the soul cannot rest but in cleaving unto him, then is there[41] something more than flesh and blood hath revealed. So that this is the way that God calleth his servants to walk in, namely, to *look* unto Christ to *turn unto this stronghold* (Zechariah 9:12), *By his blood he hath delivered his prisoners out of the pit, wherein there is no water*: our strength lieth not in our own hungering and thirsting, and poverty, though there be truth in these; and everlasting truth, by reason of the Spirit that wrought them, and the blood that bought them; yet your stronghold is not in them, but in the rock of Israel; he is the horn of salvation to his people: so that I would advise every poor soul, in whom is wrought any mourning after Christ, through sense of your need of him, make the Lord Jesus your stronghold. And this is the true work, and way of the *Son* of God to bring you to the Father; and the more you find the Lord Jesus, the more you shall discern the gifts that are given unto you, and the comfort and power of them: not that I deny that Jesus Christ doth open unto the soul, what he hath done for him; John 6:69: *We believe and are sure that thou art Christ, the Son of the living God*; so John 16:30; but he doth not show them for this end, that you should satisfy yourselves in them, but still come unto him: what though you have many gracious promises that promise many future consolations? it is, that you should seek unto the Lord, in whom they are laid up; and unto the Father of Jesus Christ, that promised them, in whose hand it is to make them all good unto us: thus in all this doth the Lord train up his servants unto an heavenly and Christian frame; and if the soul should rest in any work he doth, or gift he hath received; it is a strong jealousy[42] the work is not sound: for if it be of the grace of God, and in truth, it will still lead the soul to look up unto Christ; and the soul cannot quench his thirst in it, but comes to the Father, and earnestly beggeth, that out of his Fatherly love he would give him Jesus Christ: this is the spirit and way of a true-hearted Christian.

[*Use* 3.] Thirdly, This may teach Christians, that are in such a way as this, to hold on in that way: for truly it is a way of comfort through the grace of God; Isaiah 43:1: *Fear not, O Israel, for I have redeemed thee*; none of the redeemed of God need to fear; Luke 1:74: *We are delivered, that we might serve him without fear*: It is in the Lord Jesus that the Apostle doth so triumph; Romans 8:31, etc.: *Who can be against us? who shall lay anything to the charge of God's Elect? who is he that condemneth? it is Christ that died*, etc., and hereupon he triumpheth, saying, *Who shall separate us from the love of God?* etc., and though we may say, That he[43] was grown to a greater measure of strength than we now speak of; yet this is the work of all the *Israel* of God, to hope in the Lord, *in whom is plenteous redemption* (Psalm 130:7).

[*Use* 4.] Fourthly, This may serve to teach us to wait upon the

Lord, for this his plenteous redemption; and to bless his name for it when we find it: Psalm 103:4: *Bless the Lord O my soul, who redeemeth thy life from destruction*, etc. Let us learn to serve him with thankfulness, and to grow up therein; for this is the great redemption, wherewith the Lord hath redeemed us to himself: he that hath thus redeemed us, will still redeem and deliver us (2 Corinthians 1:10), he that hath done this, will not leave us, until he hath finished all his thoughts of peace towards us.

[*Use 5.*] In the Fifth and last place, let it exhort us to stand fast in all our Christian liberties: they cost dear; and we are redeemed from the *Covenant* and *curse* of the *Law* of God (from the *Laws* of men much more, that are not according to God); be[44] not therefore servants to lusts and passions, to the world and to the Devil: let us tread the world under foot; seeing God hath redeemed us, let us walk as his redeemed ones, redeemed from all errors of mind and judgment; *standing fast in all that liberty, wherewith Christ hath made us free* (Galatians 5:1), and *be not again entangled with the yoke of bondage*: it was a bondage that we were in before, and a bondage greater than either we or our fathers were able to bear; let us therefore stand fast in our liberty.

SELECTION III

The Sound Believer

Thomas Shepard

The first page of a sermon manuscript in the handwriting of Thomas Shepard, about 3½" by 5½". The collection from which this page is taken—Houghton bMS Am 1671(2)—contains the preaching notes for fifty-two sermons dated 1638 to 1640. The text (Heb. 11:34) appears at the top of the leaf, and the doctrine is beneath it: "That the prosperous success of the wars of the church against the armies of aliens is wrought and brought about By faith." By permission of the Houghton Library, Harvard University.

SHEPARD IN HIS AUTOBIOGRAPHY explains that the Lord revived him
from a sickness during his first years in America and "took pleasure
in me to bless my labors that I was not altogether useless nor fruit-
less."[1] The fruit of those labors was the publication of *The Sound
Believer. Or, a Treatise of Evangelical Conversion. Discovering the
Work of Christ's Spirit, in Reconciling of a Sinner to God* (1645),
treating the last three of nine "divine principles" that he had begun
in Yorkshire. The first six in that series were printed without his consent under the title of *The Sincere Convert, Discovering the Paucity
of True Believers; And the Great Difficulty of Saving Conversion*
(1640). Dissatisfied because *The Sincere Convert* "came out altered
from what was first written,"[2] Shepard nonetheless went on to complete the original design with the publication of *The Sound Believer*:
"the other three desired, I finished (the Lord helping) those at Cambridge and so sent them to England where they also are printed."[3] As
editor of the first edition, William Greenhill, a Nonconformist minister in England, prefaced it with a letter from the author in America,
attesting to the "strugglings I have had about publishing these
Notes." In the letter, Shepard cites the persuasions "both of friends
and strangers," the apparent effectiveness of the earlier volume
despite its shoddy publication, and—reflecting on the likelihood of
his early death and the certainty of his separation from friends in
England—his desire to "leave some part of God's precious truth on
record." Shepard left the details of editing and, indeed, the decision
to publish completely in Greenhill's hands. The subsequent popularity
of *The Sound Believer* (ten new editions in the hundred years after
1645) validated Greenhill's choice not to "bury it, and put it to perpetual silence."[4]

In *The Sincere Convert*, Shepard treats these six "choice and divine
principles": God exists in glory, God made humanity in a blessed
estate, men and women are miserable from their Fall, Jesus Christ
is the only redeemer, only with great difficulty are a few saved, and
people occasion their own perdition. The sermons so fully emphasize
the countless ways one frustrates one's own salvation that the last
two principles take up half the volume. *The Sound Believer* opens
with a summary of the role of Jesus Christ as Savior and a brief review of chapter 6 of *The Sincere Convert*, the four ways people ruin
themselves. Shepard numerically balances these in the first of the
three long chapters of *The Sound Believer* by an explanation of the
"fourfold act of Christ's power whereby he rescues and delivers all
his out of their miserable estate": "The first act or stroke is *Conviction of sin*. The second is *Compunction for sin*. The third is *Humiliation or self-abasement*. The fourth is *Faith*."[5] The second chapter, or
the eighth in the series of nine principles, concerns the "happy condition" converts enjoy as soon as they believe in Jesus Christ. "Six
privileges or benefits" of conversion—justification, reconciliation,

adoption, sanctification, audience for prayer, and glorification—are explained in loose sermonic form, proceeding from definition of the doctrinal term to exhortation. Chapter 3 argues that the saved are bound to live the "life of love" by "the rule of the moral law"—that portion of the Old Testament that relates to moral principles, especially the Ten Commandments.

Adherence to the Law particularly concerned Shepard because of the Antinomian conflict. He carefully explains, as he was to do often to refute the accusations of those of the Hutchinsonian persuasion, that he was not preaching a gospel of good works:

> 'Tis true indeed, obedience to the Law is not required of us now as it was of *Adam*; it was required of him as a condition antecedent to life, but of those that be in Christ it is required only as a duty consequent to life, or as a rule of life, that seeing he hath purchased our lives in redemption, and actually given us life in vocation and sanctification, we should now live unto him, in all thankful and fruitful obedience, according to his will revealed in the moral Law. 'Tis a vain thing to imagine that our obedience is to have no other rule but the Spirit, without any attendance to the Law.[6]

The section on conviction, like much of *The Sincere Convert* and the rest of *The Sound Believer*, mingles explication and exhortation instead of developing by the standard method from textual opening to uses. Although no one biblical passage principally instigates and establishes the necessity of conviction, at every turn of the analysis abundant biblical texts support the points Shepard develops. The final ten pages of the section, omitted here, include "a word of application" to ministers to preach to "this secure world" about conviction. The section concludes by advising those "that stand it out against all means of conviction" to examine their sins, judging them by God's "rule," and to take every conviction seriously, blessing God for bringing it to them: "Oh it is infinite love that he hath called thee aside and dealt plainly and secretly with thee, and will you not be thankful for this? The Lord might have left thee in thy brutish estate, and never made known thy latter end; never have told thee of thy sin or flood before it comes."[7] Curious as this gratitude may seem, it parallels the thankfulness for sin and even the Fall itself throughout Shepard's preaching; these are necessary stages for humanity's greatest joy—salvation.

The preparation for that salvation is the concern of the first three sections of the first chapter, dealing with conviction, compunction, and humiliation—those occurrences in the soul prior to conversion. Although throughout the chapter Shepard carefully describes the work as the Savior's action, rather than the individual's, Shepard, like Hooker, stresses the responsive duties of the soul in this phase of regeneration. He argues for the "renewing of the work of conversion" and thus for the importance of continually instructing saint as well as sinner about preparation. He emphasizes the experiential quality of conviction, the first stage of preparation. He preaches not only an abstract knowledge of his concept but also an active response to the reality which underlies it. From the general discontent of the questioning soul, he moves quickly to the specific response of the sinner—the recognition of a particular sin. The soul must move, however, beyond merely intellectual knowledge. Conviction occurs when the soul, guided by the powers of the Spirit, realizes the full consequences of sin—that it is an assault against God. To believe in God's power of salvation, and specifically in his power of conviction, is to believe in the reality of God: "then God comes in and appears immediately to the soul in his greatness and glory." Beginning with the simple, intellectual experience of recognizing a particular sin, Shepard shows how the soul moves to a state of belief beyond reason and discourse.

Like the other great preacher of preparation, Thomas Hooker, Shepard subdivides the work of preparation into distinct stages, cites the Law as a means of preparing the heart for conversion, and stresses the need for particular sins to be identified. The insistence in the selection on the elects' having first to understand their sin before they can grieve for it typifies the psychology commonly undergirding both the order of preaching and conversion. The selection further typifies this body of sermon literature in defining by means of the image of light the distinctive way that the saint understands.

Although this passage from *The Sound Believer* closely resembles many other sermons on conversion, it also exemplifies Shepard's distinctive strengths as a preacher. He not only structures complex arguments with architectural precision, but he also moves with natural ease into rhetorical flourishes: the brief but agonizing images of hell, the soliloquies of the distressed soul or the colloquies of sinner with saint or Lord, and the imagery of extreme contrasts intensifying his exhortations.

Hosea 13:9: *Oh Israel, thou hast destroyed thyself, but in me is thy help.*

SECTION II. *First[8] Act of Christ's power, which is Conviction[9] of sin.*

Now for the more distinct explication of this,[10] I shall open to you these 4 things.

1. I shall prove that the Lord Christ by his Spirit begins the actual deliverance of his elect here.[11]

2. What is that sin the Lord convinceth the soul thus first of.[12]

3. How the Lord doth it.[13]

4. What measure and degree of conviction he works thus in all his.[14]

1. For the first, it is said (John 16:8,9), that the first thing that the *Spirit* doth when he comes to make the Apostles' Ministry effectual is this, it shall *reprove*, or *convince the world of sin*; it doth not first work faith, but convinceth them that they have no faith (as in verse 9), and consequently under the guilt and dominion of their sin; and after this, he *convinceth of righteousness*, which faith apprehends (verse 10). It is true that the word *conviction* here, is of a large extent, and includes compunction and humiliation for sin, yet our Savior wraps them up in this word; because conviction is the first, and therefore the chief in order here: the[15] Lord not[16] speaking now of ineffectual, but effectual and thorough conviction expressed in deep sorrow and humiliation. Now the Text saith, the Lord begins thus not with some one or two, but with the *world* of God's elect, who are to be called home by the Ministry of the word; which our Savior speaks (as any may see who consider[17] the scope) purposely to comfort the hearts of his Disciples, that their Ministry shall be thus effectual to the world of Jews and Gentiles; and therefore cannot speak of such conviction as serves only for to leave men without excuse for greater condemnation (as some understand the place); for that is a poor ground of consolation to their sad hearts. Secondly, I shall hereafter prove that there can be no faith without sense of sin and misery, and now there can be no sense of sin without a precedent sight or conviction of sin; no man can feel sin, unless he doth first see it; what the eye sees[18] not, the heart rues not. Let the greatest evil befall a man, suppose the burning of his house, the death of his children, if he doth not first know, see, and hear of it, he will never take it to heart, it will never trouble him; so let a poor sinner lie under the greatest guilt, the sorest wrath of God, it will never trouble him until he sees it and be convinced of it; Acts 2:37: *When they heard this, they were pricked*; but first they heard it and saw their sin, before their hearts were wounded for it; Genesis 3:7: they first *saw*[19] *their nakedness* before they were *ashamed* of it. Thirdly, the main end of the law is to drive us to Christ; Romans 10:4: if *Christ* be the *end of the law*, then the law is the means subservient to that end, and that not *to some*, but *to all that believe*, now the law though it drive[20] to Christ by condemnation, yet in order it begins with accusation. It first accuseth, and so convinceth of sin (Romans 3:20), and then condemneth: it's folly and injustice for a Judge to condemn and bring a sinner out to his execution[21] before accusation and conviction; and is it wisdom[22] or justice in the Lord or[23] his law

to do otherwise? and therefore the Spirit in making use of the law for this end first convinceth as it first accuseth, and lays our sins to our charge. Lastly, look as Satan when he binds up a sinner in his sin, he first keeps him (if possible) from the very sight and knowledge of it; because so long as they see it not, this ignorance is the cause of all their woe; why they feel it not, why they desire not to come out of it; the Lord Jesus (who came to untie the knots of Satan, 1 John 3:8) begins here, and first convinceth his, and makes them see their sin; that so they may feel it, and come to him for deliverance out of it. Oh consider this all you that dream out your time in minding only things before your feet, never thinking on the evils of your own hearts; you that heed not, you that will not see your sins, nor[24] so much as ask this question, What have I done? what do I do? how do I live? what will become of me? what will be the end of these my foolish courses? I tell you, if ever the Lord save you, he will make you see what now you cannot, what now you will not,[25] he will not only make you to confess you are sinners, but he will convince you of sin, this shall be the first thing the Lord will[26] do with thee.

[*Question.*] But you will say, what is that sin which the Lord first convinceth of? which is the second thing to be opened.

[*Answer.*] I answer in[27] these three Conclusions.

[*Conclusion*[28] 1.] The Lord Jesus by his Spirit doth not only convince the soul in general, that it is a sinner and sinful; but the Lord brings in a convicting evidence of the particulars; the first is learnt more by tradition (in these days) by the[29] report and acknowledgment of every man, rather than by any special act of[30] conviction of the spirit of Christ; for what man is there almost but lies under this confession, that he is a sinner? the best say they are sinners; *and if we say we have no sin we deceive ourselves*,[31] and *I know I am a sinner*; but that which the Spirit principally convinceth of, is some sin or sins in particular: the Spirit doth not arrest men for offenses in general, but opens the writ, and shows the particular cause, the particular sins; Romans 3:9: *we have proved*, saith the Apostle, *that Jews and Gentiles are under sin*, but how doth the Apostle (being now the instrument of the Spirit in this work of conviction) convince[32] them of this? mark his method (verse 10,11,12,13,14,15,16, 17,18),[33] wherein you[34] shall see it is[35] done by enumeration of particulars: sins of their natures, *there is none righteous*; sins of their minds, *none understandeth*; sins in their wills and affections,[36] *none seek after God*; sins in their lives, *all gone out of the way*; sins of omission of good duties, *there is none that doth good*; their *throats, tongues, lips, are Sepulchers, deceitful, poisonful*; their *mouths full of cursing*, their *feet swift to shed blood*, etc. And this is the state of you Jews (verse 19),[37] as well as of the Gentiles; *that all flesh may stand convinced as guilty before God.* [*Question.*][38] If it be here demanded, What are those[39] particular sins which the Lord convinceth men of? [*Answer.*] I answer, in variety of men there is much variety of special sins, as there is of dispositions, tempers, and temptations; and therefore the Lord doth not convince one man at first of the same sins of which he doth another man, yet this we may safely say, usually (though not alway) the Lord begins with the remembrance and consideration of some one great, if not a man's special and most beloved sin; and thereby the spirit discovers gradually all the rest: that arrow which woundeth the heart of Christ most, the Lord makes it fall first upon the head of the sinner that did shoot it against heaven, and convinceth, and as it were hits him first with that: How did the Spirit convince those 3000, those patterns of God's converting grace (Acts 2:37)? did not the Lord begin with them for one principal sin, *viz.* their murder and contempt of Christ by imbruing their hands in his blood? there is no question but now they remembered other sinful practices, but this was the *Imprimis*,[40] which is[41] ever accompanied with many other *Items* which are then read in God's bill of reckonings where the first is set down: *Israel would have a King* (1 Samuel 8:19), *Samuel* for a time could not convince them of their sin, herein, what doth the Lord do? surely he will convince them of sin before he leaves them, and this he doth[42] by such a terrible thunder as made all their[43] hearts ache; and how is it now? what sin do they now see? they first see the greatness of that particular sin, but this came not to mind alone, but they cried out (1 Samuel 12:19), *We have added unto all our evils this, in asking to ourselves a King.* Look upon the woman of *Samaria* (John 4), the Lord Christ indeed spake first unto her about himself the substance of the Gospel, about the worth of this water of life; but what good did she get until the Lord began to convince her of sin, and how doth he that? he tells her of her secret whoredom she lived in, *the man that now she had*[44] *was not her husband*; and upon the discovery of this, she saw many more sins; and hence (verse 29) she cries out, *Come see the man that hath*[45] *told me all that ever I did in my life.* And thus the Lord deals at this day; the Minister preacheth against one sin, it may be whoredom, ignorance, contempt of the Gospel, neglect of secret duties, lying, Sabbath-breaking, etc. This is thy case, saith the Spirit unto the soul, remember the time, the place, the persons with whom you lived[46] in this sinful condition; and now a man begins to go alone, and to think of all his former courses, how exceeding evil they have been; it may be the Lord brings upon a man a sore affliction, and when he is in chains crying out of that, the Lord saith to him as to those (Jeremiah 30:15), *Why criest thou for thy affliction? for the multitude of thine iniquities I have done this*; it may be the Lord sometimes strikes a man's companion in sin dead, by some fearful judgment: and then that particular sin comes to mind, and the Lord reveals it, armed with multitudes of many other sins; the causes of it, the fruits and effects of it; as a[47] father whips his[48] child upon occasion of one special fault, but then tells him of many more which he winked at before this, and saith,[49] Now sirrah remember such a time, such a froward[50] fit, such undutiful behavior, such a reviling word you spake, such a time I called, and you ran away and would not hear me; and you thought I liked well enough of these ways, but now know that I will not pass them by, etc. Thus the Lord deals with his; and hence it is many times, that the elect of God civilly brought up, do hereupon think well of themselves, and so remain long unconvinced of their woeful estates, the Lord suffers them to fall into some foul, secret, or open sin; and by this the Lord takes special occasion of working conviction and sorrow for sin, the Lord hereby[51] makes them hang down the head and cry *unclean*, *unclean*; *Paul* was civilly educated, he turned at last a hot persecutor, oppressor, blasphemer; the Lord first convinced him of his persecution and cried out from heaven to him, *Paul, Paul, why persecutest thou me?*[52] this struck him to the heart, and then *sin revived* (Romans 7:9), many secret sins of his heart were discovered, which I take to begin and continue in special in those three days (Acts 9:9)[53] wherein he was blind and did (through sight of sin and sorrow of heart) neither eat nor drink. As a man that hath the plague not knowing the disease, he hopes to live; but when he sees the spots and tokens of death upon his wrist, now he cries out, because convinced that the plague of the Lord is upon him; so when men see some one or more special sins break out, now they are convinced of their lamentable condition: yet it is not alway (though usually thus), for some men the Lord may first convince of sin by showing them the sinfulness of their own hearts and ways; the Lord may let a man see his blindness, his extreme hardness of heart, his weakness, his willfulness, his heartlessness; he cannot pray, or look up to God, and this may first convince him; or that[54] all that he doth is sinful, being out of Christ: the Lord may suddenly let him see the deceits of his own heart, and the secret sinful practices of his life; as if some had told the Minister, or as if[55] he spake to none but him; that he is forced to fall down being thus convinced, and to confess, *God is in this man* (1 Corinthians 14:25): *Nicodemus* may first see and be convinced of the want of regeneration, and thereby feel his need of Christ;[56] the Lord may set a man upon the consideration of all his life past, how wickedly it hath been spent; and so not[57] one, but a multitude of iniquities compass him about: a man may see the godly examples of his parents, or other godly Christians in the family or town where he dwells, and by this be convinced; that if their state and way be good, his own (so far unlike it) must needs be stark naught: the Lord ever convinceth the soul of sins in particular, but he doth not alway convince one man of the same particular sins at first as he doth another; whether the Lord convinceth all the elect at

first of the sin of their nature, and shows[58] them their original sin
in and about this first stroke of conviction, I doubt not of it; *Paul*
would have been alive, and a proud Pharisee still, if the Lord had
not let him by the law see this sin (Romans 7:9), and so would all
men in the world, if this should not be revealed first or last, in a
lesser or greater measure, under a distinct or more indistinct notion:
and hence arise those confessions of the Saints, I never thought I
had[59] had such a vile heart; if all the world had told me, I could not
have believed them; but that the Lord hath made me feel it, and see
it at last; was there ever such a sinner (at least in heart, which is
continually opposing of him) whom the Lord at any time received
to mercy, as I am?

[*Conclusion* 2.][60] The Lord Jesus by his Spirit doth not only convince the soul of its sin in particular, but also of the evil, even the
exceeding great evil of those particular sins. The Lord Jesus doth not
only convince of the evil *sin*,[61] but of the great evil *of sin*.[62] Oh thou
wretch, saith the Spirit (as the Lord to *Cain*, Genesis 4:10), what
hast thou done, whose sins cry to heaven, who hast thus long lived
without[63] God, and done this infinite wrong to an infinite God, for
which thou canst never make him amends? That[64] God who could
have long since cut thee off in the midst of thy sins and wickedness,
and crushed[65] thee like a moth, and sent thee down to those eternal
flames where thou now seest some better than thyself mourning day
and night, but yet hath spared thee out of his mere pity to thee, That
God hast thou resisted and forsaken all thy lifetime; and therefore
now see and consider what an evil and bitter thing it is thus to live
as thou hast done (Jeremiah 2:19). Look as it is in the ways of holiness, many a man void of the Spirit may see and know them in the
literal expressions of them, but cannot see the glory of them but by
the Spirit, and hence it is he doth not esteem and prize them and the
knowledge of them above gold; So in the ways of unholiness, many
a man void of the spirit of conviction of sin, may and doth see many
particular sins and confess them, but he doth not, cannot see the
exceeding evil of them, and thence it is though he doth see them,
yet he doth not much dislike them, because he sees no great[66] hurt
or evil in them, but makes a light matter of them; and therefore when
the Spirit comes, it lets him see and stand convinced of the exceeding
greatness of the evil that is in them (John 16:[67]8,9). In the time of
affliction (which is usually the time of conviction of a wild unruly
sinner) *he shows them their transgressions*, but how? *that they have
exceeded*,[68] that they have been exceeding many and exceeding vile.
Oh beloved, before the Lord Jesus comes to convince, we have cause
to pray for and pity every poor sinner, as the Lord Jesus did, saying,
Lord forgive them, they know not what they do.[69] You godly parents,
masters, how oft do you instruct your children, servants, and convince them of their sinfulness, until they confess their faults? yet you

see no amendment, but they go on still; what should you now do? oh cry out for them, and say, Lord forgive them, for they know not what they do. Their sins they know, but what the evil of them is, alas! they know not; but when the Spirit comes to convince, he makes them see what they do, and what is the exceeding evil of those sins they made light of before; like madmen that have sworn, and curst, and struck their friends, when[70] they come to be sober again, and remember their mischievous ways and words, now they see what they have done,[71] and how abominable their courses then[72] were. Oh you that walk on in the madness of your minds now, in all manner of sin, if ever the Lord do good to you, you shall account your ways madness and folly, and cry out, Oh Lord, what have I done in kicking thus long against the pricks?

[*Conclusion* 3.][73] The Lord Jesus by his Spirit doth not only convince the soul of the evil *of sin*,[74] but of the evil *after sin*, I mean of[75] the just punishment which doth follow sin, and that is this, *viz.* that it must die, and that eternally for sin, if it remains[76] in this estate it is now in. Romans 4:15: *The Law works wrath*, i.e. sight and sense of wrath; Romans 7:9: *When the Law came, sin revived, and I died*: *i.e.* I saw myself a dead man by it; so the soul sees clearly God hath said, *The soul that sinneth shall die*: I have sinned, and therefore if the Lord be true I shall die, to hell I shall, if now[77] the Lord stop my breath and cut off my life, which he might justly and may easily do. *Death is the wages of sin*,[78] even of any one sin, though never so little; what then will become of me who stand guilty of so many, exceeding the number of the hairs on my head, or the stars in heaven? *Whoremongers and adulterers God will judge*, the Minister hath said so, the Lord himself hath told me so (Hebrews 13:4). I am the man, my conscience now tears me and tells me so, what will become of me? *The Lord Jesus will come in flaming fire to render vengeance against all that know not God; and that obey not the Gospel*. This I believe, for God hath said it (2 Thessalonians 2:7,8,9), and now I see I am he that hath lived long in[79] ignorance, and know not God; I have had the Gospel of grace thus long wooing and persuading my heart, and oftentimes it hath affected me, but yet I have resisted God and his Gospel, and have set my filthy lusts, my vain sports, my companions, cups,[80] and queans[81] at a higher price than Christ, and have loved them more than him; and therefore though I may be spared for a while, yet there is a time wherein Christ himself will come out against me in flaming fire. To this purpose doth the Spirit work; for beloved, the great means whereby Satan overthrew Man at first in his innocency, was this principle, although thou dost eat, and so sin against God, yet thou shalt not die. Genesis 3:4: *Ye shall not surely die*; the Serpent doth not say, *Ye shall not die*, for that is too gross an out-facing of the Word (Genesis 2:17), but he saith, *Ye shall not surely die*: that is, there is not such absolute certainty of it; it may be you shall live, God loves you better than so, and is a more merciful Father than to be at a word and a blow. Now look as Satan deceived and brought our first parents to ruin by suggesting this principle; so at this day he doth sow this accursed seed, and plant this very[82] principle in the soil of every man's heart by nature, they do not think, they cannot believe that[83] they are dead men, and condemned to die, and that they shall die eternally for the least sin committed by them. Men nor Angels cannot persuade them of it, they cannot see the equity of it, that God so merciful will be so severe, for so small a matter; nor yet the truth of it, for then they think no flesh should be saved. And thus when the old Serpent hath spit this[84] poison before them, they sup it up, and drink it in, and so thousands, nay millions of men and women are utterly undone. The Lord Christ therefore when he comes to save a poor sinner, and raise him up out of his fall, convinceth the soul by his Spirit, and that with full and mighty evidence, that it shall die for the least sin, and tells him as the Lord told *Abimelech* in another case (Genesis 20:3), *Thou art but a dead man for this*; and if the Spirit set on this, let who can claw it off.[85] I tell you beloved, never did poor condemned Malefactor more certainly know and hear the sentence of condemnation passed upon him by a mortal man, than the guilty sinner doth his, by an immortal and displeased God: and therefore those three thousand cry out (Acts 2:37), *Men and brethren, what shall we do to be saved?* We are condemned to die, what shall we[86] do now to be saved from death? Now the soul is glad to inquire of the Minister, Oh tell me, what shall I do? I once thought myself in a[87] safe and good condition as any in the Town or Country I lived in, but now the Lord hath let me hear of other news; die I must in this estate, and 'tis a wonder of mercies I am spared alive to this day. There is not only some blind fears and suspicions that it may possibly be so, but full persuasions of heart, die I must, die I shall in this estate; for if the Spirit reveal sin, and convince not of death for sin, the soul under this work of conviction being as yet rather sensual than spiritual, will make a light matter of it, when it sees no sensible[88] danger in it; but when it sees the bottomless pit before it, everlasting fire before it, for the least sin, now it sees the heinous evil of sin; the way of sin though never so peaceable before, is full of danger now, wherein it sees there are endless woes and everlasting deaths that lie in wait for it (Romans 6:21). And now saith the Spirit, you may go on in these sinful courses as others do, if you see meet, but oh consider what will be the end of them; what it is to enjoy the pleasures of sin for a season, and to be tormented forever for them in the conclusion, for be assured that will be the end: and hence the soul seeing itself thus set apart for death, looks upon itself in a far worse estate than the brute beasts, or vilest worm upon the earth; for it thinks when they die there is an end of their misery; but oh then is the beginning of mine forever: hence also arise those fears of death and[89] of being suddenly cut off, that when it lies down, it trembles to think I may never rise again, because it's convinced, not only that it deserves to die, but that it is already sentenced for to die: hence also the soul justifies God, if he had cut him off in his sin; and wonders what kept him from it, there[90] being nothing else due from God unto it: hence lastly, the soul is stopped and stands still, goes not on in sin as before; or if it[91] doth, the Lord gives it no peace. Jeremiah 8:6: Why doth the horse go on in the battle? because it sees not death before it; but now the soul sees death, and therefore stops: oh remember this all you that never could believe that you are dead condemned men, and therefore are never troubled with any such thoughts in your mind;[92] I tell you, that you are far from conviction, and therefore far from salvation: if God should send some from the dead to bear witness against this secure world concerning this truth, yet you will not believe it, for his messengers sent from heaven are not believed herein; woe be to you if you remain unconvinced of this point.

[3.] But you will say, how doth the Lord thus convince sin, and wherein is it expressed? which is the third particular.

[*Answer.*] All knowledge of sin is not conviction of sin, all confession of sin is not conviction; there is a conviction merely rational, which is not spiritual; there are three things in spiritual conviction.

[1.] There is a clear, certain, and manifest light, so that the soul sees its sin, and death due to it clearly and certainly; for so the word (John 16:9) ἐλέγκειν[93] signifies to evidence a thing by way of argumentation, nay demonstration; the Spirit so demonstrates these things as[94] that it hath nothing to object, a man's mouth is stopped, he hath nothing to say but this; behold I am vile, I am a dead man: for if a man have many strong arguments given him to confirm a truth, yet if he have but one objection or doubtful scruple not answered, he is not fully as yet convinced, because full conviction by a clear sunlight scatters all dark objections; and hence our Savior (Jude 15) will one day *convince the wicked of all their hard speeches against him*, which will chiefly be done[95] by manifesting the evil of such ways, and taking away all those colors[96] and defenses men have made for such[97] language: before the Spirit of Christ comes, man cannot see, will not see his sin nor[98] punishment; nay, he hath many things to say for himself as excuses and extenuations of his[99] sin; One saith, I was drawn unto it (*the woman that thou gavest me*),[100] and so lays the blame on others: Another saith, It is my nature; Others say, All are sinners, the godly sin as well as others; and yet are saved at last, and so I hope shall I:[101] Others profess they cannot part with sin, they would be better but they cannot, and God requires no more than they are able to perform; Another saith, I will continue in sin but a little while, and purpose hereafter to leave it; Others say, We are sinners, but yet God is merciful and will forgive it; Another saith, Though I have sinned, yet I have some good, and am not so bad as other men; endless are these excuses for sin. In one word, I know no man, though never so bad, though his sin be never so grievous, but he hath something to say for himself, and something in his mind to lessen and extenuate sin; but beloved when the Spirit comes to convince, he so convinceth as that he answers all these, pulls down all these fences, tears off all these fig-leaves, scatters all these mists, and pulls off all these scales from the eyes, stops a man's mouth, that the soul stands before God, crying, oh Lord guilty, guilty; as the Prophet *Jeremiah* told them (Jeremiah 2:23), *Why dost thou say, I am innocent? look upon thy way, etc.*, so the Spirit saith, why dost thou say thy sin is small? it is *disobedience* (as *Samuel* said to *Saul*, 1 Samuel 15:23), which[102] is *rebellion, and as the sin of witch-craft*; and is that a small matter? the Spirit of conviction by the clear evidence of the truth, binds the understanding that it cannot struggle against God any more; and hence let all the world plead to the contrary, nay let the godly come to comfort them in this estate, and think and speak well of them; yet they cannot believe them, because they are certain their estates are woeful: hence also we shall observe the soul under conviction, instead of excusing sin, it aggravates sin, and studies to aggravate sin; did ever any deal thus wickedly, walk thus sinfully, so long, against so many checks and chidings, light and love, means and mercies, as I have done? And it is wonderful to observe that those things which made it once account sin light, make it therefore to think sin great:[103] e.g., my sin is little; the more unkind thou (saith the Spirit) that wilt not do a small matter for the Lord: my sin is common; the more sinful thou that in those things wherein all the world rise up in arms against God, thou joinest with them: God spares me after sin; the greater is thy sin therefore that thou hast continued so long in, against a God so pitiful to thee, the dearest sins are now the vilest sins, because though they were most sweet to him, yet the Spirit convinceth him, they were therefore the more grievous unto the soul of God; you poor creatures may now hide, and color, and excuse your sins before men, but when the Lord comes to convince, you cannot lie hid; then your consciences (when Jesus Christ the Lord comes to convince) shall not be like the Steward in the Gospel that set down 50 for a[104] 100 pounds,[105] no, the Lord will force it to bring in[106] a true and clear account at that day.

[2.] There is a real light in spiritual conviction, rational conviction makes things appear notionally; but spiritual conviction, really:[107] the Spirit indeed useth argumentation in conviction, but it goes farther and causeth the soul not only to see sin and death discursively, but also intuitively and really: reason can see and discourse about words and Propositions, and behold things by report, and so[108] deduct one thing from another; but the Spirit makes a man see the things themselves, really wrapped up in those words; the Spirit brings spiritual things as well as notions before a man's eye, the light of the Spirit is like the light of the Sun, it makes all things appear as they are; John 3:20,21. It was *Jerusalem's* misery, she heard the words of Christ, and they were not hid from them, but *the things of her peace* shut up[109] in those words *were hid from her eyes.* Discourse with many a man about his sin and misery, he will grant all that you say, and he is convinced, that[110] his estate is most wretched, and yet still lives in all manner of sin; what is the reason of it? truly he sees his sin only by discourse, but he doth not, nay cannot see the thing sin, death, wrath of God, until the Spirit come; which only convinceth or showeth that really. A man will not be afraid of a Lion when it is painted only upon[111] the wall, why? because therein he doth not see the living Lion: when he sees that, he trembles. So men hear of sin, and talk of sin and death, and say they are most miserable in regard of both; yet their hearts tremble not, are not amazed at these evils; because sin is not seen alive, death is not presented alive before them, which is done by the Spirit of conviction only, revealing these really to the soul; and hence it is that many men *in seeing see not,*[112] How can that be? thus, in seeing things notionally, they see them not really. And hence many that know most of sin, know least of sin, because in seeing it notionally, they see it not really. And therefore happy were it for some men, Scholars and others, that they had no notional knowledge of sin,[113] for this *light* is their *darkness*, and makes them more uncapable of spiritual conviction: the first act of spiritual conviction is to let a man see clearly that he is sinful and most miserable; the second act is to let the soul see really what this sin and death is. Oh consider of this, many of you know that you are sinful, and that you shall die; but dost thou know what sin is, and what it is to die? If thou didst, I dare say thy heart would sink; if thou dost not, thou art a condemned man, because not yet a convinced man. If you here ask, how the Lord makes sin real?[114] I answer. By making God real, the real greatness of sin is seen by beholding really the greatness of God who is smitten by sin; sin is not seen because God is not seen; John 3:especially verse 11: *He that doth evil hath not seen God.* No knowledge of God is the cause *why blood toucheth blood:*[115] the Spirit casts out all other company of vain and foolish thoughts, and then God comes in and appears immediately to the soul in his greatness and glory, and then the Spirit saith, Lo, this is that God thy sins have provoked. And now sin appears as it is, and together with this real sight of sin, the soul doth not see painted fire, but sees the fire of God's wrath really, whither now it is leading, that never can be quenched but by Christ's blood: and when the Spirit hath thus convinced, now a man begins to see his madness and folly in times past, saying, I know[116] not what I did. And hence questions, Can the Lord pardon such a wretch as I, whose sins are so great? Hence also the heart begins to be affected with sin and death, because it sees them now as they are indeed, and not by report only. A man accounts it a matter of nothing to tread upon a worm, wherein there[117] is nothing seen worthy either to be loved or feared; and hence a man's heart is not affected with it: before the Spirit of conviction comes, God is more vile in man's eye than any worm; as Christ said in another case of himself (Psalm 22), *I am a worm and no man*; so may the Lord complain, I am viler in such a one's eyes than any worm, and no God: and hence a man makes it a matter of nothing to tread upon the glorious Majesty of God, and hence is not affected with it; but when God is seen by the Spirit of conviction, in his great glory; then as he is great, sin is seen great; as his glory affects and astonisheth the soul, so sin affects the heart.

[3.] There is a constant light; the soul sees sin and death continually before it; *God's arrows stick fast*[118] in the soul, and cannot be plucked out; *My sin is ever before me*,[119] said *David* (in his renewing of[120] the work of conversion). For in effectual conviction, the mind is not only bound to see the misery lying upon it, but it is held bound; it is such a Sunlight as never can be quenched, though it may be clouded. When the Spirit of Christ darts in any light to see sin, the soul would turn away from looking upon it, would not hear on that ear, *Felix*-like.[121] But the Spirit of Conviction sent to make thorough work on the hearts of all the Elect, follows them, meets them at every turn, forceth them[122] to see and remember what they have done, the least sin now is like a[123] mote in the eye, it's ever troubling. Those ghastly, dreadful objects of sin, death, wrath, being presented by the Spirit near unto the soul, fix the eye to fasten here; they that can cast off at their pleasure the remembrance and thoughts of sin and death, never prove sound, until the Lord doth make them stay their thoughts, and muse deeply on what they have done, and whither they are going. And hence the soul in lying down, rising up, lies down and rises up with perplexed thoughts, What will become of me? The Lord sometimes keeps it waking in the night season, when others are asleep, and then 'tis haunted with those thoughts, it cannot sleep; it looks back upon every day, and week, Sabbath, Sermon, Prayer, speeches, and thinks all this day, this week, etc., the goodness of the Lord and his patience to a wretch hath been continued, but my sins also are continued;[124] I sin in all I do, in all my prayers, in all I think, the same heart remains still not humbled, not yet changed.

And hence you shall observe, that word which discovered sin at first to it, it never goes out of the mind; I think saith the soul I shall never forget such a man, nor such a truth. Hence also if the soul grow light and careless at some time, and casts off[125] the thoughts of these things, the Spirit returns again, and falls a-reasoning with the soul, Why hast thou done this? what hurt hath the Lord done thee? will there never be an end? hast not thou gone on long enough in thy lewd courses against God, but that thou shouldst still add unto the heap? hast thou not wrath enough upon thee already? how soon may the Lord stop thy breath? and then thou knowest thou hadst better never to have been born; was there ever any that thus resisted grace, that thus adventured upon the sword's[126] point? hast thou but one friend, a patient, long-suffering God, that hath left thy conscience without excuse long ago, and therefore could have cut thee off, and dost thou thus forsake him, thus abuse him? Thus the Spirit follows; and hence the soul comes to some measure of confession of sin; Oh Lord I have done exceeding wickedly; I have been worse than the horse that rusheth into the battle, because it sees not death before it; but I have seen death before me in these ways, and yet go on, and still sin, and cannot but sin: Behold me, Lord, for I am very vile. When thus the Spirit hath let into the soul a clear, real, constant light, to see sin and death, now there is a thorough conviction.

But you will say, In what measure doth the Spirit communicate this light?

[4.] I shall therefore open the fourth particular, *viz.* The measure of spiritual conviction in all the elect, *viz.*

So much conviction of sin as may bring in[127] and work compunction for sin, so much sight of sin as may bring in sense of sin, so much is necessary and no more. Everyone hath not the same measure of conviction, yet all the elect have and must have so much: for so much conviction is necessary as may attain the end of conviction. Now the *finis proximus*, or next end of conviction in the elect, is compunction, or sense of sin; for what good can it do unto them to see sin, and not to be affected with it? What greater mercy doth the Lord show to the elect herein,[128] than unto the Devils and Reprobates, who stand convinced, and know they are wicked and condemned; but yet their hearts altogether unaffected with any true remorse for sin? *Mine eye,* saith *Jeremiah, affecteth my heart.*[129] *The Lord opens the ears* of his to instruction, *that he might humble.*[130] Some think that there is no thorough conviction, without some affection. I dare not say so, nor will I now dispute whether there is not something in the nature and essence of that conviction the elect have different from that conviction in reprobates and devils; 'tis sufficient now; and that which reacheth[131] the end of this question, to know what measure of conviction is necessary, I conceive the clear discerning of it is by the immediate and sensible effect of it, *viz.* So much as affects the heart truly with sin.

But if you ask, What is that sense of sin, and what measure of this is necessary? that I shall answer in the doctrine of compunction.[132]

Let not therefore any soul be discouraged, and say, I was never yet convinced, because I have not felt such a clear, real, constant light to see sin and death as others have done: consider thou, if the end of conviction be attained, which is a true sense and feeling of sin, thou hast then that measure which is most meet for thee, more than which the Lord regards not in any of his; but you that walk up and down with convinced consciences, and know your states are miserable and sinful, and that you perish if you die in that condition, and yet have no sense nor feeling; no sorrow nor affliction of spirit for those evils, I tell you the very devils are in some respect nearer[133] the Kingdom of God than you be, who see, and[134] feel, and tremble; woe, woe to[135] thousands that live under convicting Ministries whom the word often hits, and the Lord by the Spirit often meets, and they hear and know their sins are many, their estates bad, and that iniquity will be their[136] ruin, if thus they continue, yet all God's light is without heat, and it is but the shining of it upon rocks, and cold stones; they are frozen in their dregs: be it known to you, you have not one drop of that conviction which begins salvation.

SELECTION IV

The Soul's Vocation, Doctrine 3

Thomas Hooker

A genealogically constructed portrait of Thomas Hooker. This statue, in the capitol building, Hartford, Connecticut, is one of a number of historical subjects by Charles Henry Niehaus (1855–1935), including a companion statue of John Davenport. Since no seventeenth-century likeness of Hooker exists, Niehaus studied portraits of Hooker's lineal descendants to form a composite of family features. From The National Cyclopaedia of American Biography, *vol. 6 (New York: James T. White, 1929).*

BOTH *The Soul's Vocation or Effectual Calling to Christ* (1637–1638) and *The Soul's Exaltation* (1638) were published by Andrew Crooke with no prefaces or letters explaining how the manuscripts were obtained.[1] Two early accounts—the editors' prefatory letter to Hooker's Hartford-preached sermons, *The Application of Redemption* (1656), and Cotton Mather's *Magnalia Christi Americana* (1702)—identically date the preaching of the sermons and the circumstances of their publication. Hooker's "special inclination to those principles of divinity which concerned *the application of redemption*" results, in Mather's view, from Hooker's own religious experience: "he had been from his youth trained up in the experience of those *humiliations* and *consolations*, and sacred *communions*, which belong to the new creature, and he had most critically compared his own experience with the accounts which the *quick and powerful word of God* gives of those glorious things." No less than three separate examinations of the life of the "new creature" formed the substance of Hooker's preaching, one in each of the three principal locations where he preached:

> . . . he preached first more briefly on these points, while he was a catechist in Emmanuel College [Cambridge University], in a more scholastic way; which was most agreeable to his present station; and the notes of what he then delivered were so esteemed, that many copies thereof were transcribed and preserved. Afterwards he preached more largely on those points, in a more popular way, at Chelmsford [Essex], the product of which were those books of *preparation for Christ, contrition, humiliation, vocation, union with Christ, and communion*, and the rest, which go under his name; for many wrote after him in shorthand; and some were so bold as to publish many of them without his consent or knowledge . . . when he came to New England, many of his church, which had been his old Essex hearers, desired him once more to go over the points of *God's regenerating works upon the soul of his elect*; until, at last, their desires prevailed with him to resume that pleasant subject. The subject hereby came to have a third concoction in the head and heart of one as able to digest it as most men living in the world; and it was his design to perfect with his own hand his composures for the press, and thereby vindicate both *author* and *matter* from the wrongs done to both, by surreptitious editions heretofore. He did not live to finish what he intended.[2]

Winfried Herget, a contemporary scholar who has studied the textual and publishing complexities of the Hooker canon, corroborates the assignment (by Mather and the editors of *The Application of*

Redemption) of *The Soul's Vocation* and *The Soul's Exaltation* to
Hooker's ministry in Chelmsford (1625–1629).[3]

Belonging, then, to his second recitation of the redemptive process,
The Soul's Vocation and *The Soul's Exaltation* represent Hooker's
mature theology; furthermore, they demonstrate a more comprehensive treatment of specific stages in the process of salvation than does
his third coverage of the subject, published as *The Application of
Redemption*. The volumes of 1638 are also livelier than the series
Hooker himself prepared for the press (*The Application of Redemption*), perhaps because the earlier publications, recorded by notetakers, are closer in substance to the actual delivery of the sermons.[4]
They seem more spontaneous and energetic in imagery, more faithful
to an oral event, than do the cautiously phrased and balanced texts
Hooker wrote out.[5]

The Soul's Vocation is bound with "The Soul's Ingrafting into
Christ," which Hooker terms a "preface" of some nine thousand
words. He begins it with a review of his scheme, detailing "how
Christ's Merits are applied to the Soul." Throughout his preaching
career, he tended to envision redemption as a complex but regular
process. He frequently subdivides it into two main activities—
preparation and implantation—of four stages each.[6] In "The Soul's
Ingrafting," he summarizes how he has already "finished" explaining
preparation.[7] In this first half of redemption, God (1) breaks the
relation between sin and the soul and (2) draws the soul to himself;
and through his Spirit he enables the soul to experience (3) contrition and (4) humiliation.

The "heart being thus prepared," "our implantation"—or "ingrafting"—into Jesus Christ becomes Hooker's next major activity
of redemption. He explains (see selection VI) that ingrafting comprises two events: vocation and "the growing of the soul together
with Christ." Vocation consists of (5) God's call and (6) the soul's
answer; the soul's growth consists of (7) union with Christ and (8)
communion with Christ.

Working from the complete recitation of the process of salvation
in *The Soul's Exaltation* (see selection VI) and from its repetition in
many of the other series, we selected sermons of Hooker's that represent successive stages in his scheme of redemption. The two selections from *The Soul's Vocation* represent what he finds most central
to vocation: God's call by the "word of the Gospel" (the fifth stage)
and the soul's answer, by means of the four affections, to the "riches
of [God's] mercy" (the sixth stage). The very next stage, union with
Christ, is the concern of the selection from *The Soul's Exaltation*.
In summarizing the process of salvation, Hooker explains that union
follows directly upon vocation in his scheme: "The former of these
two [vocation or "the calling of the sinner"] we have largely treated
of, and fully finished in the great work of vocation, when the Lord

brings the sinner to himself by the call of mercy, and the voice of the Gospel: we are now to proceed; and we have made some entrance into the second; and that is the growing of the soul together with Christ" (see selection VI).

Hooker begins *The Soul's Vocation*, in the context of an abbreviated summary of ingrafting, with a definition of his title and intention: "Now the point at this present to be handled, is called by the stream of Divines *Vocation*, and I term it the putting in of the soul, when the soul is brought out of the world of sin, to lie upon, and to close with the Lord Jesus Christ . . . when the Lord by the call of his Gospel doth so clearly reveal the fullness of mercy, and certifies to the soul by the work of his spirit, that the soul humbled returns answer to God's call."[8] For Hooker, "vocation" most closely labels conversion. Throughout *The Soul's Vocation*, it is the answer of the wayward soul in this miracle that consumes far more of Hooker's energy than does the call of the trustworthy Lord.[9] The two doctrines that open the work and precede the selection, however, center on the action of God in vocation—how he calls the soul to answer.[10] Prior to the selection, Hooker explains the way God is the heart's "teacher" (doctrine 2); his lesson is the "sufficiency in the mercy of God" (doctrine 1). Throughout this initial section, God emerges as loving and tender in appointing the "ministry of his Gospel" as the means of conversion: "There must be hearing before coming; not of the Law, to terrify a man; but of the Gospel, to persuade and allure a man to come unto the Lord, and receive mercy and kindness from him."[11]

Because this selection emphasizes God's bountiful mercy and the soul's acceptance of that mercy, its message of conversion seems efficacious: the preacher assumes that some of his audience have experienced conversion (use 3) and implies that many others are capable of acquiring "life" (uses 4 and 5)—that is, the Spirit is seen to be at work in this audience. Like the other preachers, Hooker asserted that the Spirit is free to bring grace in any way, but he also represented typical practice in stressing the "common course" of conversion: the Spirit brings grace within the confines of the sermon.[12] The "Gospel preached," not merely the Gospel, is for Hooker the primary vehicle of the Spirit. Countering extremists—the preachers were amply prepared in England for the Hutchinsonian crisis in America—Hooker refutes "fantastical" notions that the Spirit in ordinary cases calls the soul directly rather than through the medium of the preacher.

Among the sermons in this anthology, only Shepard's approximate Hooker's in the dramatization of the soul through its soliloquies and colloquies and in the range and plenitude of imagery. Hooker is the most consistent and impressive of the preachers in amplifying his points with numerous and diverse similitudes. For example, to explain to the faithful that they may gain assurance of their conversion by meditation on the word, he analogizes from breast-feeding, then eating, and finally alchemy. He is scrupulous in using "so" or "so it is" each of the three times so that, in conformance with his rhetorical aim of keeping fact separate from fancy, his hearers know that the references are merely "plain and evident demonstrations."[13] In addition to clarifying and enlivening his points by similitudes, Hooker teaches his auditors and rouses them by rhetorical questions. Serving as guideposts for the soul in its self-examination, the six questions in the last part of the second use—beginning with "what, resist the Spirit?"—build on previous rhetorical questions on the state of the soul, soliloquies, imperatives, and imagined dialogs. The questions intensify the concluding warning and exhortation: "if thou opposest the Spirit, none can succor thee, therefore look to it."

John 6:45: *It is written in the prophets, And they shall be all taught of God. Every man therefore that hath heard, and hath learned of the Father, cometh unto me.*

[*Doctrine.*][14] The word of the Gospel and the work of the Spirit always go together; the point is grounded in the Text, after this manner: they must first hear, then learn; hear by the word, and learn by the Spirit. The hearing of the Gospel without the Spirit, is nothing else but a beating of the air, and a dead letter.[15] It is true, the Lord can work above means:[16] we know also God can appoint other means for to call the soul, but it is not our meaning, we must not look for revelations and dreams, as a company of fantastical brains do; but in common course God's Spirit goes with the Gospel, and that is the ordinary means whereby the soul comes to be called. God can make the air nourish a man, but he doth not. If a man should expect to be fed by miracle, he himself would be a miracle; Galatians 3:2; for there goes a spiritual power with it, it raiseth the dead in sin to life; it is a living word, and the word discovers also the secrets of men's thoughts. Now that word which raiseth the dead, and discovers the secrets of men's hearts, it must needs have a marvelous power with it, and accompanying of it.

For the opening of it, observe two things: first, the manner; secondly, the reasons.

[*Point 1.*][17] After what manner doth the word and Spirit go together? and you must know, I do not mean that the Spirit is in the word, no otherwise than in all other things, but in a more special manner, and that conceive in three things.

First, the Lord hath ordained and set apart the preaching of the word, he hath sanctified it, and set it apart to call the soul. Look as it is with the brazen Serpent,[18] God appointed it to heal those that were stung; now[19] if 500 men should have made another Serpent, it could not have healed one man, though they had looked their eyes out of their heads: So it is with the Gospel, there is no other usual means to call the soul: Hence it is called the word of the Gospel. Now if five hundred men make five hundred Gospels besides this, they could never convert, or comfort one soul. Or as it is with a mint, if a mint master coin money, it will go current; but if twenty other coin money, though the stamp were as good, yet it is but counterfeit coin: so it is here. 1 Corinthians 1:21. Let a man study all the arts and tongues that can be devised, he never shall, nay he never can, know one drop of God's mercy and goodness in Christ. Why but how then may a man know it? saith the Text,[20] *by the foolishness of preaching*, that is, wicked men count it foolishness.

[*Point* 2.] The Lord doth appropriate the saving work of his Spirit to go with the ordinance; not that God is tied to any means, but he tieth himself to this means. Why doth not air nourish all, as well as meat? because only God hath set meat apart for this purpose. Hence this Gospel is called *the power of God to salvation*, because the power of God ordinarily, and in common course appears therein: the waters of life and salvation run only in the channel of the Gospel. There are golden mines of grace, but they are only to be found in the climates of the Gospel. Nay, observe this, when all arguments prevail not with corruption, to persuade the heart to go to God, one Text of Scripture will stand a man in stead, above all humane learning and inventions, because the Spirit goes forth, in this, and none else.

[*Point* 3.] God doth undoubtedly, as he will, when he will, and how he will, give success to his ordinance.[21] Isaiah 55:10,11. The word of the Lord doth ever accomplish that for which it is sent. For, it is true, many a man is called after the word is delivered a long time. Why is that? it soaks into the soul, as the snow in December soaks into the earth, but the fruit of it is not seen until May. The word is *a savor of life unto life*, it is a living *savor of death to death*,[22] it is a poison, a deadly savor; and though it hardens some, yet the work goes forward.

[*Reason* 1.] Because the Lord would not have any careless of his own glory, and our good: as he will humble the soul, that he may do good to it, so he will make him use the means. If a gentleman should go after a beggar with an alms, how proud would he be, and rather think himself a master than a beggar? So, if God should follow us with mercy, we would rather go from him: but he hath laid mercy in the mine of the Gospel, that we may dig for comfort in the cistern of the Gospel, that we may draw all our consolation from thence.

[*Reason* 2.] That we may[23] not be cozened by our own fancies, the Lord would[24] prevent all inconveniences and conceits of Eatonists and Familists,[25] that think they have the power of the Spirit in themselves, whereas God's Spirit goes always with the word. 1 John 4:1. Every Minister preaches with a spirit; some out of the spirit of envy, some out of the spirit of sincerity: some hears out of the spirit of love, some with the spirit of malice, to carp at the Minister: try therefore the spirits, and if they hold not with the word, they are naught.

[*Reason 3.*] That we may be watchful and careful, lest we lose the comfort that we have: lightly come, lightly go, got with little pain, lost with less care; therefore the Lord will make us seek unto the means.

[*Use 1.*] Instruction: to teach us the worth of the Gospel above all other things in the world, for it is accompanied with the Spirit, and it brings salvation with it. What if a man had all the wealth, what if he had all the policy[26] in the world, and wanted this? he were but a fool. What if one were able to dive deep into the secrets of nature, to know the motions of stars, and yet know nothing belongs to his peace, what avails it? what if a man could speak with the tongues of men and Angels, yet without this, he is a novice in knowledge. Why do we value a mine, but because of the gold in it? and the cabinet, but because of the pearl in it? oh this is that pearl we sell all for; 2 Corinthians 2:1,2.

[*Use 2.*] For trial: a man may know whether he[27] have a spiritual heart or no: Judges 19; he that hath not the Spirit, is a fleshly sensual man. Wouldest thou know whether thou art carnal or spiritual? this doctrine tells thee. How came the Spirit? If thou hast it, it ever came with the Gospel: therefore see now how thy soul stands affected with the Gospel, and so it stands affected to the Spirit. If thou wilt none of the Gospel, thou wilt miss of the Spirit, then Christ will none of thee. Now reason with your own souls, Why, unless I take the Spirit, woe be to me, I may own myself, Christ will never own me. Is it so, that I will not suffer the word to prevail with me? remember the time will come that you must die as well as your neighbors, and then you will say, Lord Jesus forgive my sins, Lord Jesus receive my soul: then Christ will say, Away, be gone, you are none of mine, I know you not. Any man, whether noble or honorable, let him be what he will be, and let his parts be what they will, if he hath not the Spirit, he is none of Christ's: *his you are to whom you obey*;[28] but pride and covetousness you obey, and malice and spleen you obey, you are therefore none of Christ's. Pride will say, This heart is mine, Lord, I have domineered over it, and I will torment it: Corruptions will say, We have owned this soul, and we will damn it. You that heretofore have made a tush at the word, this wind shakes no corn, and these words break no bones: think what you have done; little do you think you have opposed the Spirit; Acts 7:51;[29] what, resist the Spirit? Oh think of this. Why, what shall I say? by what spirit wilt thou be sanctified? by what spirit wilt thou be saved? Can thy own spirit save thee? no, the Spirit of God must save thee; and have you resisted that Spirit? methinks it is enough to sink any soul under heaven. Hereafter therefore think this with thyself, were he but a man that speaks, yet I ought not to despise him: but that is not all, there goeth God's Spirit with the word, and shall I despise it? the Lord keep me from this: there is but one step between this and that unpardonable sin against the holy Ghost, only adding malice to thy rage; thou opposest thy Father, haply the Son mediates for thee; thou despisest the Son, haply the holy Ghost pleads for thee: but if thou opposest the Spirit, none can succor thee, therefore look to it.

[*Use* 3.] Direction. Hence we may observe the ground why many of God's faithful people understand not that they have the Spirit of God, nor yet the increase of it; they look not to the promise by which it is conveyed, but to corruption by which it is hindered; you listen not to the verdict of the Gospel.

Let everyone ask this great question, How may I know when the Spirit is in me? That you know it not, the fault is, your own; look into the word. It is with a poor soul, as with little children; the child in the night being hungry, seeks for the dug, but if he doth not lay hold of it, he gets no good by it; so thou hast been a long time muzzling about a dry chip, and hast got no comfort. Be sure therefore to lay hold upon the promise, hold it, and thy spirit shall be filled with marrow and fatness. If there be marrow in a bone, thou must break it before thou canst get any out. So it is with the promises; they are full of sweetness, but you must chew them, break them, and bestow thy heart on them. An Alchemist that distills oil, doth draw out the spirit[30] of metals, but it is by distillation: so it is with the promises, they are excellent metal, there is a great deal of comfort in them, but if you will have benefit by them, you must distill them by meditation.

[*Objection.*] Aye, but some souls may say, We have done thus often, but yet return as empty as before.

[*Answer.*] I answer, You should have stayed longer upon the promise, it must not be at your carving and disposing: in reason, a man must swallow his pills, and eat his cordials;[31] but we should do the contrary, we should chew the promises, and that is done by meditating on them: but we swallow the precious promises of Christ that should comfort us, therefore chew them, if you desire comfort, over and over again; eat these daily, and you shall find much comfort and consolation therein, and benefit thereby.

[*Use* 4.] Terror: we may see the hopeless condition of those men that live under the Gospel, and their hearts are not wrought upon.[32] If the Spirit of God, and the Gospel of God, will not work upon thee: if thou hast the eye of a man about thee, thou mayst see thy woeful and lamentable condition. If a bungling servant cannot tell how to hew a piece of wood for a building, it is no marvel; but if it be such a piece, that the master Carpenter cannot make it fit for the building, then it is good for nothing but to be burned: So it is here with the soul, if the Spirit of God can do thee no good, who can? if we, a company of bunglers, cannot do it, no marvel; but if our master Christ, if he takes a stubborn sturdy heart in hand, and cannot do it, it is fit to be damned. Is not that man miserably ignorant, that wisdom itself cannot make wise? is not he sick of sin, whom the Gospel cannot cure? 2[33] Corinthians 4:3. I desire those whose conscience to this day accuse them that yet they are blind, and those that brave it out, and say, Shall I fear the face of a man? no, no, I scorn it; I beseech you let me deal with you, do not brave it out so, for it is the greatest misery under the Sun, for thou dost as good as to say, thou wilt not have the word of God to work upon thee. James 1:21. The word of God is able to save thee, and to sanctify thee, and art thou yet polluted and defiled? Oh, take heed of it, go and bemoan thy soul to the Lord, and say, Good Lord, such a drunkard thou hast met with, such a proud heart thou hast humbled, and such a stubborn heart thou hast plucked upon his knees; and if drunkards be humbled, if the ignorant be instructed, then what a cursed heart have I, that was loose and vile, and base and profane before, and so I am now. I tell thee, what can you think of yourselves? if the Spirit go with the word, and thou mock at it, thy condition is lamentable.

[*Use 5.*] Exhortation: Then you are to be entreated, in the bowels[34] of our Lord Jesus Christ, whenever you hear the word of the Lord, and the Gospel of God, you must come trembling, and submit to that good word; Exodus 23. Whenever the word of the Lord is revealed, the Spirit of God, blessed forever, is there accompanying of it, therefore good reason the creature should submit to the Creator. We speak not a word for ourselves, we preach the good word of the Lord; and however ourselves have spoken this, if you oppose it, know it, that it is the Lord's word: therefore when you hear the word, do what you will with us, only submit to the word of the Lord; do what you please with us (as *Jeremiah* saith) only embrace the word of the Lord. It is God's word, therefore take heed of opposing and gainsaying it, labor to awe your souls, to settle all distempers, wipe out all carping and caviling at the word, as they press in upon thee.

[*Objection.*] But how shall we bring our souls to do this?

[*Answer.*] By considering these two or three means.

[1.] Labor not only to have thy soul convicted, that the holy Ghost is there accompanying the word, as it doth (or else how could it reveal thy sins?), but also persuade thy heart that it is so, apprehend the power of the Spirit of God; for as we apprehend the Spirit of the Lord to be in the word, so much the word will work upon thee; as it was with the Israelites; 1 Samuel 8:19 compared with 1 Samuel

12:18. What is the reason they do so at the one, and not at the other? why, did they fear the one more than the other? because they apprehended God to be in the one, and not in the other.

[2.] Confess and know, that not one word of God shall fall to the ground: there thou hast heard, if a man did hear thunder, and knew it would fall upon him, it would awe him. The word of the Lord is as thunder from heaven, it is not the word of man, but of God; then consider, shall not the word fail? then the word that God hath spoken shall fall upon me.

[3.] Consider, that when judgment hits, it is irrecoverable. If a man knew, that although judgment came, it would not hit him, if it did hit him, he might recover, this would comfort him a little; but if thou dost not stoop, it will hit, and that irrecoverably; therefore labor to tremble at God's word.

SELECTION V

The Soul's Vocation, Doctrine 7

Thomas Hooker

A nineteenth-century painting of Thomas Hooker and his congregation migrating to Hartford. This early work of the Hudson River artist Frederick Edwin Church (1826–1900) emphasizes the dangers and the potential of the New England wilderness as conquered by a leader like Hooker. As David C. Huntington points out (The Landscapes of Frederick Edwin Church: Vision of an American Era [*New York: George Braziller, 1966*], p. 28), *this painting is generically related to religious paintings of the flight of the Holy Family and illustrates "the painter's . . . belief in the unique destiny of New England." The painting is entitled* Hooker and Company Journeying through the Wilderness from Plymouth to Hartford, in 1636 *and is dated 1846. Courtesy of the Wadsworth Atheneum, Hartford, Connecticut.*

As we have seen in the previous selection, *The Soul's Vocation* concerns God's call to his chosen by means of the ministry of the Gospel and the soul's answer by means of its affections. Both concerns emerge from the text that initiates the eight doctrines of the volume: "Every man therefore that hath heard, and hath learned of the Father, cometh unto me" (John 6:45). At points in *The Soul's Vocation*, Hooker instructs the uncalled about conversion; more frequently, however, he shows the called how to ascertain the validity of their vocation. In other words, one of his major intentions in *The Soul's Vocation* is to reacquaint the saved with the first two stages of implantation, so that they can enjoy the saint's elusive comfort—assurance of salvation. Therefore, the sermon-series abounds in the "signs" that distinguish "a true saving faith from a false faith."[1] To help the called avoid the misfortunes of the uncalled, Hooker populates *The Soul's Vocation* with an unsavory crowd: the lazy hypocrite, the stage hypocrite, the terrified hypocrite, the whining hypocrite, the sturdy hypocrite, the glorious hypocrite, the presumptuous hypocrite, the shifting hypocrite, and the stately hypocrite.

To teach us to answer God's call, Hooker first explains the many ways God "must teach all the affections to come unto the promise"—the mercy of God manifest in Jesus Christ. Having "spoken" of the "work of God upon the understanding," he turns to the major concern of *The Soul's Vocation*: describing how the will and the four affections—hope, desire, love, joy—enable the soul to respond to vocation. The psychology of vocation is as ordered as the entire process of salvation: "what the mind hath known, and hope expected, and desire longed for, and love embraced, then cometh in the great wheel, the great commander, the will, which saith, I will have it: Go no farther, it is the best match we can make." As Hooker explains the way the will comes "to rest upon the free grace of God in Christ" (the eighth and last doctrine of *The Soul's Vocation*), he also defines faith. In a summary of the first seven doctrines, he explains: "you saw the seeds of faith before in the affections." He goes on to preview the eighth doctrine: "but now you shall see the root of faith." The sermon on the will is a sermon on belief and faith, on the benefits of faith, on the signs of faith, and on the nature of faith.[2]

On this last point, Hooker expresses his differences with "many learned godly judicious Divines . . . of another opinion": "faith is a work of effectual vocation, and no part of sanctification." He apologizes for any offense his theological quibbling occasions his auditors: "it hath ever been my care not to trouble a popular congregation with any matter of dispute." *The Soul's Vocation* demonstrates that he was energetically involved in England in settling doctrinal complexities on the stages of salvation similar to those raised by the Antinomian crisis in America. His continued emphasis in *The Soul's Vocation* on the minister's mediation is insistent enough to suggest that

threats to the preacher's authority in salvation preceded Anne Hutchinson's. A statement, prefatory to the selection, resembles orthodox
assertions made during the Antinomian upheaval: "it is not mine
intendment to persuade any to think that sanctification is before justification." Hooker goes on to clarify the process of salvation by
defining the role of love and joy in sanctification. He explains that
"desires and loves are of a double nature," one kind for vocation and
another for sanctification. Whereas in sanctification love and joy
proceed "from a principle which I have received from the power of
grace," in vocation "the Lord worketh this work upon me, I have no
power of myself." The emphasis on the Spirit's causality in this selection, then, matches that in the first: just as the Spirit inspires the
preacher of the Gospel, so the Spirit moves the affections of the soul
in vocation. When Hooker preaches that the hypocrites' "joy is a foolish imagination hammered out of their Anvil," he alludes to a recent
warning: "thou canst not hammer out a desire upon thine own
anvil." [3]

To help his auditors understand the affections, Hooker resorts to
a marvelously compelling personification of desire, involving this
"second affection" in a wearying pilgrimage. The same personification occurs in Bulkeley's *The Gospel-Covenant* and as follows in
Shepard's *The Parable of the Ten Virgins*: "*By what acts of Faith
doth* [*the soul*] *go forth?* There be two affections of the Soul that
chiefly look to a good absent, yet loving that good, go forth to meet
it, and those are Hope and Desire; like the blind man and the lame,
both together can make a shift to go. Hope like the eye goes out and
looks, Desire like the feet runs out and longs . . . Hope gets on the
top of the world, and cries, Oh I see him, Desire stands by and longs
for him, Oh come Lord. . . . by love and joy we embrace and entertain the Bridegroom, by hope and desire we go forth to meet the
Bridegroom." [4] It is possible to admire the figure as it appears in *The
Soul's Vocation* for its ingenious development but not for its originality. Its recurrence suggests that it belonged to that vast vocabulary and vision of salvation that the preachers held in common. [5]

The selection demonstrates the leisureliness and thoroughness of
The Soul's Vocation. Over half the preaching (more than 100,000
words) of the series falls to the eighth and last doctrine: how the will
comes "to rest upon the free grace of God in Christ." In the selection,
only the first sixth of the sermon on love and joy is represented. Immediately following it is the question, "But how doth the Spirit kindle
this love and joy?" and the answer in three particulars, followed by
four uses (instruction, consolation, trial, and reproof). Their principal task is to distinguish God-given love and joy from that which is
"feigned, wild, hypocritical." [6] Although Hooker announces a doctrine concerning love and joy, he wanders from its confines. The selection typifies the seeming repetitiveness of *The Soul's Vocation,*

and indeed of all the works on the process of salvation from the
Chelmsford period, in reviewing fully "the ministry of the Word" and
the exercise of the initial affections—hope and desire—in vocation.
Hooker's amplification, however, is neither careless nor purposeless.
Although the similitude of the pardoned malefactor and the called
sinner takes up two-fifths of the selection, it is remarkably precise—
each character exercises the four affections of vocation in seeking
mercy. Repetition functions as part of the plain style of preaching—
the educational needs of the auditors are foremost.

John 6:45: *It is written in the prophets, And they shall be all taught
of God. Every man therefore that hath heard, and hath learned of
the Father, cometh unto me.*

[*Doctrine.*][7] The Spirit of the Lord kindles in an humbled heart, and
enlightened sinner, love and joy, to entertain and rejoice in the riches
of his mercy: there are three passages[8] to be considered, that so we
may see the compass of the point in hand.

[*Passage 1.*] First, this love and joy is nowhere to be found but in
a heart humbled and enlightened, for unless the soul be humbled before God, it seeth no need of grace or mercy, and therefore despiseth
it, and disclaims it, and is carried with a hatred against that grace
that would master his corruptions and purge them: Nay the soul is
carried with a kind of wearisomeness, and is pestered with the power
of grace that would frame his heart anew, his corrupt heart is rather
troubled with it, than any way delighted in it; and if humbled and
not enlightened, he[9] could not be enlarged to bestow his heart thereupon, nor carry himself with that pleasure and delight which otherwise he would: this is the first passage. I know there is a wild kind
of love and joy in the world, counterfeit coin; but this is not the love
and joy we mean, we will have garden love and joy, of the Lord's own
setting and planting; those carnal hypocritical joys we will not med-
dle withal.

[*Passage 2.*] The second passage is this, this *love* and *joy* is kindled by the Spirit of the Father, he it is from whence comes all the
sparks that must kindle grace in us. So that all other love and joy
which is not spiritual and from him, cannot be acceptable to his Majesty. It is that in general which the Apostle *Paul* infers, *They which
are in the flesh cannot please God.*[10] So all the joy and love (as well as
any other action) that proceeds out of nature and flesh cannot please
God: But it must be heavenly love and joy, proceeding from the Spirit: Suffer me to express myself after this manner.[11] Look as it is with
a gentleman in the country, he will be content to leave his habita-

tion for a while, and give up his house to the *king* for a while, because he is but a mean man, and not able to entertain so great a retinue; therefore the King sends his own provision beforehand (observe it). So it is with a poor humble broken-hearted sinner; the poor soul is marvelous well content, the Lord should come to him, and dwell in him, and dispose of him; but he is such a poor beggarly wretch, he is not able to make God a fire, he cannot love God, he hath not that holy heat of *love* and *joy* to entertain and welcome the Lord as becometh his Majesty: therefore the Lord sends provision beforehand, and kindleth love and joy in the soul, that by that love and joy he may be welcomed to the heart of an humble sinner; or thus (to express myself more clearly); Take a burning glass that will receive the beams of the Sun, and heat and burn other things, the glass of itself hath no such heat in it, but when it hath received the beams of the Sun, it heats and burns other things, as flax, and such combustible matter; but it is by the heat of the beams of the Sun received, otherwise it could do nothing. So it is with an humble sinner, he lieth fit to receive the beams of God's mercy, and waits when the Sun of righteousness will shine from heaven comfortably upon his heart; and being warmed with the beams of God's love and favor effectually, he is able to reflect the heat of love and joy back again: this is the second thing.

[*Passage* 3.] Thirdly, the Doctrine saith, that love and joy are kindled, that they may entertain and rejoice in the riches of God's mercy. This last clause is added to discover the difference, and to make known the distinct nature of this love and joy here, from all the feigned and false love and joy, which hypocrites pretend to have, and seem to express to the Lord Jesus Christ. Therefore I say this love and joy is kindled not only to entertain him, and rejoice in him; for there is a kind of entertaining and rejoicing in Hypocrites. *Judas* had a hail Master, and the common people spread their garments, and welcomed Christ, crying *Hosanna, blessed is he that cometh in the Name of the most High*;[12] and the young man pretended a dear affection to Christ, *Master, I will follow thee whithersoever thou goest*;[13] And the *stony ground received the word with joy*,[14] and with love too, for they go both together, for he[15] that joys in a thing, cannot but love that he rejoiceth in: So that we see all these had a kind of joy, but it is not that kind of joy that comes from the Father, neither will it carry itself beseeming the riches of God's mercy; for he that saluted his Master *All hail*, in conclusion *betrayed him*: is this your joy and love you entertain Christ withal? So that young man that would *follow* him *whithersoever he went*, presently forsook him: And they that even now cried *Hosanna, Hosanna*, blessed be he that cometh in the Name of the Highest, anon cry as fast, crucify him, crucify him; and they that received the Word with joy, when temptation and persecution came, rejected it: This joy is a foolish imagination hammered out of their Anvil, for base ends and by-aims;[16] but they carry not themselves beseeming the riches of God's mercy revealed to them. For, *He that loveth father or mother, or brother or sister, more than me, is not worthy of me*, saith our Savior:[17] that is, he that prizeth anything more, and delights in anything more than Christ, is not worthy of him. Therefore whosoever he be that bestows his love and joy more upon anything in this world, than upon Christ; it is not a love and joy beseeming him, nor brought from heaven, but proceeds from a base rotten heart, and will fail us, and bring no profit nor comfort in the end. This then sufficeth for the sense, and proof of the point; we come now to open it a little; wherein for explication, and confirmation thereof, we will handle these two things: First we will show you the reason of the order, why after hope and desire, there comes this love and joy. Secondly, we will discover the motives and grounds, what[18] it is in the promise that will kindle and strike fire, and inflame these two affections, and bring them to the Lord.

[*Reasons.*] First, you will say how comes love and joy next after hope and desire?[19] I answer, you must know[20] there is no more but two affections in the soul, God infinitely wise having so framed it, and these two are hope and desire. The understanding saith such a thing is profitable and comfortable, if I had it, then hope is sent out to wait for that goodness, and if it comes not, then desire the second affection[21] is sent out to meet the good;[22] hope stands and waits for it, but desire wanders up and down, seeking and inquiring after a Lord Jesus, and goeth from coast to coast, from East to West; Oh that I could, and[23] oh that I might, and when shall I, and how may I come to the speech of a Lord Jesus[24] Christ. As it was with the Spouse in the[25] Canticles, when her beloved was gone, she wandered up and down, seeking of[26] him, and inquiring of the watchmen if they did not see him:[27] so desire[28] wanders from this thing to that thing,[29] from this place to that place, and never ceaseth, to see if it[30] can gain notice of Christ: It goeth to prayer to see if that will entreat a Christ: It goeth to the Word to see if that will reveal him:[31] It goeth to conference[32] to see if he can hear of a[33] Christ there: then it cometh to the congregation, and to the Sacrament, to see if it can hear any news of a Lord Jesus[34] Christ, and of mercy; and[35] the soul thus continues wandering and seeking, till at last the Lord Jesus[36] Christ comes into the soul, when the soul hath hungered[37] and longed for him. At length the Lord is[38] pleased to show himself in view: behold thy[39] King cometh; so the Lord saith, *Behold the Lamb of God that taketh away thy sins*:[40] Oh thou poor broken-hearted sinner, here is thy Savior, he is come down from heaven to speak peace to thy soul in the pardon of thy sins; thou that hungerest for a Christ, here he is to satisfy thee; thou that thirsteth for a[41] Christ, he is now come[42] to refresh thee; thou that hast long sought him, he saith, here I am, and all my merits are thine.[43] Now when the Lord Jesus is pleased to present himself to the soul; now desire hath met with the Lord: there are two other affections sent out by the Spirit to entertain Christ, and they are love and joy. Suffer me (I beseech you) to express myself after this manner, that I may discover the frame and guise of God's Spirit in this gracious work.[44]

It is in this case with a sinner,[45] as it is with a malefactor or traitor (observe what I say) who is pursued with a Pursuivant,[46] and is fled to the sea coasts, and hath taken a hold, and he is[47] there besieged. And now he seeth there is[48] no hope of favor, nor no hope of escape; therefore he is even[49] content to submit to the King's pleasure, and yields his neck to the block,[50] that he may receive punishment for his offense. Now coming to execution, he hears an inkling from the messengers,[51] there is yet hope that this man may[52] be pardoned; with that the poor malefactor in the tower,[53] his heart is stirred[54] up to hope: Nay then he hears another[55] messenger from the King himself say,[56] if he will come unto[57] the Court and seek unto his Majesty, and importune his grace for mercy and favor, it is[58] like he shall be pardoned: this is the second voice: one saith thou mayest be pardoned, the other saith, nay if thou wilt submit thyself, thou shalt be pardoned.[59] Then he makes haste, and desire carries him to the Court, to sue for favor from the King: So that he will be continually there,[60] listening and inquiring of everyone saying,[61] did you hear the King speak nothing of me, how stands the King's mind towards me, I[62] pray how goes my case? then some tells[63] him, the truth is the King hears you are humbled, and that you are sorry[64] for it,[65] you are like to hear more news hereafter.[66] At last the King looks out of the window, and seeth the malefactor and saith, is this the traitor? they say yes,[67] this is the man that is humbled and entreats[68] for mercy, and desires nothing so much as favor. The King tells[69] him the truth is his pardon is drawing,[70] and coming towards him: with that his heart leaps in his belly, and his heart is enlarged to[71] his Majesty; and he saith God bless your Majesty, never was there such a favorable Prince to a poor traitor.[72] His heart leaps with[73] joy because his pardon is coming towards him; haply it is not sealed yet: Now when it is sealed and all,[74] the King calls him in and delivers it, and that is the last stroke of faith.[75]

So it is with a poor sinner, he is this[76] malefactor: you that have committed high treason, you think not of it, but take heed, God will pursue you one day; haply the Lord lets[77] you alone for the present, but he will surprise you on the[78] sudden, and conscience will pluck thee by the throat, and carry thee down to Hell. And now the Lord pursueth him with heavy and terrible indignation,[79] and lets fly at his face, and sets conscience awork[80] as Pursuivant,[81] and that saith, these are thy sins, and to hell thou must go, God hath set[82] me to execute thy soul. Now the poor soul seeth he can by no means escape[83] from the Lord, and to purchase any favor he sees it is[84] impossible;

therefore he is resolved to lie down at God's feet, and saith,[85] I confess Lord, there is but one way, let me be damned, so thou mayest be glorified. If the Lord will show favor, so it is; but he cannot desire it almost, because he hath so sinned against him. Now comes the great voice, he hears a noise afar off by the ministry of the Gospel, thy sins are pardonable: with this the soul looks up, and hope stirs the heart, and saith, then it may be a damned creature may be saved, then it may be a *dead dog* may live, and a traitor may be pardoned: Then the soul hears another voice, if thou canst see the excellency of mercy and long for it, and seek after it, thou shalt be pardoned. Why, go then, saith Desire, and he fills heaven and earth with his cries, and his closet with his prayers, and the congregation with his tears, and will inquire of the Minister of God, and other good Christians; Sirs, you are of the bed-chamber, you are acquainted with God, I pray how goes my case? will the Lord, think you, pardon me? did you hear the Lord say nothing of me? how stands it with me? Now the Ministers of God that understand the frame of the heart aright, will say, The Lord hears you are an humble sinner, and that you long for mercy, and lie at the court gate, and will not away without mercy; we hear, God intends well towards you, you shall hear more hereafter: thus far now desire goeth.

At last, Christ presents himself to the sinner, and speaks to his soul by the ministry of the Word, he looks down from heaven, and gives him a sweet look of mercy, and that makes his heart leap again, and that is done in this manner (for still understand that God doth it by the ministry of the Word, do not now look for any strange dreams or miraculous imaginations), the Lord speaks by his Word, and saith, thou hast a broken heart, thou hast longed for my salvation, go thy ways, I have heard those prayers of thine, and observed those endeavors of thine, and thy pardon is granted, be it to thee as thou hast desired, and thy pardon shall afterward be sealed and delivered. Now when the Lord tells the soul, It is done, it wants only sealing and delivering, the heart of a poor sinner, when it finds some comfort and refreshment from the Lord in the word, he saith, The Minister said I was the sinner, and God intends good to me, and that my sins are pardoned: as the Prince saith, *Fiat*, let it be done; so the Lord saith, Mercy is coming towards thee, and mercy is granted to thee: Now the heart leaps with joy, and blesseth the Lord, let my soul bless him forever: How ought I to bless that God that hath done so great things for my poor soul? What, I pardoned? and what, my sins forgiven? What, is the pardon granted, and now sealing, only it wants delivering? why then if I never see more of it, but go down to hell, yet this is my comfort, that I have seen a smile from God, this makes my heart leap within me, though I burn in hell forever; this is the next voice.

Now that brings in love and joy: See a passage this way (Isaiah

40:2),[86] *Comfort ye, comfort ye my people, saith the Lord, speak comfortably to Jerusalem, and cry unto her, that her warfare is accomplished, and her iniquity is pardoned, tell Jerusalem she is accepted;* tell her so, saith the Lord. So the Lord speaks to poor hungry broken sinners, after he hath seen their desires to be sound and thorough; the Lord saith to his Ministers, Speak to the heart of a poor sinner, tell him from me, tell him from heaven, tell him from the Lord Jesus Christ, tell, from under the hand of the Spirit, his person is accepted, and his sins are done away, and he shall be looked upon in mercy. So (Isaiah 66)[87] the text saith, *The Lord looks to him that is of an humble and contrite heart, and that trembles at his word.* The poor creature cannot but observe every word, and tremble at every truth: Here is salvation (indeed, saith he) but it is not mine; here is mercy, but that is not mine: and so he shakes at the apprehension of it, that he should hear of it, and not enjoy it. The text saith,[88] *The Lord looks at such a trembling soul;* that is, he casts sweet intimations of his goodness and kindness upon him; and saith, Thou poor trembling sinner, to thee be it spoken, I have an eye towards thee in the Lord Jesus Christ; this, as I take it, is the meaning of the place. *Ephraim* is the picture of a soul truly humbled; we may see his behavior towards God, and God's dealing towards him; the text saith, *Surely I have heard Ephraim bemoaning himself* (here is the heart broken, and thirsting, and what more), *thou hast chastised me, and I was chastised, as a bullock unaccustomed to the yoke; turn thou me, and I shall be turned; thou art the Lord my God, surely after that I was turned, I repented, and after that I was instructed, I smote upon my thigh, I was ashamed, yea even confounded, because I did bear the reproach of my youth.* Here we see *Ephraim* lamenting himself, as if the sinner should say, I am the wretch that have seen all the means of grace in abundant measure and beauty, and yet never profited under the same; the Lord hath corrected me, but I would not be tamed; the Lord he hath instructed me, but I would not learn; Lord turn me, thou art my God, I have nothing in myself. Nay now I see the evils which before I never perceived, and I observe the baseness of my course now, which before I never considered; and I am ashamed of my former abuse of God's grace revealed; I am even confounded in regard of the abominations which my soul hath harbored; this is the mourning of a poor sinner: Now mark God's answer, *Ephraim* is my dear son, he is a pleasant child, for since I spake against him, I do earnestly remember him still, therefore my bowels[89] are troubled for him, I will surely have mercy upon him. The Lord kindled the fire of his indignation in his heart, and spake bitter things against his conscience, yet he remembered him all the while; as who should say, I observed all those desires, and considered all those tears, and heard all those prayers, and took notice of all those complaints; and my bowels earn[90] towards a poor sinner that desires my mercy in Christ, and the truth is, I will show mercy to him: thus we see the behavior of God to the soul, as also the behavior of the soul to God: and thus you see the order of the affections; when God is absent, hope waits for it, and desire longs after it; when the good is in view, love entertains it, and joy delights, and sports, and playeth with it: love is like the Host that welcomes the guest, and joy is like the chamberlain that attends upon him, and is very ready and pleasing to entertain the promise, and the Lord Jesus Christ: this is the very guise[91] of the heart, as I conceive.

SELECTION VI

The Soul's Exaltation

Thomas Hooker

The Thomas Hooker Window, First Church of Christ, Hartford. This stained-glass window from the Tiffany Studios (1900) commemorates the first pastor of the church for his double role as a religious and political leader. It presumably depicts the interior of a meeting house, with Hooker delivering a sermon. The window is the gift of Mary Turner Hooker. Courtesy of the First Church of Christ, Hartford, Connecticut.

The Soul's Exaltation comprises three relatively short sermon-series:
"The Soul's Union with Christ," on 1 Corinthians 6:17; "The Soul's
Benefit from Union with Christ," on 1 Corinthians 1:30; and "The
Soul's Justification," on 2 Corinthians 5:21. Hooker had concluded
The Soul's Vocation with the promise to continue his discussion of
salvation: "thus the soul is come home to God by vocation; now the
prodigal is come home to his father . . . thus we have heard, how
the soul is ingrafted into the stock Christ. Now afterward if the Lord
lend life and liberty, we shall come to show what the soul receives
from the stock."[1] "The Soul's Union" and "The Soul's Benefit" are
concerned with the seventh and eighth steps of salvation: union with
Jesus Christ and communion with Jesus Christ (see selection IV).
They seem to be the promised successors to the sermons in *The
Soul's Vocation* centering on the first half of ingrafting.

The selected sermon represents half of "The Soul's Union," the
first sermon of two, and focuses on the joining or "knitting" of the
believer with Jesus Christ. The second sermon goes on to disclose
the way they become one spirit (doctrine 2). That second sermon
centers on the "deep mysteries" of how the Spirit "leave[s] a super-
natural dint and power" on the soul to enable its union with Jesus
Christ, how "the words [of the Gospel] are but the shell, but the substance is the Spirit of grace," and how "the heart of a poor sinner
believes and stays itself, firstly, upon the Godhead, and Deity, and
afterwards upon the Humanity" of Jesus Christ.[2] In explaining the
mystery of union with Christ, Hooker is conscious of the inadequacy
of exact and logical explanation: between the two sermons of "The
Soul's Union," he says, "The point is difficult, and the mystery great,
and beyond the reach and room of that little light I enjoy."[3] The reasons for the lack of information lie less with Hooker's abilities than
with the inexplicability of regeneration. Like Paul (in 1 Cor. 6:17,
the text of the sermon), Hooker can hardly go beyond this miracle:
"Every true believer is joined unto Christ."

He copes with the inadequacy of logical expansion of the stated
topic in two of his typical ways—widening the focus and stressing
the uses. He expands, as he often does in *The Soul's Vocation*, beyond the doctrinal emphasis on the event to the situation after its
occurrence; that is, the sermon shifts from an initial analysis of all
the ways knitting occurs to a conclusion exhorting "the Saints knit"
in the fulfillment of their duties.[4] The second particular of the knitting of the soul to Christ epitomizes the way Hooker's preaching
pushes far beyond the announced topic: he moves in one paragraph
from a positive definition of the manner in which the soul closes
with Christ, to a contrary description of lack of closure, to an exhortation to work for union. Puritan preachers emphasized that stirring
the heart—the seat of the affections—during the uses was the most
important part of the sermon. Thus Hooker devotes over two-thirds

of this sermon to the uses. One senses that even if he could have given an extensive and detailed description of the miracle of union, the urgency to apply the theological truths personally to his auditors would have pulled him on to instruct, to instill terror, and to provide comfort.

Assiduous attention to the context of each particular is strikingly impressive throughout Hooker's preaching. The selections amply demonstrate that he never proceeds to explain a step of salvation without fully clarifying its position in the entire scheme. In this sermon on union with Jesus Christ, Hooker reviews the ordering of the soul's faculties and affections in vocation. With the images of eating and the personifications of hope, desire, love, and joy from *The Soul's Vocation*, he stimulates the auditor's memory and insures its continuance by adding a new similitude of kneading. Likewise, in the third use, he repeats previously used language regarding the way the soul is unified with Christ and goes on to reinforce it with a masterful similitude of the tree and the branch.

Such abundant catalogs of similitudes—especially the manner in which each image builds on the previous one—typify Hooker's preaching. For instance, to explain the union of the soul and Christ, Hooker employs an impressive number and variety of images of "near combination[s] of one thing with another": friendship, parent-child relationship, grafting, matrimony, union of body and soul. Even more striking is their growing applicability; Hooker's excited "nay, go yet farther" validates our experience of their increasing suitability. The most brilliant image in the sermon is this marital similitude: "when he is satisfied with her breasts, he is ravished with her love." Once again Hooker is to be admired for apt appropriation, not for daring originality. It is the Old Testament (in this case, Prov. 5:19) that provides the frank sexual imagery.

1 Corinthians 6:17: *He that is joined to the Lord, is one Spirit.*

We told you[5] that the application of the merits of Christ, consists especially in two things:

First, the preparation of the soul for Christ.

Secondly, the engrafting or the knitting of the soul to the Lord Jesus Christ.

Of this preparation we have heretofore largely treated: partly in contrition, where the soul is cut off from sin: partly in humiliation, whereby the soul is cut off from itself; whereby the Lord razes[6] the foundation of all carnal confidence, whereby a man rests upon his own privileges and performances, and makes his services his Savior; either the soul seeth no need to depart from sin, or else it thinks it can help itself out of sin: when both these are removed from the soul, then it is fitted to receive the Lord Jesus Christ.

Secondly, the soul comes to be engrafted into Christ: and that hath two parts:

First, the calling of the sinner; or the putting of the soul into Christ.

Secondly, the growing of the soul with Christ: these two take up the nature of engrafting a sinner into the stock:

First, it is put into the stock.

Secondly, being put into the stock, it grows together with the stock: these two things are answerable[7] in the soul. The former of these two we have largely treated of, and fully finished in[8] the great work of vocation, when the Lord brings the sinner to himself by the call of mercy, and the voice of the Gospel: we are now to proceed; and we have made some entrance into the second; and that is the growing of the soul together with Christ: for though the graft be in the stock, yet it cannot be fruitful, unless it grow together with the stock: now this growing together is accomplished by two means:

The first is the union which the soul hath with Christ.

The second is a conveyance of sap, or sweetness, or a communion with Christ, and all the treasures of grace and happiness that is in him: then to make up the growing together of the graft and the stock; First, the graft is put into the stock. Secondly, there must be a communicating of the moisture that is in the stock, to the graft, and so they grow together; otherways[9] it grows not at all, but withers away: now we are first to describe the nature of the work in general; and then we will descend to particulars, and the several parts of it: now we will define this union so far as it concerns our purpose, not entrenching into particulars.

It is such a joining of the faithful soul in such a means to Christ, that it becomes one spirit: these are not by way of collection[10] to be gathered, but they are plainly expressed in the text: and two points of doctrine I mean to prosecute: the first point is from the first part of the text.

[*Doctrine 1.*] Every true believer is joined unto Christ: the word in the original is, glued; he is glued, he is waxed, he is firmly and nearly combined and knit to the Lord Jesus Christ.

The second part of the description, is the second point in hand.

[*Doctrine 2.*] He is so joined unto the Lord, that he becomes one spirit: as the adulterer and the adulteress is one flesh; so he that believes in Christ, is so nearly joined to him, that he becomes one spirit: so we see the verse offers two doctrines:

First, that a faithful soul is firmly and nearly knit unto Christ.

Secondly, he is so knit that he becomes one spirit.

But first of the first doctrine.[11]

Whatever by way of comparison can be alleged, concerning the

near combination of one thing with another, they are all tied to this
knitting of the soul to Christ: look what a friend is to a friend; look
what a father is to a child; what a husband to a wife; look what a
graft is to a tree; and that is nearer than a husband to a wife: nay, go
yet farther (Galatians 2:20), what the soul is to the body;[12] the soul is
not only knit to the body, as one member to another, as the hand is
knit to the arm, and the arm to the shoulder; but the soul doth communicate itself universally thorough[13] the least part of the body: so the
Apostle saith, *Christ is the very soul of a believer, I live, yet not I, but
the Lord Jesus liveth in me*; so that look as the body liveth by the soul,
the soul closing, and communicating, and quickening of the same, so
Christ is in a Christian, and speaks in a Christian, and enableth a
Christian to the performance of that he doth; hence the body of the
faithful is called Christ (1 Corinthians 12:12), but we will open this a
little further in two passages:

First, the carriage of the soul in this closing.

Secondly, the manner how it doth close.

The carriage we shall desire to discover in three particulars, which
may be expressed in a graft, when it is put into the stock: and I say,
therein observe three particulars:

First, there is an exercise of the elements that are in the graft upon
the stock, and are so far mingled one with another, and do so far close
one with another, that they become one.

Secondly, the graft joins to the stock, and none other.

Thirdly, they do not only act thus, but are bound one to another:
and this makes them act answerably to these three particulars. There
is also an expression of the knitting of the soul to Christ in three
particulars:

First, the soul gathers up itself, and all its spirits, its faculties, that
doth exercise in the work thereof upon Christ, and that makes the soul
to grow unto the Lord: when the soul turns the promise into good
blood, it doth not only chew the meat, but disgest[14] it, and it becomes
good blood: a true believer gathers up all the faculties of his soul, and
employs them upon Christ: hope expects Christ, and desire longs for
Christ, and love and joy embrace Christ, and the will closeth[15] Christ;
thus the soul settles itself upon Christ, hoping, expecting, longing,
desiring, loving, embracing: look as it is with a woman that kneads
dough, if there be two parts of it, the molding and the kneading knits
them together, and makes them one lump: so there is the molding of
the soul to the promise, hoping, and desiring, and longing, and choos-
ing; faith kneads all these together, and knits them unto God, and
draws the soul to him.

Secondly, the soul is satisfied with Christ, and the riches of his
grace; the believer doth repose his confidence wholly thereupon: Proverbs 5:19: that which makes the love of a husband increase towards
his wife, is this, *He is satisfied with her breasts at all times, and then*

he comes to be ravished with her love: if a husband hath a loose heart, and will not content himself with the wife of his youth, but hath his back doors, and his goings out; this makes a breach in matrimonial affection; but when he is satisfied with her breasts, he is ravished with her love: so hope hath an expectation of mercy, and is satisfied therewith; desire longs for mercy, and is satisfied therewith; the will closeth Christ, and it is fully satisfied with him; and if it were to choose again, it would choose none but Christ: thus suck thou up the consolations in the promise, and be satisfied therewith, and then thou wilt grow thereupon; but if you will be resting here, and staying upon the contentments of the world, this is weak confidence, and draws the soul from God.

Thirdly, the last thing is the binding of the heart upon both these, *viz.* the keeping of the heart to the exercise.of the promise, and to be satisfied with the promise; Colossians 1:23:[16] *If ye continue in the faith*; being grounded and settled, so that a man doth stake down his heart to the promise, and holds hope, and desire, and love, and joy, and the will unto it: it receives all Christ, and none but Christ, and stays here, and continues here forever: this same covenant that binds the soul to Christ, is that which makes the union between Christ and the soul: thus we see how the soul carries itself in this union.

The second thing considerable, is the manner how it is done, and the quality of this union: and this we will discover in three particulars:

First, it is a real union, but it is spiritual, you must not conceive it grossly, as if my body were joined to Christ; but there is a real union which is spiritual: there is a union between the nature of Christ, God and man, and a true believer: that which I desire to declare is upon this ground, to difference this union from that which Divines are deceived in; viz. that it is an union more than in bare notion and apprehension of the mind; for whatever a man conceives, his understanding closeth with it; as whatever I apprehend, I close with that; there is a conveyance of the thing into my mind, and I close with it: now the union of a believer's soul with Christ is more than this: it is not a bare apprehension, a wicked man will go far in the apprehension of Christ; but this union is somewhat more, and I call it a real union, because there is a knitting and a closing, not only of the apprehension with a Savior, but a closing of a soul with a Savior.

Secondly, I say this is a total union, the whole nature of a Savior, and the whole nature of a believer are knit together: first, that it is a real union, all the places of Scripture do intimate as much: what the branch is to the vine, the soul is to Christ: now they are more than imagination; so what the husband is to the wife, the soul is to Christ. Now they are more than in understanding; for a man may conceive of another woman, as well as of his wife; but this is another union, whereby the person of the one is knit unto another: the bond of matrimony knits these two together. This is the frame and guise of knitting the soul to Christ, it is no bare apprehension but we feed upon Christ, and grow upon Christ, and are married to Christ: Hosea 2:20: *I have married thee to myself, in truth, in judgment, and in righteousness.*

Secondly, I say it is total in so much that Christ is the head, and a believer, a member; in both these regards they are joined: Christ is the head of the Church, not only according as he is God, but as he is God and man; and a believer is a member not only according to his body, but according to his body and soul: now whole Christ being the head, and the whole believer being a member, therefore a whole Christ, and a whole believer must be joined together.

The third is this, this union is inseparable: Jeremiah 32:40: *The Lord promiseth to make an everlasting covenant with the house of Israel, and I will never part away from them to do them good*: so Psalm 89:33,34. It is spoken there concerning *Solomon* as I conceive the Psalmist saith, *If he sin against me, I will scourge him, and I will visit him with stripes; nevertheless, my loving kindness I will not take away from him, nor suffer my faithfulness to fail my covenant; I will not break, nor alter the thing that is gone out of my mouth*: mark that the Lord out of faithfulness doth establish thee to him in vocation, the Lord hath made a covenant with the soul in vocation, the hand of the Lord lays hold upon the soul, and brings it home; now though the Lord correct the soul sharply, yet will he not leave it totally and finally; it is inseparably knit to Christ; what can it be, what shall it be, that can separate a poor sinner from Christ? if Satan could have hindered him from coming to a Savior, he would have then hindered him from coming to a Christ, when he had his greatest dominion over him: if sin could have let[17] him when a man had nothing else but sin, he would not have forsaken that and have been brought home to Christ. If the world could have prevailed, Christ should never have plucked him from it; but when Satan had his greatest power over him, when a man was nothing else but sin by nature, when the world most prevailed, yet then God by his good Spirit plucked thy heart from sin and self: that soul is mine, saith Christ, Satan must give way, and shall not hinder it: that soul is mine, saith Christ, sin shall not let it from coming to me: that soul is mine, saith Christ, and the world shall not stop the work of a Savior; and if Satan in the height of his malice, and the world in the top of its force, could not prevail to keep the soul from Christ; then much less shall these be able to pluck us from a Savior: the point then is undeniable, that the soul is really, totally and inseparably knit to the Lord Jesus Christ.

[*Use 1.*] We may here take notice of the high and happy privilege of poor creatures; however the poor Saints of God are despised and contemned[18] of the world, yet they are received into covenant with the Lord; they are made one with Christ, and are of the blood royal: and this is the greatest privilege that can be; this should bear up the hearts of poor Christians; ye are now in the very gate of Heaven, nay let me say as the Apostle speaks; and I see no reason why a man may not say that he is in Heaven in truth, though not in that measure and largeness of glory he shall be afterwards. 1 Thessalonians 4:17.[19] The happiness that a Christian shall have in Heaven, is this, *He shall be ever with the Lord Jesus*; Heaven were not Heaven, unless a man might be with Christ there: the place doth not make a man happy, but the union with a Savior, that[20] makes him happy, and to be joined to Father, Son, and holy Ghost, that makes him happy, and the believer is now knit to them, and therefore must needs be happy; Deuteronomy 33:the last verse:[21] as he said of the people of Israel, so may I say of all faithful souls, *Happy art thou, oh Israel*, saith the text, *who is like unto thee, saved by the Lord, the shield of thy help, and the sword of thy excellency*; so may I say, Happy are ye, oh believing souls, who is like unto you? ye are saved by God, and are married to the Lord Jesus Christ, and are the spouses of the Savior of the world; and he that is the Judge of the world, is your Husband, your beloved, and you are his: let nothing therefore dismay your hearts.

[*Use* 2.] The second use is that of terror, and it is like a thunderbolt, able to break the hearts of all those that are opposite to them that believe in Christ: that which I would have all consider on is this, that the persecution of the Saints is a sin of a high nature, it is a most heinous abominable sin in the sight of God, however the world thinks not so of it, yet they shall be sure one day to find: I know men think not thus, because haply the law of man provides not in this case to punish those that oppose the Lord Jesus Christ, and the power of his grace, because haply the Magistrate doth not, or haply cannot smite those that set themselves against those that fear God and trample upon them: therefore wicked men make the Saints of God the mark of their malice, and the aim of their rage, and all their indignation is bent that way, they glory in what they have done, and threaten what they will do; they will hang and draw, and quarter within themselves: this is that which the proud spirits of the world make their main prize, and they think thereby to procure praise unto themselves, and great preferment in their own eyes this way: let me speak a little to these, you that are guilty of this sin, see the compass of it, take notice of the reach how far this rebellion goeth: I would wish these men that persecute the Saints, I would have them understand the compass of their course, how far their wicked practice extendeth, it is not against a despised Christian; no, let them know it, their rage and malice ascends up to Heaven, and offers violence to the Lord Jesus Christ, and they labor what they can to pluck Christ from the right hand of his Father, and they endeavor what in them lies to shed his blood, and take away his life: let all know that have been professed opposers and dead haters of the Saints of God, let them know they are indicted of high treason, and that in a most heinous manner against the Lord of Heaven and Earth, against the Lord Jesus Christ, the Redeemer of the world: I would that these men would not cozen themselves, for God will not be mocked: they profess they love Christ with all their hearts, and they will do anything for him, but those nice fellows, those spruce fellows, it is those that they hate to the death: do you so indeed? thou hast said enough then, for thou hatest Christ in hating them, and thou persecutest Christ in persecuting them: Isaiah 37:23,28: *Whom hast thou reproached and blasphemed*, saith the text, *and against whom hast thou exalted thy voice, and lifted up thine eyes on high? even against the Holy one of Israel*: and in the twenty-eighth verse, *I know thy abode, and thy going out, and thy coming in, and thy rage against me*: so that however *Sennacherib* aimed at *Hezekiah* only, and those that profess the truth, yet the Lord takes it as done to himself: he that knew their hearts and their malice, he saith, *I know thy rage against me*, it was *against the holy One of Israel that they railed*. Wicked men persecute the lives of believers; now Christ lives in them, and thou hatest the life of Christ, and persecutest the life of Christ: Acts 9: *Paul had gotten letters from the Synagogue, and he would have haled to prison all the Saints of God that professed the Name of Christ*; now if a man had come to *Paul*, and asked him, *Paul* why do you persecute Christ; he would have been in great indignation; what, reverenced *Paul*, learned *Paul*, zealous *Paul*; what, he persecute the Lord of life? why, Christ proclaims it, he doth so, and he puts it to an upshot, and ends the controversy, and puts the question out of doubt, *I am Jesus*, saith he, *whom thou persecutest*: as if he had said, Poor fool; thou knowest not, and I perceive thou thinkest it not, but I receive the wound; the foot is pricked, and the head complains. I would have a man make the case his own, and be his own Judge: If any man should pretend friendship to you, and profess he loves you, and tells you he tenders your person, but yet he will torment your body; and he loves your head, but yet he will cut off your arm: there is no man so weak, but he would loathe such cursed kind of dissimulation: a man cannot love the head and hate the member; love the person and torment the body: just so these men deal with the Lord Jesus Christ; God's faithful believing servants are his eyes: Zechariah 2:8: *He that toucheth you, toucheth the apple of mine eye*; they are flesh of his flesh, and bone of his bone: thou that pretendest to love Christ, and to tender the head, and in the mean time loathest his members, and his poor Saints; know that thou dost not persecute the Saints so much, but thou persecutest Christ much more: but haply thou wilt say; I am no drunkard, nor no whoremonger; I tell thee this sin is worse than drunkenness, or whoredom: the text saith, *that Herod was an incestuous person, and married his brother Philip's wife*;[22] but he added this sin above all the rest, he put *John* in prison; therefore all that hear the Word of God: if a man did see an incestuous wretch in the congregation, whom humanity, and reason, and nature doth loathe, we would abhor and detest him, nay every man knows that it deserves death. Look upon thy own soul, and lay thy hand upon thy heart, thou that persecutest the Saints: thy sin is greater, and thy condemnation shall be far sorer than such a man's: hence it is that God threatens such men with the heaviest judgments: Psalm 52:2,5:[23] it is spoken there concerning *Doeg*; we may see the story: 1 Samuel 22: *When Abimelech gave David show-bread and Goliah's sword, Doeg saw it and told Saul, and afterwards slew eighty-five persons of the Priests*; now this Psalmist made this Psalm against this man: and he saith, *Thy tongue deviseth mischief like a sharp razor working deceitfully, and God shall likewise destroy thee forever; He shall take thee away, and pluck thee out of thy dwelling place, and out of the land of the living*; because he did oppose himself against *Abimelech*, therefore the Lord would not let him go without a punishment: nay as God threatens the sorest punishment against such persons; so the Saints of God by their prayers set themselves most against them: Psalm 129:5: *Let them all be confounded and turned back that have ill will at Sion, neither do they that go by say, The blessing of the Lord be upon you*: the poorest man that lives, that is in the meanest place, if he walks in an honest calling, the Saints wish a blessing to him; but they that oppose the Saints of God, the Saints curse them in the name of the Lord: it is true, I confess, we must be wary and wise, but being wise and wary, it is a thing we may and should do; *David* by way of Revelation knew who were implacable and obdurate; though we know not this, yet aiming at none in particular, but only in the general, at those who be incorrigible; the Saints of God curse them, and that bitterly in all their desires that they put up to God; nay the greatest indictment at the day of judgment proceeds against sinners because of the persecution of his Saints, because in them they persecute Christ himself; they tear out the very eyes of Christ, and rend his heart in pieces: Jude 14: *The Lord cometh with thousands of his Angels to execute judgment upon all, and to convince all that are ungodly amongst them of all their ungodly deeds which they have committed, and of all their hard speeches which ungodly sinners have spoken against him*: Matthew 25: the latter end: *Depart from me, ye cursed, I know ye not; I was in prison, and ye visited me not; I was naked, and ye clothed me not*: why, Jesus Christ is gone to Heaven, and haply they never saw him: but saith he, *in that you did it not to one of these, ye did it not to me*. Now Divines reason thus, that all the doom that shall pass upon the wicked at the day of judgment, shall go in this tenure:[24] because ye have not done this and that; and if those shall be condemned that did not visit the Saints when they were in prison: if those shall be damned that did not cover the naked, what shall become of those that tear their hearts, and rend the clothes off their backs? the Lord hath not only torments for them here, but he hath devils in hell to torment them forevermore: Therefore let me speak a word of advice to those that are guilty of this great sin of persecuting the Lord of life; go aside and reason with your souls, and parley with your hearts, and think with yourselves, Oh poor fool that I was, it was not any poor Christian, any poor Saint that I hated, but it was the Lord Jesus Christ, the Lord of life, and of glory, that I persecuted, that I would have plucked out of his Throne; I would have tore his flesh off his body, and rent his members asunder; and alas, I never knew it; it was not the Saints I opposed, but the Lord Jesus Christ. I speak not this to countenance faction, my aim is at those that persecute religion and sanctity of life.

[*Use* 3.] For examination and trial; we may hence see who are those that cleave unto Christ, as also those that are false and dissemble with Christ, which pretend great love, and profess great kindness unto our Savior, and how much they respect him, and how near Christ is to them. From the former Doctrine, you may discover whether this be true or false: he that is a true believer, and knit so to Christ as nevermore to be separated and parted, he takes up the whole strength of his soul, and bottoms it upon a Savior; he is sanctified with the freeness of his grace, and is resolved forever to cleave unto him, and bestow himself upon him: he that truly believes, is thus knit, thus joined to the Lord Jesus Christ: look as it is sometimes with a mighty branch of a tree, or with the arm of a man's body, however the bough of the tree may be rent sometimes, and haled aside by the violence of the tempest, or by the pulling of a man's hand, yet it will hold by the body, and when the hand is gone, it will go up again: so it is with a faithful soul, he so cleaves to Christ, that he will never be parted from him, he will never be separated, whatever provocation or opposition comes to the contrary: the believing soul is sometimes rent and strained by the weight of persecution and temptation, and with the violence of corruptions; but as soon as the temptation and the weight is gone, it clings to Christ again; and as the bough, take away the hand, and it will rise up again: so whatsoever temptations come, or corruptions come, or oppositions betide, yet it will not be plucked off from the Lord, and though it may be swayed aside, yet it grows to the Lord: therefore the first of Samuel 10:26, it is said, *The hearts that God touched did cleave unto Saul*; so it is with a believer, those that are famous in the eyes of the world, and have professed great kindness to him, in the time of persecution they will fly off; but those whose hearts God hath fully touched, they will follow Christ, notwithstanding all opposition; as it is with the needle of a dial,[25] it may be stirred and moved, but it will never rest till it come to the right place again: so it is with the soul that is knit to Christ by faith, though he may be staggering and doubting, yet he will never be quieted, till he come to be fastened the right way to Christ; but others there are that cleave feignedly to Christ, and herein it will appear; either they will off when occasion serves, or else wither in the very work of the profession of the Gospel, though they continue therein: some there be that fall away wholly from their profession; of this sort are thousands of your common protestants, that are only knit unto Christ by peace and prosperity: there are millions, if the day of trouble should come, and fire and sword should come, and make them make profession of their faith, they would fly off from their profession, and they would leave the Lord, and the Gospel, and all in the lurch, because they are not knit unto Christ by saving faith. In the second place there are others, who though they do not fall away totally, yet notwithstanding they wither, and die, and come to nothing: and these are your cunning and close-hearted hypocrites, those that are knit to Christ, and grow to him by some help, and succor, and assistance, which they have from him, by which they flourish, grow green in the profession of the Lord: there is a generation of cunning dissemblers, and close false dealers with the Gospel, that grow to Christ by some help they receive from him, and that makes them make a glorious show in the profession of the Gospel; but yet if God take away this assistance, they wither, and die, and fade, and vanish: look as it is with the hairs of a man's head, or with the leaves of a tree, the leaves grow to the tree, and the hairs to the head, but they grow not so much upon the substance of the body, nor the leaves upon the substance of the tree, as the arm and the branch doth, but they grow only by the moisture that comes from the body, and the moisture that comes from the root: or look as it is with a wen[26] in a man's body, it is no part of the body, but it grows out of the superabundant humors of the body, and that feeds the wen, and increaseth it; but if the body grow weak and feeble, and that humor be taken away, it withers and comes to a dry skin: just so it is with these cursed close-hearted hypocrites, as the hairs and leaves grow, so they grow to the Lord Jesus, namely, the Lord vouchsafeth some sap and moisture, and some assistance to the performance of some services, but they never grow to the substance of a Savior, they never grew to the holiness of Christ, they never had the Spirit of Christ powerfully prevailing with them: as it is with the wen, so it is with these glorious hypocrites, that can vent themselves very gloriously, they are wens in the profession of the Gospel, they look full bigly, and stare every man in the face, and to the appearance of the world, are men of great account; but if once the Lord take away his assistance from heaven, they are like leaves upon the tree, if they fall not, yet they wither away: I have observed sometimes, you shall have dry leaves stay upon an oak tree, till new ones come again: so these haughty-hearted hypocrites, they will take up a kind of a dying course of profession in the way of life and salvation, but they never come to be opposers and resisters of God and his grace, till there comes some to be wiser and stricter in a Christian course than they, and then he falls away.

[*Use* 4.] Is it so that the faithful soul is thus nearly knitted to Christ, as the member to the body, or the branch to the vine? then all you

that believe in Christ, observe from hence a ground of strong consolation, against all the contempt of the world, and the misery that can
betide, and against all the temptations that Satan can lay against
you, to cause you to fall finally, or totally.

First, it is a ground of great comfort and consolation to carry up
the soul, and lift up the heart against all the contempt and disgrace,
against all the troubles, and miseries, and persecutions, that can betide or befall you, or can be cast upon you, in this wandering pilgrimage of yours: when a Christian begins to turn his face heaven-
ward, and go home to the Lord, then all his friends fly away, and
depart from him: *David* complains, that his honors stood afar off,
and he was a mocking to the enemy, and a contempt to those that
were before near unto him; so it will be with you, nay, it is so with
most that live in the bosom of the Church: how often can many of
you speak of it, when the Lord hath given you a heart to walk with
him, and depend upon him? how often are you made the off-scouring
of the world? your carnal friends detest your persons, and scorn your
societies; why? raise up your hearts with the consideration of the
former truth; ye that do endure it, or may fear it, comfort yourselves:
doth man cast you off? doth man cast you out? Christ will receive
you, why then are you discouraged? what though the servant frown,
if the Master welcome? what though we be not with the wicked, if we
be with Christ, and Christ with us; why are we then discontented?
it is that which comforts a party that matcheth against her parents'
mind, when her parents frown, this comforts her heart, though she
hath not their love and society, yet she hath the love and company
of her husband, and that contents her: so it is with every believing
soul, you have matched against the mind of your carnal friends, they
would not have you take that course; Oh then they tell you, Woe and
beggary will befall you; well, though you have matched contrary to
the minds of your carnal friends, or master, or husband, yet comfort
thyself, though thou hast the ill will of an earthly husband, yet now
God will be a husband in heaven, thou mayst sing care away, and be
forever comforted and refreshed: it was that which God himself gave
for a cordial[27] to cheer up *Jacob*, in that long and tedious journey of
his, when he was going into a far country; Genesis 28:14,15: when
he was going from his own country, and had no friends to succor
him, the Lord met him, and said, *I will go with thee, and keep thee
in all places whither thou goest, and I will bring thee back into this
land, and I will never leave thee, until I have done that, which I spake
unto thee of*; this was that which lifted and bare up the heart of the
good man, though he could not but expect hard dealing; why yet
saith the Lord, *I will go with thee, and never leave thee*; think of it,
and consider of it seriously, what a ground of consolation may it be,
when we shall wander up and down, and go into caves, and holes,
and dens of the earth; when we shall go into prison or banishment,

and friends may not, nor will not go with us, yet Christ will go;
Isaiah 43:2: *When thou passest thorough the waters, I will be with
thee; and thorough the rivers, they shall not overflow thee; when
thou walkest thorough the fire, thou shalt not be burnt, neither shall
the flame kindle upon thee*; a man cannot save his wife sometimes in
the water, though she be ready to be drowned; a man cannot go into
the fire to help her, though she be ready to be burnt; but Christ will
be with thee in the water, and in the fire, that is, in the heaviest
trials and sorest troubles: what can come to us, if Christ be with us?
if misery, and sorrow, and trouble be with us, if Christ our husband
be with us, what matter? he is the husband of his spouse, and the
Savior of his people, why should we then be discouraged or disquieted?

Secondly, as it is a ground of comfort against all opposition and
troubles of the world, so it is a ground of comfort to stay our souls
against the fierceness of all temptations, whereby Satan labors to
pluck us from the Lord Jesus Christ; and our hearts sink within us,
and we shall (we say) one day perish by the hands of *Saul*, by the
hand of the enemy attempting, and corruptions prevailing; clear your
hearts and know, though temptations may outbid your weaknesses,
and corruptions may outbid your abilities, and when you would do
good, evil is present with you, and sin cleaves and sticks close to you:
why cheer your hearts with this consideration, that you have Christ
that sticks closer to you than your sins; and this should cheer up weak
and feeble ones: I know what troubles you, were I as strong as such
a christian, had I such parts, and such strength of faith; and shall
such a poor little one as I am, bear the brunt of persecution, and
endure in the time of perplexity: Why consider though thou canst not
help thyself, yet Christ can: and know this that Christ will not lose
the least member, he is a perfect Savior: the Lord will not suffer
Satan to take thee away from him, nor suffer his love to be taken
from thee: Romans 8:the two last verses:[28] it was the triumph of the
holy Apostle *Paul*; *I am persuaded* (saith he) *that neither death nor
life, nor Angels, nor Principalities, nor powers, nor things present,
nor things to come; nor height, nor depth, nor any other creature,
shall be able to separate us from the love of God which is in Christ
Jesus our Lord*: when health is separated from thy body, and light
from thy eyes, and strength from thy feeble nature, yet remember,
that when thy body is separated from thy soul, the Lord will not
separate his love from thee, neither from thy body in the grave, nor
from thy soul when it is departed out of thy body, he will love thy
body in the grave, he loves the dust of his Saints, and he will take
thy soul up into heaven; therefore cheer up thy heart, and comfort
thy soul in the consideration of God's goodness.

[*Use 5.*] Lastly, are the Saints knit to Christ thus firmly? then it
shows us our duty; we ought to take notice of the goodness of the

Lord vouchsafed unto us; hath the Lord advanced you thus highly? then walk worthy of this advancement, it is the use that the Apostle makes, *Walk worthy of the calling whereunto the Lord hath called you; are ye the members of Christ? why then behave yourselves as the members of Christ; are you joined thus nearly to Christ? then carry yourselves as beseems you; let the dog return to his vomit, and the sow to the wallowing in the mire;*[29] but let the Saints that are knit unto a Savior, walk worthy of that mercy, and union, and prerogative that God hath vouchsafed unto them; it is a shame to see, that servants of Christ's family, and the plants of his vineyard do walk after the conversation[30] of the world: what manner of persons ought we to be in all manner of holiness of conversation? we are knit unto Christ, and therefore ought to be holy, as he is holy; pure, as he is pure: we ought to do nothing, but that which may beseem and content a Savior; but ye will say, the world will hold up their hands at us, and their mouths will be open against us; why God hates the world, and ye are redeemed from the world, ye are called out of the world, therefore live not as if ye were in the world, but as God hath called you to live with himself in heaven, your conversation should be such, as if ye were in heaven: I would not have a Saint of God tamper with the least distemper, or be addicted to any base course, but walk exactly before the Lord.

SELECTION VII

The Way of Life

John Cotton

The interior of St. Botolph's Church, Boston, Lincolnshire. John Cotton was rector of this wealthy parish church from 1612 to 1633. The background shows the Jacobean pulpit (1612) from which, presumably, the sermons comprising The Way of Life *were delivered. See Nikolaus Pevsner and John Harris,* Lincolnshire *(Harmondsworth, Eng.: Penguin, 1964). From an engraving by Thomas Bolton, in Pishey Thompson,* The History and Antiquities of Boston *(Boston, Eng.: John Noble, Jr., 1856).*

ALTHOUGH THE FIRST and only edition of John Cotton's *The Way of Life* (London, 1641) appeared during his ministry in New England, the sermons most likely date from the latter part of his active tenure as rector of St. Botolph's parish in Boston, England, probably from the years 1627 to 1630.[1] In England, not yet convinced of the need for a strictly Congregational polity—a church composed only of covenanted saints—Cotton ministered both to a parish of worshipers for whom Puritan doctrines were either uninteresting or offensive and to an inner congregation of Puritan saints. Although he was famous for his skill in holding such a remarkably heterogeneous group in relative harmony, it must have been one of the inner core of loyal Puritans who recorded his delivery of these intense sermons and arranged for their publication after his emigration in 1633.[2]

The attractiveness of *The Way of Life* derives in large part from the broad applicability of these sermons. Not only does Cotton employ illustrative material drawn from a wide range of daily activities (trades, errands, household management, education), but the doctrines themselves also apply to many stages in the process of salvation. The four separate treatises that compose this largest of Cotton's sermon volumes[3] together comprise a treatment of the familiar pattern of salvation—that movement which, in outline at least, constituted the spiritual biography of every Puritan. As the title page explains, the first stage is "The Pouring Out of the Spirit" (its text is Zech. 12:10–14), God's call to the individual Christian. "Sin's Deadly Wound," part 2 (Acts 2:37), takes Christians from their original state of sin to the regeneration worked in them by the Spirit. Part 3, "The Christian's Charge" (Prov. 4:23), begins the consideration of the nature of regeneration by urging Christians to treasure and maintain their new condition. Finally, the fourth part, "The Life of Faith" (Gal. 2:19–20), describes at length the new life of the Christian, in the church, in the home, and in the community, both spiritually and temporally.

Even more than in theme or examples, the broad appeal of *The Way of Life* results from Cotton's continual specification of a heterogeneous audience, such as he had in England during his conforming ministry.[4] By alternately referring to saints and sinners, he implies that all his audience is involved in every doctrine of these sermons. For example, in applying doctrine 1 of part 2, he addresses contrite Christians in uses 1, 3, 5, and 6, ministers of the Gospel in use 4, and unsaved souls in use 2 ("such as yet find their hearts whole and unbroken").[5] The effect of such alternation is to imply that while the true congregation may be composed only of saints, the audience of the preacher represents all stages of salvation.

The audience of *The Way of Life* is not, however, treated with complete impartiality. The uses emphasize those who are moved in some degree to become saints, rather than those who mock at the life of faith, the reprobates. "To teach such Christians as are given to pray, to be sure you look to Christ in your prayers" is a typical use in these sermons.[6] Not surprisingly, the lengthiest applications refer to Christians fairly advanced in the life of salvation. The most significant use of a doctrine tends to be labeled "of trial of our own estates": it sets the preacher and certain of his audience apart as Christians who believe themselves to have passed through a given stage and who are here helped to test that passage.

The question of the preacher's audience relates to one of the crucial issues of Cotton's career—the relative actions of God and the soul in the process of conversion. The stage of salvation that Hooker terms preparation—the action of the heart in readying itself for the Spirit— was in Cotton's view a minor occurrence, not to be relied upon in cases of salvation. His doctrinal emphasis, as in parts 1 and 2 of *The Way of Life*, is on the acts of God, who pours the Spirit and pricks the hearts of his people: the *"Spirit of Grace . . . is freely bestowed on us without any desert of ours, yea without so much as our desire."*[7] Cotton's exhortations, however, do not always match his doctrines. His preaching, as his editor William Morton perceived, was itself a converting instrument, designed "to bring man unto a conformity to God, into a Communion with God"; therefore, he could not neglect to urge the unconverted part of his audience to prepare for the Spirit. "The Spirit of Grace will not come but into an heart in some measure prepared; the Spirit of Grace will not come into a cage of unclean lusts: but if God give a man a heart to lend a patient ear to a reproof, and lay down all scorning, and turn from his loose and unprofitable courses, then the promise is evident, *I will pour out my spirit upon you.*" Doctrinally, he asserts the almost incredible sufficiency of the Spirit: "God doth sometimes pour out the Spirit of grace, upon the most bloody, and most heinous, and most desperate, and most profane, and most abominable sinners." In exhortation, however, he urges "every ungodly soul, to stir up himself for the obtaining of the spirit of grace."[8]

The first two treatises of *The Way of Life* present God's order of salvation, explaining the process of conversion to those who have experienced it and recommending it to those who have not. The selection printed here begins the second half of the volume (pts. 3 and 4), which treats the more advanced stages of salvation and therefore more consistently addresses a sanctified audience. In it Cotton continually recognizes—as he did in preaching about the earlier stages of salvation—the needs of the unsanctified world. In preaching the life of faith, he refers again and again to the demands of the world, defining sainthood by showing how the saint coexists with the sinner. Much of part 4, for example, is an extended "use of instruction to all Christians, to learn how to live this life of faith . . . and also how to live a natural life in this world, and all by faith." The saint must live "a most busy life in this world," just as any unconverted person might, "yet he lives not a worldly life." By faith the saint transforms his or her natural environment while partaking of it: "by faith it is that we live comfortably in this present world."[9]

The nexus between the world and the soul of the saint is the heart—the central image of this selection. Earlier in the volume, Cotton defines the heart as a metaphor for the will, which is "seated in the *heart*"; the will is "that whereby we choose or refuse a thing."[10] The heart initiates all action; it alone is the meeting place of the sanctified motives of faith and the actual practices of the natural world. Cotton stresses the heart's ability to engage in worldly action without being part of the world: "you keep your duties constantly, your set time of prayer, and it is well, but unless you keep your heart better, all you do will be but dead works, you must keep your heart above all." As no perfection is possible short of glorification, even the saint fails to achieve the perfect life of faith. To be sure, the process of conversion has killed the natural, unregenerate heart: "The very first work of living and saving grace, gives a deadly stroke to the life of sinful nature." But there are ghosts in the heart of the saint—"the mixture of graces and corruption in every man's heart, and the strong power corruption hath to deaden grace." Therefore, the charge Cotton finds in the Book of Proverbs—"Keep thy heart"—is a twofold charge. The soul must imprison the ghosts of the unregenerate heart, lest they mingle their natural inclinations with the motives of faith (faith, not works, of course, is the test of sanctification). That message of confinement, however, is balanced by the charge to treasure the purified heart, for "All is right when the heart is right."[11] Cotton's sermon on the keeping of the heart expounds clearly and earnestly the preservation of the saint's treasure, the will to live the life of faith.

Proverbs 4:23: *Keep thy heart with all diligence* (or as it is in the Original, *Above all keepings, keep thy heart); for out of it are the issues of life.*[12]

Having formerly showed from Zechariah 12:10 and from Acts 2:37 how we might bring our hearts into a right frame;[13] Now let me show you how we may keep them so.

These words are a part of the Catechism, which *David* taught his son *Solomon*, when he was yet tender and young; verses 3, 4 of this Chapter;[14] when in the third verse he saith, he was his Father's son, he means, his dearly beloved son, or darling; he had many other sons besides *Solomon*, but he his Father's son; as if he should say, his *Father's darling, and Mother's joy*; as if he were the top and vigor of the affections of them both; And as they both did deeply affect him, so they both taught him, and led him along in his whole course. Though some Divines cut off the coherence at the tenth verse, yet indeed the whole Chapter is but one instruction. And thus you see the occasion of the words.

The words divide themselves into two parts.

First, An exhortation to the keeping of our hearts, and that exhortation amplified by an Argument from the less, *above all keepings*, as if the heart must be kept above all keepings besides.

Secondly, A reason to persuade to this work, taken from a man's life, it is as much as the life is worth.

Now first to explain the words, and then see the notes[15] that follow. First, what is meant by the heart. Secondly, What is meant by keeping it. Thirdly, To whom this duty is directed. And then what are the issues of life.

For the first, By the heart is here understood, not as sometimes it is taken, for the mind and judgment, for they are no such faculties, as out of which spring the issues of life; A man lives not by his knowledge: And therefore by the heart in this place, is not meant the mind or understanding, no, nor the affections, for a man may have good affections, as *Jehu*, and *Felix*, and *Herod*;[16] and yet not one of them live in God's sight.

The heart therefore here spoken of, is such an heart, as out of which, being well kept, springs life; evil things come out of the heart ill kept, *But a good man out of the good treasure of his heart, brings forth good things* (Matthew 12:34,35). It is the will of a man, in which his goodness lies, and from the will it is communicated to the rest of the faculties; if the will be good, then is the understanding good; Psalm 111:*ult.*;[17] then is the conscience good, the affections and speeches good; the works of our hands, and the words of our mouths, come all from a well-kept heart, that is a good will.

Now what heart is this, whether good or evil? I take it, he speaks of a good heart, because first, he speaks of such an heart, as out of which are the issues of life, and that must needs be a good heart.

Secondly, Because I take these words, as spoken to *Solomon*, and he was one of a good heart, from his tender years; 2 Samuel 12:24,25. So that this being spoken to *Solomon*, 'tis sign that even a good heart is to be kept, even the will of a man when it is regenerate and gracious.

2. What is meant by keeping? In the Original it is, *Above all keepings, keep thy heart*; but the word translated keeping, signifies two things usually in Scripture phrase; sometimes it signifies keeping a thing in custody, as it were in prison, so the word is taken, Genesis 40:3, and that hath reference to an evil heart; keep it as it were in prison, according to that (Hebrews 3:12), *Take heed lest there be in any of you an evil heart of unbelief, to depart from the living God*; as if a prisoner be ready to break loose, you will cause the Keeper to

look well to him; so look well to thy heart, hold it in durance,[18] or else it will deceive thee; yet thus far it may have reference to a good heart; A[19] man had need confine the evil of a good heart, and not to suffer it to break out, otherwise it will, and so shall a man keep himself upright; Psalm 18:23.

But secondly, sometimes it signifies the watch and charge a man hath over the holy things of the Sanctuary; Ezekiel 44:8,16; it is the same word that is here used, and you may take them both; Keep an evil heart as a prisoner, and so you shall mortify it; Keep a good heart holy and pure, and clean, even as a Sanctuary, for the holy Spirit of God to dwell in; You will keep a prisoner, but keep your hearts above a prisoner; You will keep your gardens, but keep your hearts above your gardens; You will keep your Vineyards (Isaiah 27:1,2), but keep the heart above all keepings; keep your heart above your life: It is an ill-kept life, that is kept with the loss of the heart.

Thirdly, To whom is this exhortation directed? It is spoken to *Solomon*, and he considered not only as a good man, but as a young man, so that this is considerable in this case; Here is counsel given to young men, and those whom we love best, though never so dear to us, this is the best counsel we can give them, Keep your hearts.

Fourthly, What is that which he saith? *For thereout are the issues of life*; It is as much as if he should say, For out of an heart well kept, doth spring and issue out such streams of good thoughts, and good affections, and conversations, and conferences,[20] as express the life of grace, and prepare for the life of glory. Thus you see the meaning of the words. You see then *Solomon* here speaks of a good heart, of an heart given up to God, and set in a good frame: whence observe this Note.

[Doctrine.] *When a man hath given up his heart to God, and it is set in a good frame, it is then the best and most needful work in the world to keep it so.*

For it is to an heart set in a good frame, that this charge is here given, Above all keepings, keep this; It is the greatest business in the world, no such keeping to be expressed in the keeping of a man's estate, or credit, or treasure, or prisoner, or life itself. This work of keeping the heart, is a busier work, than any in the world; Hast thou a shop, or an house, or a place, or a sanctuary to keep? why, yet above all these keepings, keep thy heart, and keep it most carefully when it is in a good frame. Now *Solomon*, now that God hath given you wisdom, and you are now beloved of God and man, when your way is paved with the blessings of God, and his mercies compass you about, now look that you keep your heart.

For the opening of this point; First, see the Reasons; and then Secondly, wherein this keeping of the heart stands.

[Reason 1.] Taken from the *deceitfulness of our hearts*, it is *deceitful above all things, and desperately wicked* (Jeremiah 17:9,10). No prisoner so slippery, no chapman[21] so cunning and able to deceive us, as a man's heart is; And though that be spoken of a carnal heart, yet though the heart be regenerate and sanctified by the Spirit of grace, yet it hath still in it a tang of its old haunts; we shall taste of the old man,[22] till death separate us, and therefore even *David*, a man after God's own heart, yet he had an heart, that could tell how to ensnare him with his neighbor's Wife, and afterwards to plot to cover his sin, which shows you, that there is nothing so deceitful as the heart is; and therefore even *David* had cause to speak this, out of the experience he had of his own unclean and deceitful heart; he that had received a better heart, than yet had *Solomon*, and yet seeing it so bad, he had good reason to give *Solomon* this charge, Above all keepings, keep thy heart. This deceitfulness of man's heart is mentioned (Jeremiah 5:22,23,24): This people hath a revolting and a rebellious heart, they are revolted and gone; Though you might think the sands would soon be fretted through by the boisterous waves, yet God by his word hath made the sand a perpetual Bulwark against the sea, that it cannot prevail against it; but the heart of man is more unruly than the great sea, and more illimitable than the sea; Hosea 11:7: Their heart is bent to backslidings, therefore they ought diligently to look to their souls (Deuteronomy 4:9), which shows you, we are apt to lose all that good God hath wrought for us; we can tell how to slip from under the power of God's grace to follow our own foolishness.

[*Reason 2.*] From the *deceitfulness of sin*, which will soon get within us; see your hearts be not unbelieving; Hebrews 3:12. Sin is deceitful, and it easily besets us; Hebrews 12:1. It gets within us at every hand, and thereupon we are ready to take some contentment in it.

[*Reason 3.*] Taken from the *daily war* which we are called forth unto, no day, but God calls us to war with some cross, or some temptation or other; now this was a strait charge God gave unto his people (Deuteronomy 23:9),[23] *Take heed there be no wicked thing found in thee, when thou goest out to war*, because, if there were but one *Achan* found among them,[24] it were enough to discomfit an whole host; Take heed therefore there be no evil thing found in us, for out of a well-kept heart, springs our preservation.

[*Reason 4.*] Taken from the approach that we are daily making towards God, we are to resort unto God to call upon his name, and to hear his word, and nothing so much hinders us, from finding God in an Ordinance,[25] as an unkept heart; Psalm 66:18; which shows you, that if there be any evil in a man's heart, it disappoints him of all the hopes and fruits of his prayers. So when we come to hear the word, if God see any Idol in your heart, he will answer us according to that Idol; we shall find something in that Ordinance, to feed and nourish that corruption in us.

[*Reason 5.*] And that is especially intended in the text; it is taken from the great command, which the heart hath over the whole man;

Keep the heart well, and you keep all in a good frame: all the senses behold not an object so much as the heart doth; Set before a man any pleasant prospect, and if his mind be on another thing, all his senses take no notice of it; if the heart be not taken up with a thing, the eye minds it not; present the ear with any sweet melodious sound, and it hears and minds it not, because the heart was otherwise taken up; but upon whatsoever the heart is set, to that the eye looks, and the ear attends, everything acts towards it, all goes freely that way, the mind, the judgment, the invention, the affection, and whatever a man hath, it all works that way, and therefore it is well said, *Out of it are the issues of life*; if you have the whole man, and not the heart, you have but a dead man, get the heart and you have all; as they say in nature, the heart is *Primum vivens, et ultimum moriens*,[26] It is the first that lives, and the last that dies; according to the temper of the heart, such is the temper of the whole man; if the heart be good, though the affections should be disordered, and the eyes wanton, if the will be right, all is right; *If I do that which I would not, it is no more I that do it, but sin that dwells in me* (Romans 7:20). If my heart be for God, it is not I that sin: If there be a Covenant made between two States, as suppose between France and England, if the Princes of both States keep Covenant, it is not some lawless subject or Pirate on either side that breaks the League, so long as the Princes do their best endeavors to punish it; so is it in the League made between God and my heart, it is not any disordered affection that breaks the league, but the sin that dwells within us.

Now wherein stands this keeping of the heart, or what is it? There be three things implied in it.

First, that we keep our hearts *clean*; God is truly good to them that are of a clean heart (Psalm 73:1). Psalm 18:23: *I kept myself from mine iniquity*; we must keep ourselves from sinful defilements; *O Jerusalem wash thy heart from thy filthiness* (Jeremiah 4:14). Keep thy heart from old and new iniquities, Psalm 4:16.

Secondly, we must keep our hearts *prepared* or *fixed*, the word signifies both; Psalm 57:7; that is, we must have our hearts fraught with all good things, fixed and set upon God, our hearts must not be like the heart of a wicked man, little worth (Proverbs 10:20). But keep hearts of worth within you, I mean prepared for the presence of the Lord, as the Church saith (Canticles 7:13). In our gates is all manner of pleasant fruits; The gates of a Commonwealth, are the gates of Judicature, but the gates of a Christian is his heart (Psalm 24:7). So that when the Church saith, our gates are full, she means, there are no graces of God, but she hath stored her heart therewith, faith, and love, and humility, and whatever grace else.

Thirdly, to keep the heart, implies, to keep the heart in *good order*, that is, ever to have right ends, to use right means to attain those ends, to have a right measure and degree of everything; we may indeed set our hearts on the blessings of this life, yet so, as therein we do God's will, build up his kingdom, honor the name of his grace, otherwise it will not be lawful for us to set our hearts upon them, no not upon lawful things; Psalm 62:10; meaning not principally, for if you set your hearts on things for themselves, you will lose your hearts, and the comfort of them together.

[*Use 1.*] It is first a just reproof to many a soul, that is more watchful in keeping any blessing in the world than their own hearts, and so are transgressors of this gracious exhortation of the holy Ghost; You have many men that can tell how to keep their purses, their credits, and estates, and it is commendable; there are men that can tell how to keep their friends, others can tell how to keep good tables, good servants, and good horses, but did we know how to keep all these and not our hearts, we shall fall short of this charge here given us; you had better lose your purses, your friends, yea which is more, your lives, than your hearts; it is but a poor thing, to be skillful in keeping all these, and to bungle at keeping the heart, which stands most need of best keeping; It was a word that *Ahab* sometimes spake against himself (1 Kings 20:39): A man brought a man unto me and said, Keep this man, if he be missing, thy life shall go for his life: and as thy servant was busy here and there, the man was gone. Why, saith the King, so shall thy judgment be. Truly God hath put this charge upon us all, God hath given thee thy heart to keep, and hath bid thee, Above all keepings, to look well unto it, upon the keeping whereof depends thy life, and without it nothing but death; and if we shall now come and say to God, whilst we had this and that business to do (as they said, Luke 14), our hearts are lost and gone; then call in any rather than those, who for the comforts of this life, have lost their hearts. I do not know what men are more careless of, than of keeping their hearts; most will teach their children to keep anything rather than their hearts; you will bid them keep their books, keep their learning, keep their hats, gloves, and points,[27] and I blame it not in you, but I pray you consider, Do not you think, that the very pins and points of your children will not one day rise up in judgment against you, when you so carefully teach them how to keep these, and not at all how to keep their hearts, for want of which, they are exposed to the ruin and destruction of their souls? And in this particular, I cannot excuse God's own servants; whence come (think you) our manifold complaints in this kind? I now speak to them, that know what it is to have the heart in a good frame: Though the heart be now in a good frame, ere long they will complain, and confess their heart is lost in a day or two's business, so as, when that they should come to the Ordinances again, in the midst of the week, or that day seven-night, their hearts are gone, and they know not in the world where to have them; whence is that we complain, Nobody hath such dead and cold, heavy, and unprofitable an heart as I have? Why, doth it not come from hence; we have been negligent to keep our hearts? have you kept your friends, and purses, and estates, and everything from losing, and only your hearts lost? what a shame is it, we can say we have lost nothing but our hearts this week? that which especially should have been kept, is the only thing we have lost, all is well, save only the heart, and that is lost, and what a shame is this? and this only through want of diligence; what a poor case was *David* in (Psalm 51:10), *Renew a right spirit within me*; Time was when God had said of him, that he was *a man after his own heart* (1 Samuel 13:14). He had an heart that was careful and watchful, but now his heart is lost; *David* could tell how his heart had given him the slip, his heart was soon gone after his lust, before he was aware, and so far, that when he should seek it up again, it is lost, and had not *Nathan* helped him, it may be he had never found it;[28] not that his grace was, or could be wholly lost forever; in his worst, there was something of the holy Spirit of grace in him; but it was so far lost, as he entreats the Lord not *to piece* it,[29] but *to create a new and right spirit within him*; he had been much defiled, and now he desires a new spirit; though he had done very wickedly, yet he was senseless and hard-hearted, and therefore is it not a shame to God's people, that we can tell how so easily to lose our hearts, that unless God extraordinarily help us to gather them up again, we should die dead-hearted? and therefore let it cast a just reproof upon us, in that we have kept everything better than our hearts; we have lived it may be 20, 30, or 40 years, and have not lost one friend, nor lost anything that could be saved by keeping, only our hearts we have lost, and many times we know not how.

[*Use* 2.] Let it therefore teach us all, to set home this charge upon our hearts, and upon all with whom we have occasion to deal. There are many good lessons in this Chapter, but above all learn this, it would not be lost labor to teach your children to learn such a Chapter, but learn first to keep your own hearts; you have been taught, that no member you have is so deceitful as the heart, it will soonest give you the slip, it is bent to backsliding, you had need keep your hearts clean, that God might preserve you in all your temptations, you will then profit by any Ordinance you partake in, and therefore let it be carefully kept. And for a Motive, if you shall thus do, it will honor you before God and man, and by keeping your hearts, you will find favor in the eyes of such friends whom you feared, by so doing, you should have lost; First, God will put honor upon you; 1 Samuel 13:14; and man will put honor upon thee; Proverbs 22:11: the King shall be thy friend; a man shall never want great friends that keeps his heart pure and undefiled; an[30] unbelieving heart is apt to think the more pure he is, the more danger he is in; but though great men should be displeased, yet it would be no small help to my spiritual estate, their checks and frowns would do us much good. But how shall this be done? First, trust not in your own keeping of your hearts; Proverbs 28:26. In the fear of God therefore resign up your hearts into God's hands, be sensible of your own insufficiency to keep them; 2 Corinthians 3:5 and 2 Timothy 1:12;[31] so Jude 24. Commend your hearts to God in prayer, and trust him with all your affairs, Philippians 4:6,7.[32] Allow not yourselves in the out-coming of any unsubjected thoughts, check yourselves for unnurtured affections; there is not a vain thought passeth without a check, but it makes a riffle in our hearts; Job 31:1. The Courts of the Lord are exceedingly broad, there is liberty enough in God's ways to do well, but not to do evil.

Again, be careful to treasure up those graces to which God hath made promise of keeping the heart.

The first is faith, that purifieth the heart (Acts 15:9). Faith ever hath the word for its warrant; Psalm 19:9; and also will derive all its daily strength from Christ; Isaiah 40:2, ult.[33]

The second is the fear of the Lord; Proverbs 16:6. When a man's heart is kept in the holy fear of God, it preserves him from evil.

Lastly, if this be done in love, it will keep all the affections and graces of the Spirit in good order, and you should labor to keep them alive, so shall you keep your hearts as they should be.

SELECTION VIII

The Parable of the Ten Virgins

Thomas Shepard

The parish church of Thomas Shepard's childhood. The Church of St. Laurence, in Towcester, Northamptonshire, was probably the site of the sermons of Shepard's schoolmaster, William Cluer, who—in Shepard's words—"was an eminent preacher in those days and accounted holy but afterward turned a great apostate," presumably by abandoning the Puritan cause. Although Shepard thought Towcester a "profane, ignorant town," he acknowledges that "by God's good providence . . . this man stirred up in my heart a love and desire of the honor of learning." Shepard later set up a lectureship in Towcester—"the Lord's mercy following me to make me a poor instrument of sending the gospel to the place of my nativity." See God's Plot: The Paradoxes of Puritan Piety, *ed. Michael McGiffert (Amherst: University of Massachusetts Press, 1972), pp. 39–48. Courtesy of the Shepard Historical Society, Cambridge, Massachusetts.*

THE PREACHING AND PUBLISHING circumstances of Thomas Shepard's *The Parable of the Ten Virgins Opened and Applied: Being the Substance of Divers Sermons on Matthew 25:1–13* are recorded by Jonathan Mitchell, successor to Shepard in the Cambridge pulpit, in the prefatory letter to the reader. The sermons, Mitchell reports, "preached by the Author, in a weekly lecture, were begun in *June* 1636 and ended in *May* 1640." They "are now transcribed by industrious and intelligent persons, and have been carefully reviewed and corrected. They are written out of the Author's own Notes, which he prepared for preaching." Mitchell goes on to explain that Shepard, at his death, appeared to have just barely begun the process of writing out the sermons. The preacher himself failing to publish the series, the effort was further delayed until 1660, because of the "work being Somewhat lengthy, and fitting Scribes not easily attainable in this Wilderness."[1]

The Parable of the Ten Virgins is indeed "somewhat lengthy." By far Shepard's longest work (close to 300,000 words), it treats progressively each of the first thirteen verses of Matthew 25, often with several sermons and many chapters explicating one verse. The focus of Shepard's treatment is the second coming of Christ. At the beginning, Shepard explains that part 1 deals with the "Church's preparation to meet with Christ (called here the Bridegroom)" and that part 2 examines the "Bridegroom's coming forth to meet" the church.[2] Many topical concerns may have prompted Shepard to choose and interpret the text as he did. *The Parable of the Ten Virgins* suggests a general fear that the New England congregations, despite the requirement of evidence of conversion for church membership, may have had hypocritical converts or, more probable and even worse, complacent and therefore backsliding saints within the ranks. American prosperity engenders "security" and thereby endangers readiness for the coming of Jesus Christ: "Take heed the Lord find not many of you foolish, take heed you that are not so, that in time you grow not secure; you have the pillow of peace to lie on, and the cares of the world to make you dream away your time, and you have no pinching persecutions to awaken you, and if no wrestlings within, look for security there." Although Shepard suspected that the "last Judgment" was "not far off," he was cautious about the heavenly calendar; but he was bold enough to utilize the uncertain occurrence of the final judgment or natural death to keep saints from their greatest danger—"carnal security." Arriving in America in the midst of the Antinomian crisis, he began these sermons almost immediately after his church congregated and continued them while he organized the synod to refute the heresy and sat on the court to try Anne Hutchinson. Hence, as Mitchell explains, "the Reader will meet with sundry passages tending to reprove and refute some of those conceits." For instance, Shepard deplores "private meetings too frequent," so-called union "with the

Lord Jesus Christ by the power of immediate Revelation, without the *medium* of the Word," and the use of "Grace itself" to fight "the Ministers of the Gospel of Christ." [3]

In addition to explicating the parable and addressing contemporary problems, Shepard provides yet another survey of the life of faith in this period of preaching. He obviously sees a need to identify for his audience of saints the nature of true conversion. Many converts may in fact be conscious or unconscious hypocrites, whose treacherous guises and continual presence receive comprehensive analysis. He also sees a need to emphasize the essential incompleteness of any stage in the process of salvation. The preparation of the sinner is succeeded by that of the saint; the temporal communion a saint enjoys with Jesus Christ during life on earth, by an everlasting communion during life in heaven. Shepard explains these duplications by an analogy between the first coming of Christ, which he calls the conversion of the elect, and the second coming. In the imagery and language of the parable, conversion represents espousal (that is, betrothal) to Christ, and the final judgment or death represents marriage. Just as a sinner must prepare for the first coming of Christ, so must a saint prepare for his second coming. Hence, throughout *The Parable of the Ten Virgins* Shepard teaches the saints, who experience a tentative communion with Jesus Christ, how to be "wise virgins" so that they can progress to an "eternal communion" with him after judgment.[4] This series emphasizes the uncertainties of the state of grace, the incompleteness of sanctification.

The selection itself demonstrates further important analogizing. Like the other first preachers, Shepard compared the state of the church with that of each saint, the condition of the community with that of each soul. The wise virgins represent the visible church, specifically the congregations of professed believers in New England. Hence, in the last part—the fifth use—of the sermon immediately preceding this selection, Shepard addresses "all the churches of the Lord Jesus here planted in these Western parts of the World" and warns them: "maintain your Church-chastity and Virginity . . . Open whoredom is too gross, too shameful, to yield to man's inventions, to open the door for all comers unto the Church." [5] But the remedy for communal declension is individual endeavor; consequently, the way the piety of each Christian can be nurtured becomes the topic of the next sermon—the selection here printed.

As in *The Sound Believer*, action to amend depends upon knowledge of the way backsliding occurs. That knowledge is found at the core of the selection—the question-and-answer section following the doctrine and preceding the four reasons and the two uses of the doctrine. Here the saint learns, by a negative phrasing of the qualities of "readiness to enjoy Christ," the signs of unpreparedness for death or the day of judgment. Here through dramatization of the unready soul, Shepard engages his auditors to identify with this unprepared saint. Here he stresses how unstable are both the assurance and the sanctification of the converted. Having seemingly exhausted the four ways "a man is unprepared for the Lord Jesus his [Jesus'] coming," Shepard has merely begun. He sets himself up to preach in the next chapter "a four-fold exhortation to believers." Here he will repeat in positive form, in seven times the length of the printed selection, the four ways to be in "readiness to enjoy Christ." Christians can (1) seek assurance, if they doubt the love of Christ; (2) "set" their love on Christ; (3) "do the work of Christ"; and (4) "be ever humble," giving honor to the Lord. Such infinite ramifications for one stage in the life of faith demonstrate its centrality for this preacher and his New England auditors.

Matthew 25:1–13: *Then shall the kingdom of heaven be likened unto ten virgins, which took their lamps, and went forth to meet the bridegroom. . . .*

CHAPTER VIII.[6] *Concerning*[7] *a Christian's Duty of being constantly and continually ready to meet Christ, and to enjoy Communion with him.*

2. *Took their Lamps.*[8]

SECTION I.

Much dust is raised, and much Dispute is made, especially by Popish Interpreters, What the Lamps, what the Oil, what the Vessels should be?[9] The general conceit of most of them is: that by Oil is meant good works, and by Lamps Faith; answerable to their own conceit,[10] that not Faith but good works chiefly save: Whereas if we consider the thing rather *e contra*,[11] that by lighted Lamps are meant good works, or external[12] shining profession, according to that of Christ (Matthew 5), *Let your light so shine before men*, etc., and that by Oil should be meant Faith, because 'tis inward, and is the nourishment of works and outward profession. And in this sense some of our Divines do take this Scripture; and the *Rhemists*[13] likewise, who understand by Lamps lighted, good works; by Oil a good intention: To which 'tis answered by *Cartwright*[14] (that burning and shining light of our Times), that rather by Lamps lighted is to be understood, *watchful minds alway lifted up in attending for the coming of Christ* (according as 'tis verse 13).[15] And I doubt not but this is one thing aimed at, that they *took their Lamps, i.e.* were watchful for Christ's coming. But when I weigh other circumstances, methinks there is somewhat else more plainly and principally intended, of which I scarce read any Divine, but he gives a hint of, *viz.* that by lighted Lamps, and taking of them, is meant nothing else but the readiness of the Churches to meet and to have fellowship with the Lord Jesus. And my Reasons are these:

1. Because the Lord Jesus to teach his people watchfulness, and to put them to a narrow search of themselves, borrows a similitude from the custom of those Times, wherein their Marriages were celebrated in the Night, and hence the Virgins (the only children of the Bride-chamber, and some think their number never exceeded Ten) being to walk out in the Night, took their Lamps: and when they had kindled their Lamps (usually the last thing that is done), now they are ready to go out, and this is that which Christ aims at.

2. From [16] Luke 12:35, *Let your loins be girt, and lamps burning;* it's evident that thereby is meant nothing else but readiness to meet the Lord whenever he comes; for when loins are girt, then one is fit for travail,[17] but seeing 'tis in the Night, hence lamps must be burning too.

3. Because 'tis said plainly (verse 10),[18] when their lamps were kindled again, *they that were ready went in;* I know the Word is called a lamp for our feet (Psalm 119), and so by lamps may be meant minds enlightened and kindled by the word. The eminent profession and excellencies of the Church is like a lamp (Isaiah 62:1), and more particularly may be here included and aimed at: but in this verse lamps are spoken of in general, including light, Oil, Vessels; and hence I give this general Interpretation here, intending Particulars if need be afterward: So that now I shall only raise this Point.

SECTION II.

Doctrine. *That all those that are Espoused unto Christ, ought to be in a constant or continual readiness to meet Christ, and to have immediate communion with Christ.*

A Woman may be Espoused to another, and yet she may be sometimes not ready to meet him, her foul apparel is on. So here, therefore 'tis not enough to be espoused unto Christ, but being espoused,[19] now you ought to be in a continual readiness to clasp the Lord in your arms, and to lay your heads in his bosom in Heaven: this is commanded by Christ; Matthew 24:44. This was the mighty power of God's Grace in *Paul*, when others were weeping to think of his Bonds, *Why do you break my heart, I am ready not only to be bound, but to die for Christ,* and so doubtless to be with Christ; much more ready to meet Christ whenever he shall come, ready to welcome Death, much more ready to welcome Christ (Acts 21:13). This also is the end of *John's* Ministry (Luke 1:17), To make ready a people prepared for the Lord, to meet with Christ on earth; Now he is gone, our work is to prepare a people to meet the Lord in Heaven. Hence this is put in[20] as the difference between Vessels of wrath, and Vessels of Glory: the one are fitted for destruction, the others are fitted, prepared, or made ready for Glory, and the glory of a christian is chiefly to enjoy fellowship immediately with Jesus Christ. There is many a soul dear unto Christ, and espoused to him, and hath his heart affected to think of the good time that is coming, when we shall ever be with the Lord: but ask, are you ready yet for to go to him, though it be through fires, waters, thorns, sorrows, death itself? who can say yes: but (say men's hearts) shut the Lord out a little longer, let not the door stand open yet; yet this must be: And therefore for explication's sake, let me, 1. show you when the Soul is in a[21] readiness for the Lord Jesus. 2. The reasons why there must be a continual readiness.

SECTION III.

[*Question.*] *When is the Soul in a*[22] *readiness to enjoy Christ?*

[*Answer.*] As there are four things which make a christian unready, so this readiness consists in Four things contrary.

1. That which makes a christian unready for him, are those strong fears, and jealousies, and damping[23] doubts of the love of Christ to him. The soul haply[24] hath made choice of him, is content with him, melts into wonderment and love to think that he should love him: what me? and Christ hath writ[25] him on his heart, and on the palms of his hands; *but*[26] *Israel saith, my God hath forsaken me, my God hath forgotten me* (Isaiah 49:14). Is it possible? is it credible? one that hath been so vile, one that still hath such a heart, for him to set his heart on me? surely no: hence the Soul is afraid to die, and desires too much to live still: and the more he thinks of that time, and blessedness of following the Lamb wherever he goes; the more he sees and fears this[27] may possibly never be my portion: there may be some falseness in my heart towards him that I never yet saw, some secret knot that was never yet unloosed: and hence not yet ready. Hence many a christian saith, if I had a little more assurance, let him come when he will: Thus some think it was with *Hezekiah*, who though he had[28] walked before God with a *perfect heart*, yet bitterly complained that he was cut off (Isaiah 38:*per totum*).[29] So therefore then the soul is prepared and ready for[30] him, when he hath some comfortable assurance of the love of Christ towards him, that it can say, if I live he loves me, though he kills me by Death, yet I know that he loves me: nay, then he loves me most, when he puts an end to my sins, and to my sorrows too. And[31] therefore now saith as one ready to receive a Prince, now let him come to me, or

send for me when he will: why so? *Who can separate me from the love of Christ?* (Romans 8:35). That look as 'tis with a Soldier that is to go to war, where many bullets and arrows are like to fall about him, and hit him while[32] he hath no armor on; call him to the Captain, and he will say he is not ready yet, but when he hath his armor on of proof,[33] and such armor that he knows let him receive never so many wounds, yet he shall escape with his life, and triumph with his Captain afterward: Now give him but his watchword he is ready, though never so weak, yet I am sure I shall escape with my life, nay not so much as hurt. So a christian wanting his assurance, wants his armor; he is weak, and powers of darkness will assault him, and he is slain by them, now he is unready: but if assured, though weak and feeble, he is now at Christ's watchword, I know I shall live, I may fall, but I shall rise again, this puts courage and spirit into a christian; Daniel 3:17,18; Hebrews 11:35: Others were tormented (and so ready), *not accepting deliverance*; why so? to *obtain a better Resurrection*, which they are said to see by the eye of Faith, and this was by poor weak Women;[34] therefore labor for this, else not prepared. The Lord would have his people look death and dangers in the face, and triumph in sorrows, and not faint-hearted (which cannot be done without this), that the world may see that there is more than men in them; 2 Corinthians 4:16,17,18, and 5:1; who would be without this? yet may we not complain, as Christ of his Disciples, *Oh foolish and slow of heart to believe all that is written*,[35] so many promises yet not assured, so many experiences yet not established, and therefore not yet prepared and ready for the coming of the Lord. A man that hath a fair estate and house befallen him, so long as he is in Suit for it, dares not dwell in it, but makes a shift where he is: but then he is ready when quiet possession is given him. So get the Lord to pass sentence for assurance of your everlasting habitation, then are you ready to dwell therein.

2. Then a man is unprepared for the Lord Jesus his coming, while he wants affections suitable to the Majesty, and according to the worth and love of the Lord Jesus: Suppose a Woman knows her Husband's love, yet if she have lost her love to him, or if she love him, 'tis only as she loves another man, not according to the worth of her Husband's person, or the greatness of his love: Is she fit now to appear before him, when no[36] heart to receive him? so although you question not Christ's love to you, and thank God you doubt little of it, yet where is your heart? your love to him? have you not lost your love, your first love, or second love? if you have love, is it not[37] divided to other things, as Wife, Child, Friends, hopes of provision for them, and too much care hereupon for that? or if you do love him, 'tis with a carnal love, he hath no[38] more than a lust hath had, and it may be not so much, 'tis with a cold love; now you are unfit for him: hence the Lord (Luke 21:34), *Take heed your hearts be not over-*

charged; 1 Peter 4:7. Now therefore then the soul is prepared to meet Christ, when if the soul hath lost its affections, it recovers them out of the hands of all creatures that stole them away from Christ; and hence *David* prays, *Oh spare that I may recover my strength*:[39] and when it breaks out with such love unto[40] Christ as is fitting for him; 2 Timothy 4:8; There is the righteous Judge ready to give the Crown, when Christ's appearing is loved, *i.e.* they are so taken with him, as that they love the looks of him, it would rejoice my heart to see, which shall make others tremble to behold him; Oh it must be a dear love, a spring of running love without measure, for this is the difference between affections of Saints and Hypocrites to Christ, the one ariseth like a morning dew which is soon licked up by the Sun; Hosea 6:4; the heat of affections after other things licks it up; but the love of Saints to Christ is like a spring which riseth to everlasting life: a spring is but little, but yet the farther it goes, the wider 'tis, till at last swallowed up in the sea,[41] and there is no measure of water: so Saints have but a little love, but the longer they live, the more enlarged for Christ, and there is no measure, but all is too little, they never can, never do love enough, so that look as 'tis said in another case (Psalm 102:13,14), *'Tis time for thee to build up Jerusalem, i.e.* to return to thy people in thy Ordinances, for *they love the stones*; so then it's time for Christ to come, and then the set and fit time[42] is come for a people to meet with Christ out of Ordinances,[43] when the set time is come when they love Ordinances, and love Christ much more. When a man is gone beyond Sea, and all his Friends and estate are at home, they long for him, and he is left among enemies: why comes he not to them? why send not they for him? why they know he is sickly, and cannot live on the diet of the country; hence he is unfit to come, but when that is once come[44] to pass that he can live only on it, then he is ready whenever they send; so when men can live with, and be content alone with Christ and his love, now they are fit. With what face can a man appear before Christ, when he requires nothing but love, and he hath not that?[45]

3. Then a man is unready for Christ, whiles he neglects the work of Christ, for suppose a man hath some inward love to Christ, yet neglects and hath no heart to do the work of Christ: he is as yet no more fit to meet Christ, than a Steward who hath had much betrusted him, to improve for his Lord's use, and he hath let all seasons go wherein he might have traded for him, and gained somewhat to him. How can he appear before him when no fair account's[46] to be seen? So[47] the Lord hath betrusted thee with many Talents, times, strength, means, etc., and you are not Lords, but Stewards of all these. Now do you not let many fair seasons and winds blow by? you[48] have (if espoused to Christ) every man some work. Now how can you stand before Christ if that be neglected? Oh[49] thus 'tis with many christians; hence those sad alarums[50] of conscience, and shakings of

God's Spirit, after many loose days dipped in some good duties. What dost thou that others do not that never shall see God's face in Heaven?

Now therefore then the soul is ready for the Lord, when 'tis daily at it, finishing God's work: hence John 17:5: *I have finished my work, now glorify me*: Christ hath given us our lives' work,[51] days' work, every hour's work, for Christ hath ever employment; now though a soul may live long, and cannot finish its life's[52] work, yet if it finish its day's work, or hour's work, it may have comfort then if the Lord should come. That look as 'tis with a Mariner when he hath his Freight, now let the wind come to drive him out of the Haven, he is ready to depart: so here (2 Peter 1:8,9,10,11): *If ye do these things, and abound, an open entrance shall be ministered unto you, i.e.* when a christian is ever acting for Christ, and adding one Grace to another in his course, then he is so ready that an open entrance is made for him: Therefore look after this. 'Tis with most Professors[53] commonly, as 'tis with a Woman that loves her Husband, and begins to dress herself, but so much business to do, that she doth it but by starts; hence call her never so late, she will say she is not yet ready, she hath so much to do she cannot; so 'tis here: Or as 'tis in a house where all things are in a lumber,[54] and many things wrapped up and put into holes, so long as all things be in a lumber, there is no readiness. So many a soul hath a heart fit to receive Christ, but all things are in a lumber, in a confusion, out of place and order, and hence not yet ready to entertain Christ, but when this work is done, then ready. Oh betimes do this work, set things to rights in your souls.

4. Then a man is unready, when having done his work he grows puffed up with it: for let all the three former be wrought in the soul, if now the soul be puffed up, thinks highly of itself, attributes anything to itself: as he said in another case, *they are too many for the Lord*; so he is too big for the Lord. And truly this we shall find, it's[55] pretty easy to be mean in our own eyes, after we have been indeed careless and vile before the Lord; but when the Lord hath mightily assisted, enlarged, assured, enabled, comforted, quickened, now to be as nothing, this is difficult. Hence *Knox* on his deathbed had this Temptation of Meriting.[56] When *Hezekiah* was sick, he was cast down, but when well, and God gave him great Treasures, his heart was lifted up;[57] now he was unfit. Now therefore when a christian is ready to give all to free Grace, and to adore that, now he is ready for the Lord; Psalm 108:1: *My heart is prepared, I will sing and give praise.* God's last end is to bring the soul to the praise of the riches of his Grace, not only to enjoy God as *Adam*. Now the great reason why Christ comes not to his people presently after they are espoused to him, 'tis to make them ready to attain that end. Hence he leaves sins, temptations, sorrows, desertions, on purpose that they may at conclusion look back, and see if ever saved, pardoned, it's Grace. Now therefore when the soul is brought to do this, when he hath this rent in his

hand, now the Lord is ready to receive him, and it too, and he is prepared for the Lord: he that hath not his Rent ready, himself is not
as yet at all ready to meet with, and see his Landlord. So that you
think you boast not, Oh the Lord sees you do, or have not hearts so
enlarged towards Grace as you should, it's certain you are yet unready then, but when empty, and poor, and cast down, and makest
an infinite matter of a small sin, and settest a high price on a little
love, much [58] more on infinite, now you are prepared: Hence *David*
falls a-praising when near to death, and the Lord near to come to him.

SECTION IV. [*Reasons.*]

1. The law of Respect and Love requires this of us: when *Peter*
would express his love unto Christ (Luke 22:33), he professeth he
was *not only ready to go to prison, but to die with him.* Christ hath
poor respect and love if men will not so much as be alway ready to
receive him: it certainly argues a careless heart that slights Christ,
that is not ever prepared to receive Christ.

2. Because the time of Christ's coming is then when we least look
for him; verse 13.[59] Hence a christian ought to be ever ready to receive him. Many of eminent parts,[60] when the Church had most need
of them, then are cut down: Many at their first conversion, before
they or others almost could tell what to make of them, the Lord hath
cropped them in the bud. Men find their hearts unfit and unready,
they think hereupon that hereafter they shall get their hearts into
better order and tune, when these businesses are over, but yet will
live at liberty a little while: why then it's most likely is the Lord's
time of coming, even now when they think least of it; Luke 12:40.

3. Because the Lord hath set apart everyone that is espoused to the
Lord Jesus, only for the fruition of Christ, and use of Christ; 1 Corinthians 3:*ult*:[61] *You are Christ's, and Christ is God's.* A Woman
that is not chosen, nor set apart for the fellowship of a Prince, she
may go how she will, and do what she will, any base drudgery work;
but she that is chosen to be next unto him, and only to behold and
love him, she is not to plead she hath so much business to do, and
so many Friends to speak with, that she cannot make herself ready:
she is set apart for a better person, and for more noble employment.
So here men of the world not loved of God, nor chosen and set apart
for him, may do what they will; but when the Lord hath chosen and
set you apart of purpose for this end; Ephesians 1:4: *Chosen to be
holy before him in love, i.e.* to stand ever in his presence before him,
with a spirit of dearest love unto him. Hence the Lord hath taken the
care of all things else; 1 Peter 5:7; that we might mind and do this
thing; If in danger, he will deliver, if in want, he will provide, if weak,
he will strengthen, only now be ready for the Lord; Psalm 45:10:

Forget thy Country, and thy Father's house, so shall the Lord desire thy beauty. You are not now free to love and follow whom you please, the Lord hath bound you to himself by love, and you have bound yourself by promise to the Lord again: Therefore now a christian after once espoused to Christ, is better than all the world, being the Bride of the Lamb; and he hath a better and greater good for to enjoy: therefore he should scorn and abhor to match himself to, or to do anything for any other creature; and therefore methinks should sit as one upon a watchtower, looking out, and telling the clock [62] now day is near, waiting only for Christ, Oh let it be so: If in Heaven, you shall have only Christ, Oh prepare for him much more now. As a Woman that is Matched to a rich man, all the servants attend on her, and follow her, she is wholly and only for her Husband: so it should be here.

4. Because he hath prepared and made all things else ready for the soul, it's hard if he hath prepared a place in Heaven, and Grace in Heaven, not to prepare an heart, and make it ready for him; John 14:1,2,3; his Kingdom was ready long ago, and his Father ready to accept and entertain thee, and his heart loves and desires, all are ready after thee: hence be ready to meet with him. *I am my Beloved's.* [63]

SECTION V.

[*Use 1.*] Hence see the great unkindness of many a soul immediately after his espousing to Jesus Christ, who having once given himself to Christ, and received comfort thereby, presently grows more careless than before he was matched unto the Lord Jesus, who should now stand in a holy watchfulness and readiness to receive Christ, as 'tis Psalm [64] 85:8: *Let them not turn again to folly,* because they are very [65] apt so to do. Many say when in some distress, and after long waiting, if the Lord would pity once, then happy I; I would give away anything, all I have unto him: well, the Lord pities the soul when in its low estate, and then it blesseth God, but like the *Israelites,* soon forgets his works, his love, and after great peace from God, comes greatest carelessness: can this stand with Grace, and Christ? very hardly; but yet it may, for there are Two things that make for it.

1. Because at first conversion there is much seeking of Christ, for healing the horror and smart of sin, as well as for the curing of the wound and scar of sin: hence when espoused, and horror being past, that wheel [66] being broken, a man draws [67] more heavily now, and neglects seeking; now the Knife is out of his heart he cries not so earnestly.

2. Because when espoused, and much affected, commonly a man trusts to his affections, when he hath a fullness of them: hence the

Lord lets Satan prevail (Luke 22:31,33): *Satan hath desired to win-now thee as wheat*, and *I* (saith *Peter*) *am ready to die with thee*: but you see he fell, and then when the Lord looked upon him, he *went out and wept bitterly*: How shamefully hast thou fallen, should any love him more than you if ever he pity? well, for his Name-sake [68] he hath done it. But how oft hast thou broken Covenant? how forgetful of the Lord's kindness? The Lord looks upon thee this day, why hast thou so soon forgot me, and forsaken me? have I not took [69] thee from the Dung-hill, nay from Hell? and whereas I had so many thousands to set my love on, I chose thee: and whereas thou couldest not love me when I offered myself, thou couldest not return me love again, I gave it therefore to thee, yea and have given myself to thee forever: Hast thou thus forgotten me, whenas I take little wrongs from thee more heavily than great ones from others? Oh that this might make you go out and mourn bitterly: so if ever you have tasted that love as *Peter* did, Christ's looks will humble you.

[*Use* 2.] Hence see the reason why some Godly People die so un-comfortably, and with such distress of spirit; why they have not lived in an expectation of Christ, and hence they cry out of [70] themselves, not knowing whither [71] they go, insomuch as some have not been comforted by all former experiences, and by all present consolations of Ministers: Oh no, 'tis now too late to speak, they thank them for their love, but God hath otherwise thought of them; yet if any hope be given them 'tis ever picked out from some word, and they cry, Oh I thirst for a little mercy, and then die; and what is the reason of it? what need I speak? Themselves will tell you, and have done it, Oh I have lived thus and thus before you, but my heart in secret hath gone after the world, *etc.* I have neglected the Lord secretly, I have seldom thought of, or prepared for Death, and I had thought to have been better, but the Lord hath met with me: I know violence of Disease may do it sometime, but I speak how 'tis many times; whereas other-wise an open entrance should be made; 2 Peter 1:8,9,10,11. And as it hath been with some, so take warning lest it be so with you; you may be saved alive, yet to suffer wrack on the shore is uncomfort-able, and know it if your conscience be awake, it cannot but be so. Therefore do not conclude they were damned without Christ, but they were not made ready for Christ; and it may be your time draws nigh, and what have you to say? now a world for half an hour will a dying distressed man say.

SELECTION IX

The Saint's Anchor-Hold

John Davenport

The first meeting house in New Haven. This building, used from 1640 to 1670, was almost certainly the site of the preaching of The Saint's Anchor-Hold. *It was typical of New England meeting houses of the period in having a hipped roof, entrances on three sides, a bell turret, and a gallery (implied by the second row of windows). See Edmund W. Sinnott,* Meeting House and Church in Early New England *(New York: McGraw-Hill, 1963). From George H. Ford, "The Town of New Haven 1638–1784,"* Connecticut Magazine 5, *no. 12 (December 1899): 630.*

JOHN DAVENPORT HIMSELF probably had a large part in the publication, soon after their delivery in New Haven, of the sermons that constitute *The Saint's Anchor-Hold, in All Storms and Tempests*: when it appeared from a London press in 1661, the volume had a preface signed by two reputable and distinguished preachers, Joseph Caryl and William Hooke (Davenport's former associate in the New Haven church), neither of whom would be likely to condone an edition unauthorized by Davenport. The preface implies that Davenport had written these sermons in something like their printed form and that Caryl and Hooke were not relying wholly on a reported text.[1] Davenport expressed some pride in the published volume, for he sent it as a present to his influential London friend, Thomas Temple.[2] The volume, apparently meeting with some general approval, was twice republished in the forty years after its first appearance.[3]

The sermons of *The Saint's Anchor-Hold* seem to have been preached during the months of the disintegration of the Puritan Commonwealth in England and the restoration of the Stuart monarchy. Caryl and Hooke's preface emphasizes the political disturbance of the times, and the sermons reflect that emphasis. The text, from the Lamentations of Jeremiah (3:24), recounts the consolation of Israel in captivity when "greatly afflicted and tossed with Tempests": "The Lord is my portion, saith my soul; therefore will I hope in him." The historical context of the biblical text parallels the occasion of the preaching—the Puritan collapse in England. Davenport exhorts his congregation to consider the grave "calamities of the Church": "Brethren, it is a weighty matter to read letters, and receive intelligence in them concerning the state of the Churches. You had need to lift up your hearts to God, when you are about to read your letters from our native Country, to give you wisdom and hearts duly affected, that you may receive such intelligences, as you ought." His letters of 1659 and 1660 indicate that he was very much concerned with the news from England: he frequently received letters and newspapers and carefully pondered them "to see how things work towards the Accomplishm[en]t of the prophecies that concern these times [i.e., omens of the apocalypse], and to know how to pray suitably to changes of providence."[4] That purpose—understanding how to pray in times of affliction or transition—underlies the consolation of *The Saint's Anchor-Hold*.

Not only the news of the English political upheavals but also the occasion of an extensive sickness in New Haven in the years 1658 to 1660 contribute to the topical nature of *The Saint's Anchor-Hold*. Davenport's letters to his friend and physician, John Winthrop the younger, increasingly concern themselves in this period with disease as well as politics, and the preaching of these sermons obviously engaged the congregation by reference to this immediate affliction.[5] Because of their local interest, the sermons provide a clear and moving

example of an important strain of Puritan thought—the reenactment
in present-day life of the biblical history of Israel. Referring first to
the anger of the Lord exercised against Israel (Isa. 9:12), Davenport places the affliction of his time in its Old Testament context:
"So hath the Lord dealt with us, in this place; for sundry years past,
he hath visited us with returns of sicknesses, every following year
sharper than the former; because whatever purposes men and women
had, and whatever promises they made, when God's hand was upon
them, all wore off and came to nothing, after he had released them:
So that we, in this wilderness, may be justly charged for dealing with
God, as the people of *Israel* did in the wilderness." [6] For Davenport,
as for the other preachers, the word of God interpreted from the pulpit was literally and exactly a guide to life in America.

Despite Davenport's accusatory tone in the above quotation, the
sermons of *The Saint's Anchor-Hold* deal with affliction as an occasion more for consolation and hope than for blame. Introducing the
text, he considers the movement of its contexts (Lam. 3:17–23) from
"deep dejection and despondency" to hope in God's mercy. "In my
Text, [the Jews] are as men that find rest, after their dangers and
tossings at Sea, by casting Anchor upon firm ground, in a safe Har-
bor." The five sermons, dealing with distinct phrases from the text,
establish a foundation and a method for that hope. The first is an
assertion, beginning on the level of the understanding: the intellectual foundation of consolation is the knowledge that a saint "is a
Citizen of heaven; there is his inheritance." To prove that knowledge, Davenport in the next sermon demonstrates its epistemological
source: "The Lord is my portion, *saith my soul*." The saints know that
the Lord is their portion because their souls, working by the two
means of knowledge—revelation and reason—declare so. The third
sermon, the selection here printed, treats the single word "therefore"
as a transition from the faculty of understanding to the will. By the
addition of will to intellect, Davenport completes the psychology of
consolation. In the fourth sermon (on the text "I will"), he deals with
the faculty of the will itself as the necessary complement to knowledge, and in the last sermon (on "hope in him"), he expounds on the
specific action of the will in the case of affliction. As he says, his text
is "not so much an Argument to convince the judgment [intellect]
(though it contains that also, as we have before proved) as a motive
to induce and incline the will to hope in God." [7] All knowledge is useless unless it moves the soul toward God; therefore, the last sermon
fills more than half the volume with a threefold practical instruction: understanding hope, testing hope, and exercising hope.

In treating his text throughout these five sermons, Davenport moves
from knowledge to will and from despondency to hope. The pivotal
sermon on "therefore" demonstrates the emphasis on logic and reason that characterizes Davenport in particular and Puritan preach-

ing of the first generation in general. The preachers believed that although the state of sin inevitably muddles the faculties of the soul, the corruption of reason is not total. The regenerate soul, supplementing the gift of grace in salvation with training in logic, prayer, and careful thought, can regain its right reason, its ability to understand the truth and to act on it. Such rational enlightenment was for these preachers a real and blessed gift of the Spirit.

Enlightenment is the theme and the central image of this selection. The clarity of Davenport's language perfectly fits his assumption that the saint is capable of reasonable knowledge and action. With careful exegesis, Davenport treats the text with reverence for the precision of its thought and language and for its applicability to the saint's plight. The similitudes are skillfully introduced to help the listeners without distracting them—particularly memorable is Davenport's extended treatment of "the full and powerful light" of the Spirit.

Finally, Davenport's method in the sermon matches his imagery and his theme. His language is an example of the plain style of preaching at its best: all his rhetoric acts to persuade and move his listeners to recognize the action of the Spirit in themselves. This sermon, like most Puritan preaching, places the final test of its efficacy on the listeners themselves and their examination of their spiritual life. The exhortation to earnest and difficult action is the refrain of the sermon: "study the grounds of hope, and improve them for your help."

Lamentations 3:24: *The Lord is my portion, saith my soul; therefore will I hope in him.*

We have already spoken[8] of two parts of the Text; the Assertion, *the Lord is my portion*, and the proof of it; *saith my soul*. We now proceed to the third, the inference, which the Church draws from the premises; *therefore will I hope in him*. In which words three particulars are to be noted. 1. The reason, whereupon their hope was grounded (*therefore*). 2. The resolution of their will to act according to that reason (*I will*). 3. The act itself resolved upon, together with the proper object of it (*hope in him*). For the first, the reason, whereupon their hope was grounded. This illative[9] particle, *therefore*, notes the result of a discourse in the minds of believers, whereby they compare one thing with another, and gather one thing from another; and thence conclude to act suitably to the truest and best reason. Faith is an understanding grace, and knows what use to make of the soul's interest in God. When a man hath God for his portion, and knows it, thence faith inferreth it is my duty, and it is for my good to hope in him: Therefore I will hope in him. Reason of itself, in this corrupt state of fallen man, cannot teach men to hope in God. But when God hath in the word of promise given himself to us to be our portion, and faith hath closed with him, as our portion; and the word telleth us it is our duty, and for our good to hope in him, then faith seeth good reason that we should hope in him. Faith useth reason, though not as the ground, yet as a sanctified instrument, to find out God's grounds, that it may rely upon him. He[10] believes best, who best knows, why he believes, and he best hopes in God, who can give the best reasons for his hoping in him. The affections, though they have not reason grafted in them, yet they are thus far reasonable, that, in all that are godly-wise, they are raised up, and laid down, guided, and actuated, by sanctified reason, which is the highest and best reason.

Doctrine. They that hope in God aright, have their hope in him raised, and strengthened by good and strong reasons. Reasons fetched from God, and from the soul's[11] knowing its interest in him, as his portion, are good and strong reasons, for our hoping in him; and[12] such are the reasons which the Church, in my Text, gives of their hoping in God. They considered God's All-sufficiency, in himself, and to every one that hath him for his portion, and what interest themselves had in him, through faith in Christ, and thereupon conclude; therefore will I hope in him. So may all believers.

Reason 1. From the inseparable connection of hope with faith: Faith believes in Christ, and in God through Christ, upon God's authority in his word, and what faith believes, hope expects. The reasons for a believer's hoping in God, are as good and strong, as for his believing in him. For, as, naturally, beams come from the Sun, and branches from the root; so, by spiritual discourse, one truth issueth from another; and, as the Sun and its beams, the roots and branches, are all of one nature; so the grounds of comfortable truths, and reasons taken from those grounds, are both of the same divine authority in themselves. Though in us, discourse is apt to be so troubled, in times of Temptation, that we cannot see how one truth ariseth upon another; yet so far as faith sees God to be our portion, the soul sees good and strong reason for our hoping in him for all good, that we may suit all our needs, in the best season.

Reason 2. From the convincing light, which the spirit of God bringeth into the soul, when he worketh faith and hope in it. It is the office and work of the spirit, to convince, and, by convincing, to comfort; John 16:7,8. Conviction is a clear and infallible demonstration, and comfort is a demonstration, with application unto us, of better and stronger reasons to raise us up, than those are which tend to cast down our souls. When the spirit convinceth, he bringeth such a full and powerful light into the soul, as silenceth all disputes and cavils, and causeth the soul to yield, as overcome by the evidence and authority of the light and truth brought into it. Light hath a convincing property and force in it. When we see the light of the Sun, we know it is day, and will not believe those that shall deny it, though they were ten thousands,[13] because the conviction hereof is undeniable, it is an unreasonable thing to deny it. So the spirit of God brings an undeniable light into the soul, which discovers the vanity of those windings, and turnings, whereof men's deceitful hearts are so full, that there can be no thorough conviction, and effectual to salvation, without the efficacy of the Holy Spirit. A common conviction there may be, by the light of nature, or of a natural conscience, or of some common transient work of the Holy Spirit, but that is but weak: For either it discovers but little, as a little spark shows little light, not enough to lighten the room, by overcoming the darkness, and turning it into light; or the light, which it shows, it shows but weakly, like a flash of lightning, or a blaze in straw, that is soon out again. But saving conviction is a greater and stronger light, like the light of the Sun, which is a full and powerful light. This is only from the sanctifying spirit of God. This light shows the evil of sin, and the good of the contrary, in their spiritual nature, and compass, and draws the will answerably, from the one to the other, by converting grace; Acts 26:18. This light is abiding in the renewed soul. Thus the Church, in my Text, was convinced and comforted, in their great distress, by the spirit and word of God, so as they could hold forth good and strong reasons, whereupon their hope was strengthened, and their hearts were comforted in sad hours.

Use 1. For Instruction, twofold: 1 Learn hence to examine and try the reasons, whereby you are moved to act; whether they[14] be good, or not good. Reason[15] is a beam of God's light. What comes from God, carrieth the soul to God; Therefore that which draws the soul from God cannot be a good reason, it is not right reason, but falsely called reason, it is not from faith, but from[16] unbelief, not good but evil; Hebrews 3:12. Hence, no good reason can be given for any sin: Whatever reasons are pretended for it, they are not according to God's Logic, but the Devil's Sophistry; James 1:22: παραλογιζόμενοι ἑαυτούς,[17] They deceive themselves with false Syllogisms. You may find in James 3:15 three Topics,[18] from whence all such arguings are fetched, the World, the Flesh, and the Devil, the three great enemies of God's glory, and of Christ's Kingdom in us; yet they will pretend their good intention for God's honor, when they seek to themselves worldly profits by disobeying God's commandment. So did *Saul,* but *Samuel* refuted all his false pleas; 1 Samuel 15:21,22,23. See how the Scripture reproves such as encourage themselves to do evil, that good may come thereon; Romans 3:7,8. *Job* sharply took up his friends for this (in Job 13:7): *Will you speak wickedly for God, and talk deceitfully for him?* yet thus the Devil deceiveth his active instruments against Christ, *the time cometh* (saith Christ, in John 16: 2) *that whosoever killeth you, will think he doth God service*: There are that argue from worldly advantages to encourage men to sin; Proverbs 1:13. But Christ shows the pernicious delusion of such reasonings, in Matthew 16:26; others from the pleasure of carnal liberty, but *Peter* shows the falseness of that plea, in 2 Peter 2:19; others from worldly preferment of wicked men (Malachi 3:15), which the Prophet confuteth in verse 18. Some from God's patience, which God himself answereth, in Psalm 50:21,22. Such as these are the διαλογισμοί,[19] the reasonings of natural men; Romans 1:21; which should warn all men to deny their carnal wisdom, which is enmity against God; Romans 8:7. 2. Learn hence to examine and try the goodness and strength of the reasons, whereupon it is grounded, remembering that rule in[20] 1 Peter 3:15, *Be ready always to give an answer to every man that asketh you a reason of the hope that is in you.* You say, you hope in God, If you have no reason for it; it's a foolish unreasonable hope. If you have but slight reasons; it's a vain hope. And such is hope of the most: one grounds his hope of salvation upon his creation; saying, I am God's creature, and he hath not made[21] me to damn me: Therefore, I hope he will save me. See the delusion of this plea, 1. Are not the Devils God's creatures? yet they are damned. 2. Though God's end in making you, was not to damn you, yet your impenitency in sin, and unbelief will damn you. 3. See the Lord's own refutation of this plea, in Isaiah 27:11. Another grounds his hope of blessedness upon God's blessing him, as he calls it, with worldly success, and prosperity. But Christ shows the vanity of this hope in that rich man in Hell; Luke 16:25; and by telling us that *it is that they shall*[22] *be destroyed forever* (Psalm 92:7). God's end in prospering such in the world, is like *Hester's* end in feasting *Haman.*[23] Another grounds his hope that he shall have heaven hereafter, because he hath had his Hell, through afflictions, in this life. But such consider not what the Word saith concerning *Sodom* and *Gomorrah* (Jude 7): *Suffering the vengeance of eternal fire.* What misery wicked impenitent sinners suffer here, is but a beginning and pledge to them of Hell hereafter. Another grounds his hope upon his Christian privileges and performances. But this is plentifully refuted in Scripture, by *John's* speech to the *Pharisees* (Matthew 3:9), and *Paul's* to the *Romans* (Romans 2:28), and concerning himself (Philippians 3:7). Others ground their hope upon God's mercy, though they continue in their sins. This indeed is a good reason for hope, in those that confess and forsake their sin; Proverbs 28:13. But for those that abuse this mercy to the hardening of themselves in sin by it, see how the Lord thunders against such, in Deuteronomy 29:19,20. Others ground their hope upon their own self-flattering and self-deceiving thoughts of themselves. Such may see their own folly and madness, by what the Scripture saith, in Proverbs 28:26 and Galatians 6:3. Let all such, and the like, renounce their ungrounded hope, which, like *that broken reed of Egypt* (Isaiah 36:6), will at once both fail them, and ruin them. Till you have an interest in God and Christ, as your portion, you are *without hope* (Ephesians 2:12). Therefore the first work of the Spirit, in the soul, by the Gospel, and one great end of the ministry thereof, is, to make way for true faith and hope, by *casting down* those λογισμούς,[24] *reasonings*, and *bringing into Captivity every thought*, πν νόημα,[25] every sophistical reasoning, *to the obedience of Christ* (2 Corinthians 10:5).

Use 2. For Exhortation to believers, being under temptations and afflictions, whether outward or inward, to improve the reasons, which faith supplieth, for the quickening and strengthening of their hope in God. For, in such times, faith is put to it to use reasons. Indeed the soul needeth not that help so much, when it is in a clear and quiet state, for upon its close and sweet communion with God, in Christ, and from some likeness between the renewed soul and God, it present-ly, and without previous discourse, runneth to God, as by a super-natural instinct; as, by natural instinct, the child runneth to his nat-ural parents in danger, and distress, with confidence. But, in dark times of great afflictions, and temptations, faith is put to use Argu-ments, and reasons to quicken and strengthen hope. Accordingly, study the grounds of hope, and improve them for your help. 1. Such as may be supplied from the inward store laid up in the soul, as the Church did in my Text. 2. Such as are, or may be, suggested by others: Harken, and yield to them, and close with them. For, thus you will show that you have a frame of spirit suitable to any holy and com-fortable truth, that shall be presented and applied to it. There is a principle in every renewed spirit, that closeth with whatever cometh from God's spirit, that readily claims acquaintance and kindred with it, as coming from the same blessed spring, the holy Spirit. When *Asaph* found the contrary in himself, that his *soul refused comfort, and he remembered God and was troubled* (Psalm 77:2,3),[26] he saw, and *said, this is mine infirmity* (verse 10). He saw that it arose from a sickness, a spiritual disease, and distemper in his soul. While pas-sion and temptation disturb the soul, they hinder the exercise of spiritual reason: As we see in *David*, who *said, in his haste, all men are liars* (Psalm 116:10,11). This he saw afterward, when his spiritual reason had recovered itself, which before by his distemper was hin-dered in its working; then he admired God for his benefits toward him, notwithstanding his provocation of him to have taken a contrary course with him (verse 12). Labor therefore, 1. That your mind, which is the seat of principles, be well furnished with divine and spiritual truths. For false principles can never produce true comforts. As only truth sanctifieth; John 17:17; So truth only truly comforteth. There is the same reason of both. For it is the peculiar office of the Holy Spirit, both to sanctify, and to comfort: And the Holy spirit is the

Spirit of Truth; John 16:13. Therefore he will not work by a false-hood, but only by Truth, either sanctification, or consolation. 2. See that your understanding διάνοια,[27] the dianoetical, discoursing faculty, which is the seat of conclusions, be used to deduce from spiritual principles, such spiritual conclusions[28] as they are apt[29] to beget. For, by false reasonings, in times of affliction and temptation, 1.[30] Believers hinder their faith and hope, when they reason too much from sense and present feeling; Isaiah 40:27 and 49:14, Ezekiel 33:10. 2. Others have false comforts from the light of a fire kindled by themselves; Isaiah 50:11. But, if, renouncing such reasonings, you fly to Christ and his righteousness alone, for your acceptance with God, through faith in his blood, with true repentance; then you may reason with God; Isaiah 1:18; though not in your own strength or[31] worth; Job 9:14,15;[32] yet you may reason with him in faithful fervent prayer, in Genesis 32:10,11,12: whereby he[33] prevailed and got both a new blessing and a new name (verse 28). Fervent prayers are strong reasonings with God, in Christ's strength, and for his sake. This will be well pleasing to God. For, as, when God calls for our obedience, he adds persuasives to his precepts, and reasoneth with us as well as commandeth us; so he alloweth us, in prayer, to add persuasions to our petitions, and to reason with him as well as entreat him. Only, it must be our care that we reason from right Topics, and heads of Arguments; Such as these, 1. From the infiniteness and freeness of God's mercy and grace. 2. From the immutable firmness of his Covenant and promises in Christ. 3. From our indigence and dependence upon him. 4. From the concernments of his glory, and our necessary good. In such reasonings of faith and hope, the spirit, strength, and life of prayer consisteth.[34] Such pleadings, in the name of Christ, God approveth and requireth; Isaiah 43:26. 3. See that the heart, which is the seat of practical knowledge be fitted to order the conversation and practice, by sound principles, in the mind, and right conclusions, in the understanding; that mental discourse may not vanish in mere empty speculation. As, in my Text, *The Lord is my portion*, is the principle laid up in their mind, *saith my soul*, is the proof of[35] it; the conclusion to be from thence inferred, is, Therefore it is my duty to hope in him. This knowledge becomes practical, when the heart so receiveth it, that the will comes to a resolution; *therefore I will hope in him.*

Appendix A

Biographies of the Preachers

Both Cotton Mather's *Magnalia Christi Americana* (1702) and the *Dictionary of American Biography* provide ample outlines of the lives of the five preachers represented in this volume. For the three hundredth anniversary of the founding of Concord, Elizabeth Lowell Everett wrote a brief biography, *Peter Bulkeley and His Times* (Leominster, Mass.: Goodhue Printing Co., 1935). Cotton's life has been the only one so far to receive recent book-length studies. Larzer Ziff's *The Career of John Cotton: Puritanism and the American Experience* is a traditional biography and Everett H. Emerson's *John Cotton* an intellectual biography, examining "what Cotton was up to in his sermons and in his Congregational and other writings." Davenport's life is treated by Franklin B. Dexter in an extensive essay, "Sketch of the Life and Writings of John Davenport," in *Papers of the New Haven Colony Historical Society*, vol. 2, pp. 205–238, and by Isabel MacBeath Calder, ed., in her impressively detailed "biographical sketch," in her edition of *The Letters of John Davenport, Puritan Divine*. At the end of the last century, George Leon Walker prepared a biography, *Thomas Hooker: Preacher, Founder, Democrat* (New York: Dodd, Mead, & Co., 1891), subsequently reprinted in 1969 by the Garrett Press. George H. Williams provides a very thorough biographical essay on Hooker's life prior to his emigration to America in *Thomas Hooker: Writings in England and Holland, 1626–1633*, ed. Williams, Norman Pettit, Winfried Herget, and Sargent Bush, Jr. John A. Albro, Thomas Shepard's first editor, wrote a brief biography, first published as *The Life of Thomas Shepard* (Boston: Sabbath School Society, 1847) and later reprinted in *The Works of Thomas Shepard*, ed. Albro. Shepard is the only preacher for whom we have an autobiography, now impressively edited by Michael McGiffert, who introduces it with a spiritual biography of this famous early preacher. See *God's Plot: The Paradoxes of Puritan Piety, Being the Autobiography and Journal of Thomas Shepard*.

Peter Bulkeley

Peter Bulkeley (1583–1659) was born in Bedfordshire into a distinguished family, his mother of noble birth and his father a clergyman of independent means. He attended St. John's College, Cambridge, where he took the M.A. in 1608, and he returned home in 1620 to succeed his father in the parish of Odell and to inherit the family estate. Although he was even more extreme than his father in his dissenting opinions, he nonetheless preached undisturbed for fifteen years. In 1635, however, Laud suspended him; and Bulkeley with his wife and children, servants, and followers emigrated to Massachusetts. Stopping briefly in Newtown, later called Cambridge, they went west and founded Concord in 1636, there settling the twelfth church of the colony. Bulkeley served the church and town faithfully for over twenty years, notably involved in affairs beyond Concord only when he served with Hooker as moderator of the Hutchinsonian Synod in 1637. Although he occasionally expressed a longing to return to England to die, he was still preaching in Concord when he died at the age of seventy-six. He endowed the Harvard Library with a considerable number of his books and left only one published sermon-series, *The Gospel-Covenant*.

John Cotton

Born into a comfortable professional family in Derbyshire, John Cotton (1584–1652) took his B.A. at Trinity College, Cambridge, in 1603 and his M.A. at Emmanuel College in 1606. During the next six years, after he became head lecturer at Emmanuel, he found himself effectually converted by the forceful Puritan preacher, Richard Sibbes. In 1612 he was made vicar of the large parish church of St. Botolph's in Boston, Lincolnshire. From about 1615 on he simplified the liturgy and ceremonies to align them more with Puritan practices. It appears an assistant was appointed to conduct services more in line with traditional forms. Cotton himself thrived for twenty years, protected by powerful friends, but was finally forced to resign for Nonconformity and sought refuge in New England. Upon arrival in 1633, he became teacher of the church in Boston, a post he held until his death twenty years later. He managed to survive his involvement with Anne Hutchinson in the early years and went on to become one of the most distinguished leaders of Massachusetts. He spent long hours over his scholarly endeavors, publishing not only a voluminous number of sermons but also extensive writings on the Congregational system of church governance.

John Davenport

John Davenport (1597–1670) of Coventry attended Oxford but did not receive his B.D. degree until 1625, having interrupted his study to serve as a private chaplain and then as vicar of St. Stephen's in London. Some time during the 1620s, he appears to have become familiar with Puritan practices, but he consistently denied any Nonconformist leanings. In 1632 it was John Cotton, in London on his flight to America, who persuaded Davenport to take off the surplice. Davenport went first to Holland but, disagreeing with the practice of baptism of the English church there, resolved to emigrate to Massachusetts. On arrival he stayed in Boston about nine months, trying to help the colony resolve the upheaval over the Antinomian controversy. In 1638 he became pastor of the new colony of New Haven in Connecticut. In 1661 he hid the regicide judges in his house. In that same decade he vigorously opposed the Halfway Covenant, a more moderate policy on church membership. Called in 1667 to fill the pastorate of the First Church in Boston, following the death of John Wilson, Davenport misrepresented his church's willingness to release him. That strategy occasioned the split of the First Church and probably hastened his death in 1670. He can be vindicated, in Isabel Calder's estimate, on the grounds that he consistently held to a vision of church polity that gave supremacy to the elect.

Thomas Hooker

Born in Marfield, Leicestershire, Thomas Hooker (1586?–1647) received the B.A. in 1608 and the M.A. in 1611 from Emmanuel College, Cambridge. Influenced by such leading Puritans then at Emmanuel as Richard Sibbes and William Ames, Hooker remained in that center of Puritan thought as lecturer and catechist from 1611 to 1618. In the first half of the 1620s he was a minister to the small parish of Esher, Surrey; and in the last half of the 1620s he served as a lecturer in Chelmsford, Essex, where he began preaching for a popular audience and attracted great public acclaim. Deprived by Laud of his lectureship in 1629, he fled to Holland, where he was associate pastor in the English Nonconformist church at Delft and collaborated with William Ames in his writings. In 1633 he sailed for Massachusetts with John Cotton and Samuel Stone, soon to be the teacher of the congregation Hooker himself would serve as pastor. They settled in Newtown, later called Cambridge, but were discontent with this location. Although many in the colony opposed the removal of Hooker's group, it went in May of 1636 to Hartford. The reasons for removal seem to go beyond the group's stated desire for more land. In the unclear record are many hints, including the suggested difficulty of Cotton and Hooker's coexisting so closely and Hooker's supposed dislike of the strict practices of church membership in the Bay. Hooker remained a principal leader of the colony at large, however, returning to Massachusetts to serve as a moderator of the Hutchinsonian Synod in 1637 and again as a participant in Hutchinson's trial in 1638. He continued to come back for important meetings held to articulate the Congregational position. He also led in framing a civil government in Connecticut that many see as more democratic than those of the Massachusetts towns. A great preacher and leader, Hooker died in the epidemic of 1647, at the age of sixty-one.

Thomas Shepard

Thomas Shepard (1605–1649) was born in Towcester, Northamptonshire, the son of a grocer. Orphaned at the age of ten, he was adopted by his older brother John. Shepard was educated by a local schoolmaster before he went to Emmanuel College, Cambridge. There he experienced a painful and protracted spiritual conversion under the ministry of Laurence Chaderton and John Preston. He took his B.A. in 1623, and six months before receiving his M.A. in 1627, he went to live in Essex. There he was moved by the preaching of Thomas Hooker and served in Earles-Colne as a lecturer until Laud suspended him in 1630. Then began five years in which, as he says in his autobiography, he was tossed "from the south to the north of England." He went to Yorkshire as private tutor and chaplain to the family of Sir Richard Darley. In 1633 he was forced into hiding and in 1635, after an unsuccessful attempt to sail for Boston in 1634, landed in America. He and his followers went to Newtown (later called Cambridge), where Hooker's followers were willing to sell their land before departure for Connecticut, and there in the early winter of 1636 he established a church. He was active during the Antinomian crisis, organizing the Hutchinsonian Synod; and in 1638 he took part in Hutchinson's church trial. Harvard College, of which he was an unofficial chaplain and founding officer, was located in Newtown partly because Shepard had preserved his own congregation from Antinomian opinions. Sickly all his life, he died in his mid-forties, revered as one of the three great founding preachers of New England.

Appendix B

Checklist of the Earliest Authoritative Editions of the Sermons and Sermon-Series of the Preachers

"Earliest Authoritative Editions" designates the earliest appearance of the latest revision or edition by the preacher or reliable editor; but all editions are cited, as with Cotton's *The New Covenant*, if differently worded titles lead to confusion. Details of the subtitle that do not significantly advance understanding of the contents are deleted, but phrasing giving substantive information—such as where the sermon was preached or on what biblical text it is based—is retained. Spelling and capitalization are normalized; italicization has been ignored. Unless otherwise stated, the place of publication is London.

This listing has been compiled by a variety of means. Whenever possible, the original or a microfilm has been examined. We have consulted the *National Union Catalogue*, primarily to insure as complete a compilation as is possible at this date, and double-checked our findings with previous bibliographical work on these preachers. Babette M. Levy, in *Preaching in the First Half Century of New England History*, gives the first bibliography of published sermons for early major preachers. Everett H. Emerson in *John Cotton* provides a bibliography, arranged by order of composition, of Cotton's writings, sermonic and other. Franklin B. Dexter, in "Sketch of the Life and Writings of John Davenport," in *Papers of the New Haven Colony Historical Society*, vol. 2, pp. 234–238, compiles the writings of Davenport. "A 'Trial' Shepard Bibliography" appears in *Publications of the Colonial Society of Massachusetts* 27 (1932): 347–351. The bibliography, pp. 390–425, in *Thomas Hooker: Writings in England and Holland, 1626–1633*, ed. George H. Williams, Norman Pettit, Winfried Herget, and Sargent Bush, Jr., is impressively comprehensive in citing all the currently known editions and reprints of Hooker's writings. It provides a useful summary of the contents of each work. Helpful information on the delivery and publication of sermons can be found in that volume in "Establishing the Hooker Canon," by Sargent Bush, Jr., pp. 378–389, and in Winfried Herget's essay, "Preaching and Publication—Chronology and the Style of Thomas Hooker's Sermons," *Harvard Theological Review* 65, no. 2 (April 1972): 231–239. Only Hooker's and Shepard's sermons have been substantially edited. *The Works of Thomas Shepard*, ed. John A. Albro—an inadequate compilation from the nineteenth century—has recently been reissued by AMS Press and G. Olms. The abovementioned *Thomas Hooker* makes available some of his early sermons but not either of the English-preached series represented in our volume.

Peter Bulkeley

The Gospel-Covenant; Or the Covenant of Grace Opened . . . The Second Edition, Much Enlarged, and Corrected by the Author. 1651.

John Cotton

A Brief Exposition . . . of Canticles, or, Song of Solomon. 1642.

A Brief Exposition . . . of Ecclesiastes. 1654.

Christ the Fountain of Life: Or, Sundry Choice Sermons on Part of the Fifth Chapter of the First Epistle of St. John. 1651.

The Church's Resurrection, or the Opening of the Fifth and Sixth Verses of the 20th Chap. of the Revelation. 1642.

The Covenant of God's Free Grace, Most Sweetly Unfolded, and Comfortably Applied to a Disquieted Soul, from That Text of 2 Sam. 23. Ver. 5. 1645.

The Covenant of Grace Discovering the Great Work of a Sinner's Reconciliation to God. 1655. Reedited and published as *A Treatise of the Covenant of Grace* (q.v.).

An Exposition upon the Thirteenth Chapter of the Revelation. 1655.

God's Mercy Mixed with His Justice, or, His People's Deliverance in Times of Danger. 1641. Reprinted as *The Saint's Support and Comfort*. 1658.

God's Promise to His Plantation. 1630.

The New Covenant. 1654. Reprinted as part of *The Covenant of Grace* (q.v.). Reedited and published as *A Treatise of the Covenant of Grace* (q.v.).

The Pouring Out of the Seven Vials: Or an Exposition, of the 16. Chapter of the Revelation . . . Preached in Sundry Sermons at Boston in New England. 1642.

A Practical Commentary . . . upon the First Epistle General of John. 1656.

A Sermon Preached . . . at Salem, 1636. Boston, Massachusetts, 1713.

A Treatise of the Covenant of Grace . . . Sermons Preached upon Act, 7.8. 1659.

The Way of Life; Or, God's Way and Course, in Bringing the Soul Into, Keeping It In, and Carrying It On, in the Ways of Life and Peace. 1641.

John Davenport

God's Call to His People to Turn unto Him; Together with His Promise to Turn unto Them. Opened and Applied in II. Sermons at Two Public Fasting-Days Appointed by Authority. Cambridge, Massachusetts, 1669.

The Knowledge of Christ Indispensably Required of All Men That Would be Saved . . . in Sundry Sermons on Acts 2.36. 1653.

A Royal Edict for Military Exercises: Published in a Sermon Preached to the Captains, and Gentlemen That Exercise Arms in the Artillery Garden at Their General Meeting. 1629.

The Saint's Anchor-Hold, in All Storms and Tempests. 1661.

A Sermon Preached at the Election of the Governor, at Boston in New-England, May 19th 1669. Cambridge, Massachusetts, 1670.

Thomas Hooker

"Abstracts of Two Sermons by Rev. Thomas Hooker. From the Shorthand Notes of Mr. Henry Wolcott," *Collections of the Connecticut Historical Society* 1 (1860): 19–21. Hartford, Connecticut.

The Application of Redemption, by the Effectual Work of the Word, and Spirit of Christ, for the Bringing Home of Lost Sinners to God. The First Eight Books. 1656.

The Application of Redemption by the Effectual Work of the Word, and Spirit of Christ, for the Bringing Home of Lost Sinners to God. The Ninth and Tenth Books. 1656.

The Christian's Two Chief Lessons, Viz. Self-Denial and Self-Trial . . . In Three Treatises on . . . Matt. 16.24. 2 Cor. 13.5. John I. 12,13. 1640.

A Comment upon Christ's Last Prayer in the Seventeenth of John. 1656.

The Covenant of Grace Opened . . . Being Several Sermons Preached at Hartford in New-England. 1649.

The Danger of Desertion: Or a Farewell Sermon of Mr. Thomas Hooker, Sometimes Minister of God's Word . . . in Essex; But Now of New England. Preached Immediately before His Departure out of Old England. 1641. Reprinted as *The Signs of God's Forsaking a People.* 1657.

The Faithful Covenanter. A Sermon Preached at the Lecture in Dedham in Essex. 1644.

Four Learned and Godly Treatises; Viz. The Carnal Hypocrite. The Church's Deliverances. The Deceitfulness of Sin. The Benefit of Afflictions. 1638.

The Pattern of Perfection: Exhibited in God's Image on Adam: And God's Covenant Made with Him. 1640. Reprinted as *God's Image on Man.* 1653.

The Poor Doubting Christian Drawn unto Christ. 1629.

The Saint's Dignity, and Duty. Together with The Danger of Ignorance and Hardness. 1651.

The Saint's Guide, in Three Treatises; I. The Mirror of Mercy, on Gen. 6.13. II. The Carnal Man's Condition, on Rom. 1. 18. III. The Plantation of the Righteous, on Psa. 1. 3. 1645. Reordered, revised, and expanded version of *Three Godly Sermons* (q.v.).

Sermon of June 20, 1647, preached at Windsor, Connecticut, in *History of the First Church of Hartford, 1633–1883,* by George Leon Walker. Hartford: Brown & Gross, 1884. Appendix 4, pp. 429–434.

The Sinner's Salvation. 1638.

The Soul's Exaltation. A Treatise Containing The Soul's Union with Christ, on 1 Cor. 6.17. The Soul's Benefit from Union with Christ, on 1. Cor. 1.30. The Soul's Justification, on 2 Cor. 5.21. 1638.

The Soul's Humiliation. 1637.

The Soul's Implantation into the Natural Olive. 1640.

The Soul's Ingrafting into Christ. 1637.

The Soul's Possession of Christ . . . Whereunto Is Annexed A Sermon Preached at the Funeral of That Worthy Divine Mr. Wilmott. 1638.

The Soul's Preparation for Christ. Or, a Treatise of Contrition. Wherein Is Discovered How God Breaks the Heart and Wounds the Soul, in the Conversion of a Sinner to Himself. 1632.

The Soul's Vocation or Effectual Calling to Christ. 1638.

Spiritual Munition: A Funeral Sermon. 1638.

Spiritual Thirst: A Sermon Preached upon John 7.37. 1638.

The Stay of the Faithful: Together with The Properties of an Honest Heart. 1638.

"A Thomas Hooker Sermon of 1638," ed. Everett Emerson, *Resources for American Literary Study* 2 (Spring 1972): 75–89. College Park, Maryland.

Three Godly Sermons. 1638. First version of *The Saint's Guide* (q.v.).

The Unbeliever's Preparing for Christ. 1638.

Thomas Shepard

"Election Sermon, in 1638," an outline from the original manuscript, now lost, in *New England Historical and Genealogical Register and Antiquarian Journal* 24 (1870): 361–366. Boston, Massachusetts.

The Parable of the Ten Virgins Opened and Applied: Being the Substance of Divers Sermons on Matth. 25.1,–13. 1660.

The Saint's Jewel, Showing How to Apply the Promises; And The Soul's Invitation unto Jesus Christ. 1642.

The Sincere Convert, Discovering the Paucity of True Believers; And the Great Difficulty of Saving Conversion. 1640.

The Sound Believer. Or, a Treatise of Evangelical Conversion. Discovering the Work of Christ's Spirit, in Reconciling of a Sinner to God. 1645.

Subjection to Christ in All His Ordinances, and Appointments, the Best Means to Preserve Our Liberty. Together with A Treatise of Ineffectual Hearing the Word. 1652.

Theses Sabbaticae. Or, the Doctrine of the Sabbath . . . Which Were First Handled More Largely in Sundry Sermons in Cambridge in New-England in Opening of the Fourth Commandment. 1649.

Wine for Gospel Wantons: Or, Cautions against Spiritual Drunkenness. Being the Brief Notes of a Sermon Preached at Cambridge in New-England, upon a Day of Public Fasting and Prayer throughout the Colony, June 25. 1645. in Reference to the Sad Estate of the Lord's People in England. Cambridge, Massachusetts, 1668.

Appendix C

Recommended Background Reading

If a brief summary of the book is not provided, the title can be taken as descriptive.

Battis, Emery. *Saints and Sectaries: Anne Hutchinson and the Antinomian Controversy in the Massachusetts Bay Colony.* Chapel Hill: University of North Carolina Press, 1962. Drawing on a knowledge of "individual and social psychology," the author attempts "to determine what sort of person Mrs. Hutchinson was and what circumstances impelled her to press such radical conclusions."

Bercovitch, Sacvan. "Horologicals to Chronometricals: The Rhetoric of the Jeremiad." In *Literary Monographs*, edited by Eric Rothstein, vol. 3, pp. 1–124. Milwaukee: University of Wisconsin Press, 1970. A broad consideration of the parallels drawn between New England and Israel in the jeremiad, with emphasis on millenarianism and the more important theme of affirmation rather than that of denouncement.

————, ed. *The American Puritan Imagination: Essays in Revaluation.* New York: Cambridge University Press, 1975. Compilation of major essays in these categories: literary issues like genre and aesthetic, major figures, and historical continuities of Puritanism.

————. *Typology and Early American Literature.* Amherst: University of Massachusetts Press, 1972. An anthology of essays on an important style of biblical hermeneutics, whereby certain Old Testament signs and events (types) are interpreted as foreshadowing certain New Testament happenings (antitypes).

Collinson, Patrick. *The Elizabethan Puritan Movement.* London: Cape, 1967; Berkeley & Los Angeles: University of California Press, 1967.

Coolidge, John S. *The Pauline Renaissance in England: Puritanism and the Bible.* Oxford: Clarendon Press, 1970.

Cotton, John. *John Cotton on the Churches of New England.* Edited by Larzer Ziff. Cambridge, Mass.: Harvard University Press, 1968. Includes three key works on Congregational polity, two of which are tracts; the third is the sermon preached at Salem in 1636.

Dexter, Henry Martyn. *The Congregationalism of the Last Three Hundred Years, As Seen in Its Literature.* 1880; rpt. New York:

Burt Franklin, 1970. The first and most complete study of the origins and development of New England Congregationalism.

Elliott, Emory. *Power and the Pulpit in Puritan New England.* Princeton: Princeton University Press, 1975. A study of the "myths and metaphors" in the sermons of 1660 to 1700.

Emerson, Everett H., ed. *English Puritanism from John Hooper to John Milton.* Durham, N.C.: Duke University Press, 1968. An anthology of primary texts of twenty leaders of the English Puritan movement from its beginning to 1641.

Hall, David D. *The Faithful Shepherd: A History of the New England Ministry in the Seventeenth Century.* Chapel Hill: University of North Carolina Press, 1972.

―――, ed. *The Antinomian Controversy, 1636–1638: A Documentary History.* Middletown, Conn.: Wesleyan University Press, 1968.

Haller, William. *The Rise of Puritanism.* 1938; rpt. New York: Harper Torchbooks, 1957. A study of the Puritan preachers in England until 1643, based on what the Puritans themselves wrote about their intents.

Hill, Christopher. *Society and Puritanism in Pre-Revolutionary England.* New York: Schocken Books, 1964. A study of the ramifications of Puritanism in English life, with chapters focusing on such issues as lecturing, Sabbatarianism, "preaching of the Word," and "spiritualization of the household."

Levy, Babette May. *Preaching in the First Half Century of New England History.* Hartford: American Society of Church History, 1945. First comprehensive look at the theology and preaching style and content of the first-generation preachers.

McGiffert, Michael. "American Puritan Studies in the 1960's." *William and Mary Quarterly,* 3d ser. 27 (January 1970): 36–67. A bibliographical essay reviewing all the major scholarship on Puritanism during the 1960s.

Miller, Perry. *Errand into the Wilderness.* Cambridge, Mass.: Harvard University Press, 1964. Compilation of his essays written over a wide period, discussing issues like covenant theology and democracy in Hooker's Connecticut.

―――. *The New England Mind: The Seventeenth Century.* 1939; rpt. Boston: Beacon Press, 1961. The chief intellectual history of the Puritan civilization in New England, widely treating learning and religion, with chaps. 9 to 12 examining many aspects of preaching.

―――. *Orthodoxy in Massachusetts, 1630–1650.* 1933; rpt. New York: Harper Torchbooks, 1970. A study of the way Congregationalism emerged, with emphasis on its European origins.

―――, and Thomas H. Johnson, eds. *The Puritans: A Sourcebook of Their Writings.* 2 vols. Rev. ed. 1938; rpt. New York: Harper Torchbooks, 1963. Most thorough anthology of Puritan writings: histories, journals, sermons, poetry, aesthetic tracts, political essays, and letters.

Mitchell, W. Fraser. *English Pulpit Oratory from Andrewes to Tillotson: A Study of Its Literary Aspects*. London: Society for Promoting Christian Knowledge, 1932.

Morgan, Edmund S. *Visible Saints: The History of a Puritan Idea*. New York: New York University Press, 1963. An examination of how the Puritans determined eligibility for church membership, with particular focus on the requirement of experiential evidence.

Murdock, Kenneth B. *Literature and Theology in Colonial New England*. Cambridge, Mass.: Harvard University Press, 1949. An exploration of the relation between the New England Puritans' fundamental theological ideas and their literary theory and practice.

Pettit, Norman. *The Heart Prepared: Grace and Conversion in Puritan Spiritual Life*. New Haven: Yale University Press, 1966. A study of all five preachers represented in this anthology in terms of their views of the conversion experience, specifically the stage of preparation and their theology of baptism.

Piercy, Josephine K. *Studies in Literary Types in Seventeenth Century America (1607–1710), in Two Parts*. 1939; rpt. Hamden, Conn.: Shoe String Press, 1969. A useful early study of genres—such as personal essay, meditation, sermon, satire—and influences— such as classical inheritance, prose style.

Walker, Williston, ed. *The Creeds and Platforms of Congregationalism*. 1893; rpt. Philadelphia: United Church Press, 1960. Documents by the developers of Congregational polity from the 1580s to the 1880s.

Walzer, Michael. *The Revolution of the Saints: A Study in the Origins of Radical Politics*. Cambridge, Mass.: Harvard University Press, 1965. A description of Puritanism as the earliest form of political radicalism, presupposing such theories as the rise of the gentry, the crisis of the old aristocracy, and the winning of the initiative.

Wright, Thomas G. *Literary Culture in Early New England: 1620–1730*. New Haven: Yale University Press, 1920. A study of education, libraries, and the publishing business.

Ziff, Larzer. *Puritanism in America: New Culture in a New World*. New York: Viking Press, 1970. The most recent full-scale study of the entire movement, with an attempt to view the "history of American Puritanism as a culture" by synthesizing "the special concerns of intellectual, social, and economic history."

Notes to the Introduction

1. John Cotton, *The Way of Life* (London, 1641), p. 164.
2. John Calvin, rooting his arguments in Paul's vision of the way the Old Testament shadowed forth redemption by Jesus Christ, explains as the preachers do—particularly Bulkeley in *The Gospel-Covenant*—the gradual unfolding of God's plan of salvation: "although it was always the will of the Lord that the minds of his people should be directed, and their hearts elevated, towards the celestial inheritance, yet, in order that they might be the better encouraged to hope for it, he anciently exhibited it for their contemplation and partial enjoyment under the figures of terrestrial blessings. Now, having by the gospel more clearly and explicitly revealed the grace of the future life, he leaves the inferior mode of instruction which he used with the Israelites" (*Institutes of the Christian Religion*, ed. John Allen, 2 vols. [Philadelphia: Presbyterian Board of Publication, 1841], 1:405).
3. Of course, the preachers believed that God in the person of the Spirit actually converted the elect. The doctrine of the means simply denoted that God commonly chose to work the spiritual regeneration of the elect through the channel of the preacher and his sermon. The five preachers in this volume varied over how predominant a role they assigned the sermon in conversion. All certainly saw it as important and for that reason defended the centrality of preaching throughout their lives. In fact, the majority of their auditors, especially in New England, were assumed to have been converted already. Such repeated assertions about the means of conversion reminded and instructed the faithful about aspects of their progress in the stages of salvation should they doubt whether they had grace. For further discussion of this issue, see our introductory essays to Hooker, *The Soul's Vocation* (doctrines 3 and 7), and Cotton, *The Way of Life*. For a general discussion of the sermon as the means of conversion, see Perry Miller, *The New England Mind: The Seventeenth Century* (1939; rpt. Boston: Beacon Press, 1961), chap. 10, and David D. Hall, *The Faithful Shepherd: A History of the New England Ministry in the Seventeenth Century* (Chapel Hill: University of North Carolina Press, 1972), chap. 1.
4. Christopher Hill, *Society and Puritanism in Pre-Revolutionary England* (New York: Schocken Books, 1964), p. 32.
5. Alan F. Herr, in *The Elizabethan Sermon: A Survey and a Bibliography* (Philadelphia: University of Pennsylvania Press, 1940), p. 67, estimates that in Elizabethan times 40 percent of all publications were

religious and that sermons account for a large percentage of this. William Haller, citing the "abundant use which the Puritan preachers made of the press," explains that the "press itself prospered at such a rate and to such a degree that, from being an adjunct to the pulpit, it rapidly became a distinct organ of expression in its own right" (*The Rise of Puritanism* [1938; rpt. New York: Harper Torchbooks, 1957], pp. 5–6).

6. Hill, *Society and Puritanism*, p. 32.
7. W. Fraser Mitchell, *English Pulpit Oratory from Andrewes to Tillotson: A Study of Its Literary Aspects* (London: Society for Promoting Christian Knowledge, 1932), p. 255.
8. Calvin's distinction between pastor and teacher is explained by Hall, *Faithful Shepherd*, p. 11. He observes (p. 95) that like the office of ruling elder, the "distinction between pastor and teacher also vanished in a few years" after settlement. But during the ministry of the first clerics, most—notably Cotton as teacher and Hooker as pastor—shared the pulpit with another preacher, so that their congregations received a double fare of sermons.
9. See Hill, "The Ratsbane of Lecturing," in *Society and Puritanism*, pp. 79–123, and Patrick Collinson, *The Elizabethan Puritan Movement* (London: Cape, 1967; Berkeley & Los Angeles: University of California Press, 1967).
10. Cotton Mather, *Magnalia Christi Americana; or, The Ecclesiastical History of New England*, ed. Thomas Robbins (1702; rpt. Hartford: Silas Andrus & Son, 1855), p. 265.
11. Larzer Ziff, *The Career of John Cotton: Puritanism and the American Experience* (Princeton: Princeton University Press, 1962), p. 41.
12. Ziff (*Career of John Cotton*, p. 107) cites John Winthrop, *Journal 1603–1649*, ed. James Kendall Hosmer, 2 vols. (New York: C. Scribner's Sons, 1908), 1:135–136.
13. Hall (*Faithful Shepherd*, p. 145) cites *Massachusetts Records*, 1:73.
14. Edmund S. Morgan (*Visible Saints: The History of a Puritan Idea* [New York: New York University Press, 1963], p. 123) cites *Records of the Massachusetts Bay Company*, 3:99; *Records of the Colony or Jurisdiction of New Haven, from May, 1653, to the Union*, ed. C. J. Hoadly (Hartford, 1858), p. 588; and *The Public Records of the Colony of Connecticut, Prior to the Union with New Haven Colony*, ed. J. Hammond Trumbull (Hartford, 1850), p. 524.
15. Howard H. Martin reports that about 40 percent of the American publications in the first one hundred years were sermons ("Puritan Preachers on Preaching: Notes on American Colonial Rhetoric," *Quarterly Journal of Speech* 50 [October 1964]: 285–292).
16. Hall, *Faithful Shepherd*, p. 72.
17. Mather, *Magnalia*, p. 332.
18. See William T. Costello, *The Scholastic Curriculum at Early Seventeenth-Century Cambridge* (Cambridge, Mass.: Harvard University Press, 1958).
19. See Haller, *Rise of Puritanism*, chap. 2, "The Spiritual Brotherhood."
20. See Hall, *Faithful Shepherd*, chaps. 1 and 2; Morgan, *Visible Saints*, chaps. 1 and 2.

21. See Haller, *Rise of Puritanism*, p. 230.
22. See Miller, *Mind: Seventeenth Century*, chap. 9. Miller also argues (chaps. 5 and 6) that the logical and rhetorical principles of Peter Ramus (1515–1572) were a chief influence on the form of preaching in early New England. An important qualification is made by Eugene E. White, *Puritan Rhetoric: The Issue of Emotion in Religion* (Carbondale & Edwardsville: Southern Illinois University Press, 1972), p.17: "Despite the attractiveness of Ramus's teaching, the Puritans were not the thoroughgoing Ramists that Perry Miller and Wilbur Howell [in *Logic and Rhetoric in England, 1500–1700* (Princeton: Princeton University Press, 1956)] have contended. In their academic training in rhetoric and logic, the English Puritans studied principally from texts in the neoclassical tradition. Therefore, they were exposed to an integrated and functional system of training in oral communication."
23. Calvin, *Institutes*, 1:179, 180.
24. Our introductory essay to Cotton, *The Way of Life*, discusses the centrality of the heart.
25. Thomas Hooker, *The Application of Redemption . . . Ninth and Tenth Books*, 2d ed. (London, 1659), p. 204.
26. For a selection that in bulk and emphasis is weighted heavily to the uses, see Hooker, *The Soul's Exaltation*, and our introductory essay commenting on that emphasis.
27. Bruce A. Rosenberg argues that southern Baptists and Methodists keep alive a "Christian tradition of considerable antiquity" by using the " 'text-context-application' pattern" of preaching, practiced by preachers in medieval and Renaissance times as well as by the first New England ministers (*The Art of the American Folk Preacher* [New York: Oxford University Press, 1970], p. 32).
28. Richard Bernard, *The Faithful Shepherd* (London, 1607), pp. 17–18. Throughout this manual, Bernard bases arguments for the method of preaching on biblical precedent. The use of instruction "to bring us to the exercise of Christian duties to God and man" follows "the example of our Savior in his Sermons" (p. 63). Application of the word—distinguished from the use as "a nearer bringing" of the point in either the second or first person—is a practice of biblical preachers, such as David, Nathan, Jesus, and Peter (pp. 70–71). The application, Bernard advises, can be followed by the "prevention of objections," which originates in the examples of Jesus in his preaching and of Paul in his letters (p. 77).
29. William Perkins, "The Art of Prophesying," in *The Work of William Perkins*, ed. Ian Breward (Foxton, Eng.: Sutton Courtenay Press, 1970), p. 349; Bernard, *Faithful Shepherd*, p. 16. The preachers used both the King James version and the translation of the Marian exiles, the Geneva Bible (1560).
30. Bernard, *Faithful Shepherd*, p. 20. See the selection from Shepard, *The Parable of the Ten Virgins*, for the most thorough example of the opening of a text.
31. Bernard, *Faithful Shepherd*, p. 23.
32. William Ames, *The Works of the Reverend and Faithful Minister of*

Christ William Ames (London, 1643), pp. 156–157.

33. Bernard, *Faithful Shepherd*, p. 42; Perkins, "Art of Prophesying," p. 340.
34. "Gathering" has various labels, such as "collection" and "genesis." Perkins ("Art of Prophesying," p. 340) explains that the preacher might employ collection when "the doctrine not expressed is soundly gathered out of the text. This is done by the help of the nine arguments, that is of the causes, effects, subjects, adjuncts, dissentaries, comparatives, names, distribution, and definition." Genesis is the recombining of the divided elements of the text (Miller, *Mind: Seventeenth Century*, p. 341).
35. Ames, *Works*, p. 157.
36. Bernard, *Faithful Shepherd*, pp. 42, 43, 77, 63–69.
37. Ibid., pp. 70, 77, 71; Ames, *Works*, p. 159.
38. Bernard, *Faithful Shepherd*, p. 77; Ames, *Works*, p. 159.
39. Bernard, *Faithful Shepherd*, pp. 77, 80, 81.
40. It was through the note-taking and shorthand skills of the auditors that many of the sermons were published, as this title of a sermon-series by Cotton acknowledges: *An Exposition upon the Thirteenth Chapter of the Revelation . . . Taken from His Mouth in Short-Writing, and Some Part of It Corrected by Himself Soon after the Preaching Thereof*. See our introductory essays to the selections from Cotton, *A Treatise of the Covenant of Grace*, and Hooker, *The Soul's Vocation*, doctrine 3.
41. See Winfried Herget, "The Transcription and Transmission of the Hooker Corpus," in *Thomas Hooker: Writings in England and Holland, 1626–1633*, ed. George H. Williams, Norman Pettit, Herget, and Sargent Bush, Jr., Harvard Theological Studies 28 (Cambridge, Mass.: Harvard University Press, 1975), pp. 253–270, for a discussion of the flexibility of the text-through-uses sequence. We thank Norman Pettit and George Williams for permitting us to study this work prior to its publication.
42. See the selections from Bulkeley, *The Gospel-Covenant*, and Cotton, *A Treatise of the Covenant of Grace*, for deviation from the four-part presentation, and see the selection from Shepard, *The Sound Believer*, for mingling of parts.
43. Bernard, *Faithful Shepherd*, pp. 79–80.
44. Millar MacLure, *The Paul's Cross Sermons, 1534–1642* (Toronto: University of Toronto Press, 1958), p. 145; Mitchell, *English Pulpit Oratory*, p. 114.
45. Robert Cushman, "Cushman's Discourse," in *Chronicles of the Pilgrim Fathers of the Colony of Plymouth, from 1602 to 1625*, ed. Alexander Young, 2d ed. (Boston: Charles C. Little & James Brown, 1844), pp. 260–261.
46. John Dod (1549?–1645), revered English Puritan, is frequently cited by the first American preachers as an authority on the plain style. Repeating the metaphor of archery, Charles Chauncy, in the preface to *Plain Doctrine of the Justification of a Sinner in the Sight of God* (London, 1659), sig. A3ʳ, writes: "*It was piously and prudently spoken by Reverend Mr. Dod*, That too many Ministers deal like

unskillful Archers, that they do shoot over the heads, much more the hearts of their hearers, and miss their mark, whilst they soar so high, either by handling deep points, or by using of obscure and dark expressions or phrases, in their writing or Preaching of these things."

47. Increase Mather, "The Life of Richard Mather" (Cambridge, Mass., 1670), in *The Puritans: A Sourcebook of Their Writings*, ed. Perry Miller and Thomas H. Johnson, 2 vols., rev. ed. (1938; rpt. New York: Harper Torchbooks, 1963), 2:494. Normalization ours.

48. Ames, *Works*, p. 162.

49. See Haller, *Rise of Puritanism*, chap. 4, "The Rhetoric of the Spirit."

50. Charles Chauncy, *God's Mercy, Showed to His People in Giving Them a Faithful Ministry* (Cambridge, Mass., 1655), p. 37.

51. On opening a text Thomas Hooker explains: "By Faith synecdochically we are to understand all the graces or virtues which are mainly necessary to set a man in the state of grace" (*The Christian's Two Chief Lessons, Viz. Self-Denial and Self-Trial* [London, 1640], p. 202). In the same exercise of clarifying the Scripture, John Davenport preaches: "*House* is put for Nation, or People by an usual Metonymy" (*The Knowledge of Christ Indispensably Required of All Men That Would Be Saved* [*London*, 1653], p. 3).

52. Perkins, "Art of Prophesying," p. 341.

53. Bernard, *Faithful Shepherd*, pp. 66–67. Richard A. Lanham, in *A Handlist of Rhetorical Terms* (Berkeley & Los Angeles: University of California Press, 1969), defines most of the figures as follows: exclamation—strong statement expressing emotion; interrogation —rhetorical question implying strong affirmation or denial; optation—a wish exclaimed; prosopopeia—personification; apostrophe —breaking off discourse to address directly some person or thing either present or absent; dialogism—speaking in another's person.

54. Cotton Mather, *Manuductio Ad Ministerium* (1726; rpt. New York: Columbia University Press, 1938), p. 104.

55. Bernard, *Faithful Shepherd*, p. 53.

56. John Davenport, *The Saint's Anchor-Hold* (London, 1682), p. 213.

57. John Cotton, *A Practical Commentary . . . upon the First Epistle General of John* (London, 1656), p. 8.

58. These topics demonstrate the Pauline basis of the preachers' theology, for the same images—except merchandising and water—predominate in the writings of the apostle. Calvin and the writers of the sermon manuals had instructed the preachers to begin their biblical study with Paul, especially his epistle to the Romans. See Perkins, "Art of Prophesying," p. 338. The subject index of Herbert M. Gale, *The Use of Analogy in the Letters of Paul* (Philadelphia: Westminster Press, 1964), pp. 277–280, lists these as the principal images of Paul. For a discussion of the rhetorical influence of Paul and the Bible in general on the preaching of the first New England pastors, see Phyllis M. Jones, "Biblical Rhetoric and the Pulpit Literature of Early New England," *Early American Literature* 11, no. 3 (Winter 1976–77).

59. Calvin, *Institutes*, 1:82.

60. See Hall, *Faithful Shepherd*, p. 54. Because the most important qualification for the ministry was conversion, Mather in *Magnalia Christi Americana* emphasized the experience of conversion in the biography of each first-generation preacher.
61. John Norton, *The Orthodox Evangelist* (London, 1654), π3.
62. Thomas Hooker, *The Application of Redemption . . . The First Eight
Books* (London, 1656), pp. 205, 213.
63. Thomas Hooker, *The Soul's Vocation* (London, 1638), p. 515.
64. See an example of the same pattern in Shepard, *The Parable of the
Ten Virgins*, selection VIII.
65. For an extensive study of the jeremiad—the common label for the sermons centering on communal declension frequently preached in
the last half of the seventeenth century in New England—see Sacvan Bercovitch, "Horologicals to Chronometricals: The Rhetoric of
the Jeremiad," in *Literary Monographs*, ed. Eric Rothstein, vol. 3
(Milwaukee: University of Wisconsin Press, 1970), pp. 1–124.
Bercovitch emphasizes that the "counter-theme of exaltation and
affirmation" is more important than the "theme of declension."
A. W. Plumstead, ed., *The Wall and the Garden: Selected Massachusetts Election Sermons, 1670–1775* (Minneapolis: University of
Minnesota Press, 1968), provides a helpful general introduction to
the jeremiad as well as examples of it. Emory Elliott, in *Power
and the Pulpit in Puritan New England* (Princeton: Princeton University Press, 1975), examines "the myths and metaphors" in the
sermons of 1660 to 1700, finding the jeremiad to be the dominant
form between 1665 and 1675.
66. Paul (Gal. 3:24), as cited by Peter Bulkeley, *The Gospel-Covenant* (London, 1651), p. 63. The selections from *The Gospel-Covenant* and
Shepard's *The Sound Believer* emphasize the need for the Law
after conversion as well.
67. These definitions are given in the last half of Shepard, *The Sound Believer* (London, 1645).
68. Thomas Hooker, *The Soul's Implantation* (London, 1640), p. 20.
69. See Norman Pettit, "The Order of Salvation in Thomas Hooker's
Thought," in *Thomas Hooker*, ed. Williams et al., p. 125, for a discussion of gradual conversion; see the entire essay, pp. 124–139,
for an analysis of the stages of redemption. David D. Hall, ed., *The
Antinomian Controversy, 1636–1638: A Documentary History* (Middletown, Conn.: Wesleyan University Press, 1968), p. 13, states in
his introduction that "the problem of achieving assurance" of salvation was a major one that the Puritans brought with them.
The problem was intensified during a revivallike "period of exag-
gerated piety" in 1633.
70. For a discussion of narratives of conversion, see Morgan, *Visible
Saints*, pp. 88–92. Thomas Shepard's is an excellent example of a
spiritual autobiography modeled on the pattern of conversion out-
lined in the sermons of the first preachers. The most helpful edition is *God's Plot: The Paradoxes of Puritan Piety, Being the Autobiography and Journal of Thomas Shepard*, ed. Michael McGiffert,

Commonwealth Series, vol. 1, gen. ed. Winfred E. A. Bernhard (Amherst: University of Massachusetts Press, 1972).

71. For discussion of the Antinomian controversy, see Hall, ed., *Antinomian Controversy*; Norman Pettit, *The Heart Prepared: Grace and Conversion in Puritan Spiritual Life*, chap. 5, "Early Criticism and the Antinomian Controversy" (New Haven: Yale University Press, 1966). These works—Bulkeley, *The Gospel-Covenant*; Cotton, *A Treatise of the Covenant of Grace*; and Shepard, *The Parable of the Ten Virgins*—and our introductions to these selections speak directly to the conflicts of this crisis. According to Hall, "Antinomianism in its root sense means 'against or opposed to the law.' In theology it is the opinion that 'the moral law is not binding upon Christians, who are under the law of grace' " (p. 3).

72. John Davenport did not arrive until June of 1637, well after the two sides had formed.

73. Although his study centers on issues of church membership and baptism, Pettit's report (*Heart Prepared*, pp. 133–139) on the way Cotton varied from the other preachers on the order of salvation and the experience of conversion is very thorough. See also Ziff, *Career of John Cotton*, pp. 117–148, and Everett H. Emerson, *John Cotton* (New York: Twayne, 1965), pp. 112–125.

74. For an expanded discussion of Cotton's treatment of the stage of preparation, see our introductory essays to *A Treatise of the Covenant of Grace* and *The Way of Life*.

75. McGiffert, in his introduction to Shepard's autobiography, states this paradox and argues that doubts regarding his assurance are the central theme of both Shepard's autobiography and his journal.

76. Pettit, *Heart Prepared*, p. 135, provides this statement of Cotton's, published in 1646: "Though the Lord giveth himself freely to the soul, without respect unto any work of the Law, yet the Law is of special and notable use, working fear in the heart."

77. For a discussion of the definition of faith, see our introduction to *The Gospel-Covenant*, note 14, and the selection itself.

Notes to The Texts of the Sermons

1. Discussions of the relationship between preaching and publication in the seventeenth century are found in John Sparrow, "John Donne and Contemporary Preachers: Their Preparation of Sermons for Delivery and for Publication," in *Essays and Studies by Members of the English Association*, vol. 16 (1930; rpt. Oxford: Clarendon Press, 1931), pp. 144–178; in W. Fraser Mitchell, *English Pulpit Oratory*, pp. 14–38; and in two essays by Winfried Herget: "Preaching and Publication—Chronology and the Style of Thomas Hooker's Sermons," *Harvard Theological Review* 65, no. 2 (April 1972): 231–239, and "The Transcription and Transmission of the Hooker Corpus," in *Thomas Hooker*, ed. Williams et al.

2. Sparrow, "Donne and Contemporary Preachers," pp. 147, 151, 153.

3. Ibid., pp. 152–154; Mitchell, *English Pulpit Oratory*, p. 26; see also Plumstead, ed., *The Wall and the Garden*.

4. "Throughout the whole century the Puritans favoured the carefully written sermon, delivered *memoriter*, although some of their number considered notes sufficient, and probably only wrote up their sermons for printing after they had been preached. Where the sermon was written *in extenso* for memorization naturally a reliable text was available for publication" (Mitchell, *English Pulpit Oratory*, p. 26). See also Babette M. Levy, *Preaching in the First Half Century of New England History* (Hartford: American Society of Church History, 1945), p. 83.

5. Evelyn M. Simpson, *A Study of the Prose Works of John Donne* (Oxford: Clarendon Press, 1948), p. 258.

6. Mitchell, *English Pulpit Oratory*, p. 21, quoting from Samuel Clarke, *A General Martyrologie*, 3d ed. (London, 1677), p. 169.

7. Mitchell, *English Pulpit Oratory*, pp. 26–30.

8. The example of Richard Baxter also shows the intimate relationship between treatise and sermon: "His 'Treatise of Conversion,' he informs us, consisted of 'some plain Sermons on that Subject, which Mr. *Baldwin* (an honest young Minister that had lived in my House, and learnt my proper Characters, or Shorthand, in which I wrote my Sermon Notes) had transcribed out of my Notes'" (ibid., p. 27).

9. Recalling the year 1638, Shepard writes (*God's Plot*, ed. McGiffert, p. 69):

> And when I was very low and my blood much corrupted, the Lord revived me and after that took pleasure in me to bless my labors that I was not altogether useless nor fruitless.
>
> And not only to speak by me to his people but likewise to print my notes upon the nine principles I intended to proceed

on with in Yorkshire but never intended them or imagined
they should be for the press. Yet six of them being finished
in old England and printed [*The Sincere Convert* (London,
1640)], and the other three desired, I finished (the Lord helping) those at Cambridge and so sent them to England where
they also are printed [*The Sound Believer* (London, 1645)],
which I do not glory in (for I know my weakness) that my
name is up by this means, but that the Lord may be pleased
to do some good by them there in my absence, for I have seen
the Lord making improvement of my weak abilities as far as
they could reach and of myself to the utmost, which I desire
to bless his name forever for.

10. That the practice of writing in church was widespread is evident from
an educational handbook of 1627, which encourages educators to
require the lower forms of their schools to record the outline of the
weekly sermon and the higher forms to take down the whole sermon (Mitchell, *English Pulpit Oratory*, pp. 30–38).

11. Sparrow, "Donne and Contemporary Preachers," p. 161.

12. Giles Firmin, *The Real Christian, or a Treatise of Effectual Calling*
(London, 1670), p. 214.

13. Winthrop's journal for July 28, 1642, quoted by Levy, *Preaching*, p. 85.

14. Sparrow, "Donne and Contemporary Preachers," p. 162.

15. Mather, *Magnalia*, quoted by Julius H. Tuttle, "Writings of Rev. John
Cotton," in *Bibliographical Essays: A Tribute to Wilberforce Eames*
(Cambridge, Mass.: Harvard University Press, 1924), p. 364.

16. Everett H. Emerson, ed., *Redemption: Three Sermons (1637–1656)
by Thomas Hooker* (Gainesville, Fla.: Scholars' Facsimiles & Reprints, 1956), p. xi. See also Herget, "Transcription and Transmission of the Hooker Corpus."

17. Such motives may in part lie behind the statements of the editors of
Hooker's later work, *The Application of Redemption*, declaring that
his earlier works were published without his consent or knowledge.

18. A courtly poet, for example, not wishing to appear ungentlemanly or
professional, might pretend that the printer unscrupulously stole
the work; therefore, "one is forced to conclude that more often
than not unauthorized publications had the silent blessings of the
authors concerned" (Edwin H. Miller, *The Professional Writer in
Elizabethan England: A Study of Nondramatic Literature* [Cam-
bridge, Mass.: Harvard University Press, 1959], pp. 137–149). So,
too, in the publication of sermons: "That contemporary 'pirating'
at times was carried on with an amount of connivance seems clear
from the remarks of certain preachers. . . . The pretence is a familiar one where secular literature is concerned, and it emphasizes
the theological bias of the age to note that it was employed to excuse or facilitate the issue of sermons in printed form" (Mitchell,
English Pulpit Oratory, p. 37).

19. *The Letters of John Davenport, Puritan Divine*, ed. Isabel MacBeath
Calder (New Haven: Yale University Press, 1937), pp. 83–85.

20. See the discussion of the relationship between note taking and publication in terms of style in Herget, "Transcription and Transmission of the Hooker Corpus."

Notes to the Selections

Notes to the sermons are of four types: documentation of the introductory essays; explanation of unfamiliar and ambiguous words and constructions as well as identification of biblical references and quotations; marginal data from the copytext (modernized); and textual information. The first three types are self-explanatory. Notes containing a year date in italics (for example, *1638*) are textual notes. If a year date appears as the first information in a note or if the only year date to appear is the date of the copytext, an emendation to the copytext is indicated. For example, in selection V, note 64 ("*1684* / and you sorry *1638*") means that our reading, "you are sorry," is an emendation of the 1638 copytext on the authority of that of 1684. Similarly, note 15 in the same selection ("he] *omit 1638*") means that on the authority of no other edition, we have added the word "he" in our text. When one or more year dates other than that of the copytext are given in the note, one or more variant readings are indicated: the reading as found in a variant edition or editions is given, and the year date gives the earliest appearance of that reading. Except in the case of selection III, where there are several "families" of editions, variant readings are regularly perpetuated in succeeding editions, unless otherwise noted. When necessary, to avoid ambiguous readings, we have included invariant words for context. Except when essential to the sense, we have ignored italicization in the textual notes.

At the head of the notes for each selection is a brief section giving the title page of the copytext (unedited, except for regularization of italics and of words in full capitals and except for omissions as indicated), the publication data of other editions, and a summary of our editorial policy. The names in brackets indicate the location of the copies consulted: [Harvard] = the Houghton Library, Harvard University; [Yale] = the Beinecke Library, Yale University; and [BPL] = the Boston Public Library.

SELECTION I. THE GOSPEL-COVENANT

Copytext: 1651. The Gospel-Covenant; Or The Covenant of Grace Opened. Wherein are explained; 1. The differences betwixt the Covenant of grace and Covenant of workes. 2. The different administration of the Covenant before and since Christ. 3. The benefits and blessings of it. 4. The Condition. 5. The properties of it. Preached in Concord in New-England by Peter Bulkeley, sometimes fellow of Saint John's Colledge in Cambridge . . . The second Edition, much enlarged, and corrected by the Author. And the chiefe heads of Things (which was omitted in the former) distinguished into Chapters. London, Printed by Matthew Simmons, dwelling in Aldersgate-street next doore to the Golden Lyon. 1651. [Harvard]

1646. London, Printed by M. S. for Benjamin Allen, and are to be sold at the Crowne in Popes-head Alley. 1646. [BPL, Yale]

1653. London, Printed by Matthew Simmons, and are to be sold by Thomas Kembe at the Harrow in Duck-lane, and Andrew Kembe at Saint Margarets Hill in Southwarke. 1653. [Yale]

The edition of 1674, apparently in the Clark Library, Los Angeles, was not consulted. The 1651 edition was chosen as the copytext on the basis of external evidence of Bulkeley's hand in revision and also on internal evidence: the regularization of quotations, the significant correction of errors, and the introduction of only slight errors show the hand of someone—perhaps Bulkeley himself—closely associated with the sermons.

1. The dedication of the volume, presumably written at the time of the preface, is dated December 3, 1644. Bulkeley writes, "It is now some five or six years since I began to handle this doctrine now published" (*The Gospel-Covenant Opened* [London, 1646], sig. A4^v).
2. Ibid.
3. Ibid., sig. A5^r.
4. A third edition, apparently based on the second, appeared in 1674. A variant of the second edition, dated 1653, was printed from the same forms as the 1651 edition.
5. Bulkeley, *Gospel-Covenant* (London, 1651), sig. A4^v. In the last topic, Bulkeley refers to a theological controversy of the first years of settlement. The Concord pastor found baptism to be far more instrumental in salvation than many of his contemporaries did. Of "such children as do spring from godly and faithful parents," he contends, "In confidence hereof, they may draw nigh to God with much hope of acceptance, considering that the promise of the Covenant doth extend even to themselves" (ibid., p. 164). Finding baptism to be only a privilege rather than a near promise of God's acceptance, Thomas Shepard nonetheless wrote a commendatory letter for the first edition of *The Gospel-Covenant*; it was reprinted, after his death, in the second edition, that made even more explicit a view of baptism he would find too liberal (see Pettit, *Heart Prepared*, chap. 4).
6. Shepard, in Bulkeley, *Gospel-Covenant* (1651), sig. B2^v. Punctuation modernized.
7. Ibid., p. 47.
8. Ibid., sig. O1^r. Here and elsewhere in the volume the pagination is confused.
9. Ibid., sig. Kkk3^r.
10. In the prefatory letter, Shepard explains that out of love for humanity God made himself more understandable: "the Lord's heart is so full of love (especially to his own) that it cannot be contained so long within the bounds of secrecy, *viz.* from God's eternal purpose to the actual accomplishment of good things intended, but it must

aforehand overflow and break out into the many streams of a
blessed covenant" (ibid., sig. B1ʳ).

11. Ibid., sig. Cc3ʳ.
12. Ibid., p. 29.
13. Ibid., p. 333.
14. David Hall, ed., in his introductory essay to *The Antinomian Contro-
    versy*, p. 19, shows the definition of faith to be at the heart of the
    controversy: "Could faith be considered the 'condition' of the cove-
    nant of grace, the response man must make to the offer of the Gos-
    pel before God would grant him grace? Or was faith an aftereffect,
    a consequence of justification?"
15. The text is taken from the title page of the second edition, where it is
    followed by a related passage from Isaiah 55:3; the passage from
    Genesis may not have been the sermonic text in delivery, but Bul-
    keley obviously considered it central to his explication of the
    covenant.
16. The selection constitutes the whole of chap. 4 of pt. 4 of the work; the
    italicized lines are the argument of the chapter.
17. Margin: "Acts of faith about the covenant of two sorts."
18. Responsible, accountable.
19. Margin: "Two grounds tending to show how faith closeth with the
    Covenant."
20. Reasons, foundations.
21. Margin: "The first ground."
22. Ruined.
23. Acts 16:14, Acts 16:23, Luke 19:2.
24. I.e., before.
25. Hos. 5:15.
26. *1651* / into a Covenant *1646*.
27. Margin: "The second ground."
28. promise) First *1651*.
29. Margin: "How Faith closeth with the Covenant."
30. be a God *1646*.
31. us submitting *1651*.
32. Margin: "1. With the first part of it" / *no paragraph 1651*.
33. Margin: "Isaiah 56:6."
34. people? It *1651*.
35. *Ultimo versu* (?), "in the final verse": Ps. 144:15.
36. it, we seem *1646*.
37. him! this *1646*.
38. Margin: "Matthew 13:44,45."
39. Luke 15:11.
40. 1 Chron. 11:17.
41. to *1646*.
42. Isai. 56 *1646*.
43. Margin: "Luke 18:13."
44. Margin: "Jonah 2:4."
45. Margin: "Exodus 20:18."
46. *1646* / & *1651*.
47. *1646* / open *1651*.

48. Esther 4:11.
49. *1646* / answer *1651* / margin: "Psalm 27:8."
50. say; Come *1651*.
51. Margin: "Jeremiah 31:19."
52. Margin: "Lamentations 3:29."
53. me thou *1651*.
54. 14.3 *1651*.
55. 1 Kings 20:31.
56. and *1646*.
57. 1 Kings 2:28.
58. she he had *1646*.
59. Gen. 32:24.
60. *1646* / more; saith *1651*.
61. Margin: "Deuteronomy 3:24."
62. Margin: "Luke 2:28."
63. Margin: "2. How faith closeth with the second part of the Covenant."
64. Margin: "Those that will have God's blessing, must be under his do-
    minion."
65. ver. 6,7,8 *1651*.
66. Margin: "It is no more than equal that we be subject unto God."
67. only] *omit 1646*.
68. Margin: "Matthew 21."
69. they) unto him, and *1651*.
70. Bulkeley uses Apocalypse to signify Revelations; 4:7 may be a mis-
    transcription of 4:11.
71. Margin: "God's government is a merciful government."
72. they see] *omit 1646*.
73. Margin: "Faith reconciles us to God, and to his Law."
74. and] *omit 1646*.

SELECTION II. A TREATISE OF THE COVENANT OF GRACE

Copytext: 1659. A Treatise of the Covenant of Grace, As it is dispensed to
the Elect Seed, effectually unto Salvation. Being The Substance of divers
Sermons preached upon Act, 7.8. by that eminently holy and judicious
man of God, Mr. John Cotton, Teacher of the Church at Boston in N. E.
The second Edition, by a Copy far larger than the former; and Corrected
also by the Authors own hand. This Copy was fitted for the Press, by Mr.
Tho. Allen Minister in Norwich. London, Printed by Ja. Cottrel, for John
Allen, at the Rising-Sun in Pauls Church-yard. 1659. [BPL]

1671. The Third Edition, Corrected, and very much Enlarged, by the
Authors own Hand. London, Printed for Peter Parker, in Popes-head-Ally,
next Cornhill, 1671. [Harvard]

Since the 1671 edition shows no evidence of authorial changes (Cotton
died in 1652) and since this selection does not appear in the first edition
(*The Covenant of Grace*, 1655), the 1659 edition has been chosen for the
copytext. A possible variant of the 1659 edition (*A Treatise of the Covenant*,
2d ed., 1662) in the Library of Congress has not been consulted.

1. John Cotton, *The Covenant of Grace* (London, 1655), sig. A7ʳ. *The Covenant of Grace* is the major title of a composite volume; in it this sermon-series appears as *The New Covenant*, with a separate title page dated 1654.

2. John Cotton, *A Treatise of the Covenant of Grace* (London, 1659), sig. A3ᵛ.

3. The selection printed here does not appear in the 1655 edition. There are two subsequent editions, dated 1662 and 1671.

4. Everett Emerson, in *John Cotton*, p. 85, includes them among Cotton's earliest American sermons. David Hall, in *The Faithful Shepherd*, p. 160, places them in the mid-1630s.

5. For example, this passage makes a contrast between America and England, an unlikely topic before Cotton's emigration: "it is the faithfulness and tenderness of the grace of God unto his people, that when Christians come into this Country, though they have been marvelous eminent in our native Country, they cannot pray fervently, nor hear the word with profit, nor receive the seals with comfort: they wonder what is become of their old prayers, and hearings, and Sacraments, and of their lively spirits in holy duties; truly the Lord hath disenabled them (as it were) from such things, because they did build their union and fellowship with Jesus Christ upon them" (Cotton, *A Treatise* [1659], pp. 100–101).

6. Emerson (*John Cotton*, p. 104) cites *The Journal of John Winthrop*, ed. James Kendall Hosmer (New York: Scribner's, 1904), 1:116.

7. Cotton, *A Treatise* (1659), p. 43. Emerson, *John Cotton*, p. 86, notes that Cotton's American sermons are intended "for a congregation more theologically sophisticated than Cotton's English audiences; there is a precision and care about knotty points of theology not found earlier." The points of controversy and emphasis, in many cases, parallel the points of dispute recorded in the documents of the Antinomian crisis. Of the material in Hall, ed., *Antinomian Controversy*, the early Cotton-Shepard and Cotton-Bulkeley exchanges seem particularly close to Cotton's treatise.

8. See, for further explanation, the articles collected by Sacvan Bercovitch, ed., in *Typology and Early American Literature* (Amherst: University of Massachusetts Press, 1972).

9. For example, in the following sentence, Cotton treats a present-day spiritual conversion in terms of its type—the ancient bodily mark: "And as God required it of them to circumcise the outward man, even the foreskin of their children; so he will also circumcise them, taking possession of them, and circumcising their hearts, taking away the stoniness of them, and so fitting them to be a Temple for himself to dwell in" (*A Treatise* [1659], p. 5).

10. Bulkeley, *Gospel-Covenant* (1651), p. 29.

11. See Pettit, *Heart Prepared*, pp. 133–139, and Emerson, *John Cotton*, pp. 85–90.

12. Cotton, *A Treatise* (1659), sig. A4ʳ.

13. Since the treatise is repetitive in structure, points from each doctrine appear in each section.

14. Cotton, *A Treatise* (1659), pp. 41–42.

15. Ibid., p. 4.
16. Ibid., p. 173.
17. The scriptural texts of the sermons bear out this focus. Emory Elliott, in *Power and the Pulpit*, p. 14 n., writes: "before 1650 passages from the New Testament concerning mercy and grace predominate; between 1650 and 1680 there were fifty-seven published sermons based on Old Testament texts and only fifteen on texts from the New Testament."
18. Norman Pettit, "The Order of Salvation," in *Thomas Hooker*, ed. Williams et al., p. 137. Pettit refers the reader to John S. Coolidge, *The Pauline Renaissance in England: Puritanism and the Bible* (Oxford: Clarendon Press, 1970).
19. This selection, the answer to the "ninth Question," constitutes a small part of use 4 of the first doctrine derived from this text.
20. 15,] *omit 1671*.
21. 15.6 *1659*.
22. to] *1671/ omit 1659*.
23. Comprehensive.
24. *1671* / me *1659*.
25. 2.12 *1659*.
26. and] *omit 1671*.
27. it? and *1671*.
28. The second liberty is found further on: "liberty of *hope*."
29. Refreshments, reanimations.
30. Delirious fever.
31. it] *omit 1671*.
32. comfort *1671*.
33. 6.7,13 *1671*.
34. to *1671*.
35. I shall shall *1671*.
36. or *1671*.
37. Advances, sends forward.
38. Gathering for discussion of Scripture and of preaching.
39. Church practice such as prayer, preaching, baptism, and communion.
40. comfort? it *1671*.
41. then there is *1671*.
42. Suspicion.
43. St. Paul.
44. God) be *1659*.

SELECTION III. THE SOUND BELIEVER

Copytext: 1645L. The Sound Believer. Or, A Treatise of Evangelicall Conversion. Discovering The work of Christs Spirit, in reconciling of a sinner to God. By Tho: Shepard, sometimes of Emmanuel Colledge in Cambridge, Now Preacher of Gods Word in New-England . . . London, Printed for R. Dawlman. 1645. [Harvard]

1645E. Edinburgh, Printed by Robert Bryson. 1645. [Microfilm in the possession of Harvard University]

1649. London, Printed for R. Dawlman, and are to be sold by Andrew Crook, 1649. [Harvard]

1650. Edinburgh, Printed by Gedeon Lithgow Printer to the University of Edinburgh. Anno Dom: 1650. [Harvard]

1653. London, Printed for Andrew Crooke at the Green-Dragon in Paul's-Church-yard, M.DC.LIII. [Harvard]

1658. Edinburgh, Printed by Gedeon Lithgow. Anno Dom 1658. [Harvard]

1659. London, Printed for Andrew Crooke at the Green-Dragon in Pauls-Church-yard, M.DC.LIX. [Harvard]

1671. London, Printed by Ja. Cotterel, for Andrew Crooke, M.DC.LXXI [or M.DC.LXX (inking unclear)]. [Harvard]

1736. Boston: Printed by J. Draper, for D. Henchman, in Cornhill. 1736. [Harvard]

1742. Boston: Printed by Green, Bushell, and Allen, for D. Henchman, in Cornhil. 1742. [Harvard]

1853. The Works of Thomas Shepard, First Pastor of the First Church, Cambridge, Mass. [Ed. John A. Albro;] With a Memoir of his Life and Character. Vol. I. Boston: Doctrinal Tract and Book Society. 1853. [Harvard]

The 1645 London edition was chosen to be the copytext. No later editions show authorial variants. A London edition dated 1652 [BPL] seems to be virtually identical with the 1653 edition. An edition printed in Aberdeen in 1730 [British Museum] was not consulted. To simplify the textual notes, variants are here represented only by their first appearance in a "family" of editions. There are four such families, clearly demarcated by the relationship of variants and the place and manner of publication— London: 1645L, 1649, 1653, 1659, 1671; Edinburgh: 1645E, 1650, 1658; Boston: 1736, 1742; and the Albro edition of 1853. Thus, if a variant is listed as "1653," it can be assumed to appear in succeeding editions of its London family and not in later editions of other families, unless so indicated. We have not cited the few occasions when a listed variant disappears from a family for one or two editions.

1. McGiffert, ed., *God's Plot*, p. 69.
2. Giles Firmin, quoting from a letter from Shepard, in *The Real Christian*, p. 214.
3. McGiffert, ed., *God's Plot*, p. 69.
4. Thomas Shepard, *The Sound Believer* (London, 1645), sigs. A3^r–A4^v.
    The London printers, Robert Dawlman and Andrew Crooke, followed their first edition with editions in 1649, 1652–1653, 1659, and 1670–1671. Three editions were printed in Edinburgh, in 1645, 1650, and 1658, and one in Aberdeen in 1730. Two editions appeared in Boston, in 1736 and 1742. The 1853 edition, prepared by Shepard's much-removed successor in the First Church of Cambridge, John A. Albro, has recently been reissued (New York: AMS Press, 1967; Hildesheim: G. Olms, 1971).

5. Shepard, *Sound Believer* (1645), p. 4.
6. Ibid., pp. 330–331.
7. Ibid., pp. 34, 36, 43.
8. The first 1649, 1736, 1853/ the selection consists of part of sec. 2 of chap. 1. It contains, approximately, the doctrine and reasons sections of this sermonic unit; the uses follow immediately after the end of the selection.
9. the conviction 1736.
10. I.e., conviction of sin.
11. I.e., on earth.
12. of? 1659.
13. it? 1659.
14. his? 1659.
15. order; here the 1736, 1853.
16. is not 1736.
17. considers 1649, 1853.
18. the Eyes sees 1736 / the Eyes see 1742.
19. 1649 / first saw saw 1645L.
20. it drive us 1649, 1853 / it drives us 1653, 1736.
21. sinner to execution 1736.
22. and it is wisdom 1653.
23. of 1659.
24. not 1736.
25. what you cannot, what you now will not 1736.
26. shall 1650.
27. in] *omit* 1650.
28. Cons: 1645E.
29. the] *omit* 1659.
30. act of] *omit* 1736.
31. 1 John 1:8.
32. Spirit,) in this work of conviction convince 1853.
33. Margin: "Romans 3."
34. 1649 / wherein you you 1645L.
35. is] *omit* 1736.
36. affection 1659.
37. 14 1736.
38. Margin: "What those particular sins are, which the Lord convinces men of in their conversion."
39. those that 1653 / those but 1853.
40. The first item in a bill of goods.
41. was 1659.
42. he doth] *omit* 1736.
43. as shall make their 1736.
44. that she now had 1649, 1853.
45. hath] *omit* 1742.
46. whom thou livedst 1659, 1853.
47. the 1736.
48. a 1653, 1736, 1853.
49. tells him 1736.
50. Perverse.

51. hereby] *omit 1742.*
52. Acts 9:4.
53. 3.9 *1659, 1736, 1853.*
54. that] *omit 1736.*
55. if] *omit 1736.*
56. John 3:1.
57. nor *1649.*
58. show *1659, 1736, 1853.*
59. had] *omit 1659, 1736, 1853.*
60. *No paragraph 1645L.*
61. convince the evil of *sin 1650* / convince the evil of sin *1658* / convince of the evil of *sin 1659* / convince of the Evil of Sin *1736.*
62. of *sin 1659, 1736.*
63. with *1659, 1853.*
64. amends! That *1649, 1853.*
65. crush *1736.*
66. sees not the great *1736.*
67. Ioh. 36 *1645L* / Job xxxvi *1853.*
68. Job 36:9.
69. Luke 23:34.
70. friends, and when *1659, 1853.*
71. and words . . . done] *omit 1736.*
72. then] *omit 1736.*
73. *No paragraph 1645L.*
74. of *sin 1649, 1650, 1736.*
75. of] *omit 1736.*
76. remain *1653, 1853.*
77. now] *omit 1736.*
78. Rom. 6:23.
79. have long lived in *1659.*
80. *1659* / companions cups *1645L* / companions cup *1645E.*
81. Harlots.
82. accursed *1736.*
83. that] *omit 1671, 1736, 1853.*
84. his *1736.*
85. I.e., get rid of it.
86. I *1736.*
87. a] *omit 1649.*
88. Perceivable by the senses.
89. and] *omit 1671.*
90. there] *omit 1659.*
91. he *1736.*
92. minds *1736.*
93. Translated immediately following; reference is to John 16:8.
94. as] *omit 1736, 1853.*
95. will be chiefly done *1736.*
96. Pretenses, excuses.
97. their *1659, 1853.*
98. for *1653, 1853.*
99. his] *omit 1659, 1736, 1853.*

100. Gen. 3:12.
101. hope I shall *1736*.
102. 15.)23. which *1645L*.
103. greater *1736*.
104. every *1736*.
105. Luke 16:1.
106. in] *omit 1659*.
107. The contrast is between perception by intellectual use of symbols ("notionally," "discursively") and perception by direct experience ("really," "intuitively").
108. to *1653, 1736, 1853*.
109. I.e., obscurely expressed / margin: "Luke 19:41."
110. and *1653, 1853*.
111. painted only on *1736* / painted on *1742*.
112. Margin: "Isaiah 6:9."
113. of sin] *omit 1736*.
114. Margin: "How God gives a real sight of sins."
115. Hos. 4:2 / margin: "Hosea 4:4."
116. knew *1736*.
117. here *1853*.
118. Ps. 38:2.
119. Margin: "Psalm 51:3."
120. of] *omit 1736*.
121. Acts 24:27.
122. them] *omit 1659*.
123. sin is now a *1736*.
124. but my sins also are continued;] *omit 1736*.
125. of *1645E*.
126. sword *1659, 1736*.
127. may begin *1736*.
128. therein *1659, 1736, 1853*.
129. Margin: "Lamentations 3:51."
130. ears of men and sealeth instruction, that he may hide pride from men *1853* / margin: "Job 33:16,17."
131. teacheth *1659, 1853*.
132. The doctrine of compunction is not included in this selection.
133. some respects nearer *1649, 1853* / some respect nearer to *1671*.
134. and] *omit 1671*.
135. unto *1645E*.
136. *1649* / there *1645L*.

SELECTION IV. THE SOUL'S VOCATION, DOCTRINE 3

Copytext: 1638. The Soules Vocation or Effectual Calling to Christ. By T[homas] H[ooker]. London, Printed by Iohn Haviland, for Andrew Crooke, and are to be sold at the Black Beare in S. Pauls Church-yard. 1638. [Harvard]

1638 appears to be the only edition containing the first Hooker selection. An "edition" of *The Soul's Effectual Calling to Christ* (1637), listed in the

National Union Catalogue, appears to be identical to that of 1638, which
has an interior title page so dated and entitled.

1. *The Soul's Vocation* (1638) has a second title page: *The Soul's Effectual Calling to Christ* (1637).
2. Mather, *Magnalia*, p. 347. Similarities in the phrasing indicate that
   Mather drew much of his account from that of Thomas Goodwin
   and Philip Nye, the editors of *The Application of Redemption*
   (London, 1656, sigs. B1ʳ–D1ʳ).
3. Winfried Herget, "Preaching and Publication." After pointing out that
   the 1629 edition of Hooker's *The Poor Doubting Christian Drawn
   unto Christ* was included in *The Soul's Vocation*, Herget summarizes (p. 232):

> If it can be assumed that *The Poore Doubting
> Christian* as published in 1629 was part of the longer
> series of sermons published in 1637 as *The Soules
> Effectual Calling* [and in 1638 as *The Soul's
> Vocation*], the latter must have been preached by
> 1629. On the other hand, *The Soules Effectual Call-
> ing* itself is part of a large cycle of sermons on
> the *ordo salutis* [order of salvation], in which
> Hooker showed how effectual calling or vocation
> had to be preceded by humiliation and prepara-
> tion. Sermons on *The Soules Preparation for
> Christ* were published by Dawlman in 1632. They
> had been entered in the Stationers' Registers as
> "out of Actes 2d vers 37 and Luke.15" on October
> 29, 1631. Dawlman never published any sermons
> on Luke 15, but several years later, again in
> 1637, Crooke published *The Soules Humiliation*
> on Luke 15:14–15.
>
> Thus it appears that the whole cycle—to
> which at least should be added *The Soules Exal-
> tation* (London, 1638) as the final stage, and
> *The Unbeleevers Preparing for Christ* (London,
> 1638) as the beginning—was preached before
> Thomas Hooker left England.

Herget comments on the time lag between the preaching and the
publishing of these sermon-series (pp. 233–234):

> It is difficult to determine what was responsible
> for the great interest in Hooker's sermons in 1637,
> the year in which Laud was successful in estab-
> lishing censorship of the press (on July 11), the
> year in which New England was embroiled in the
> Antinomian Controversy, the year after Hooker
> had left Massachusetts Bay for Hartford in Con-
> necticut. Whatever the reasons, except for *The
> Soules Preparation* recorded in 1631, none of
> Hooker's sermons appeared in the Stationers'

Registers before 1637. But then they were entered in rapid succession.

Herget notes that between February 28 and November 13, 1637, there appear eight entries of significant sermonic works by Hooker, including *The Soul's Effectual Calling* and *The Soul's Exaltation*.

4. Herget, in "Transcription and Transmission of the Hooker Corpus," pp. 256–257, demonstrates the accuracy of the notes of an auditor when compared to the same sermon supposedly written out by Hooker (*The Application of Redemption*). Auditors, accustomed to the method of preaching, probably rendered precisely the main sections and subunits of the sermons; the amplification doubtless reflected the literary efforts of either the notetaker or the editor, or both, as well as of the preacher. Herget shows how it is likely that several notetakers could well have passed on their outlines of a sermon-series like *The Soul's Vocation* to an editor.

5. Nye and Goodwin (in Hooker, *Application*, sigs. C3^v–C4^r) report that Hooker himself wrote out this series. Herget, in "Transcription and Transmission of the Hooker Corpus," p. 258, reaches the same conclusion about the readability of the texts after collating similar passages in *The Soul's Implantation* (from the Chelmsford cycle of preaching) and *The Application of Redemption*.

6. In his essay, "The Order of Salvation," Norman Pettit discusses thoroughly Hooker's early development of the *ordo salutis*. It is also discussed as an eight-stage process by Alfred Habegger in "Preparing the Soul for Christ: The Contrasting Sermon Forms of John Cotton and Thomas Hooker," *American Literature* 41 (November 1969): 342–354.

7. Hooker is probably referring to the sermons, apparently preached in Chelmsford, published under these titles: *The Soul's Preparation* (1632), *The Soul's Humiliation* (1637), and *The Unbeliever's Preparing for Christ* (1638).

8. Thomas Hooker, *The Soul's Vocation* (London, 1638), pp. 33–34.

9. A summary of the main points of *The Soul's Vocation* introduces the next selection.

10. Nine thousand words precede the selection; altogether there are 200,000 words in *The Soul's Vocation*.

11. Hooker, *Soul's Vocation*, p. 34.

12. John Cotton similarly explains: "Sometimes indeed where ordinary means fail, God his Spirit [i.e., God's Spirit] can do it alone, without the breath of the word, but this [the word] is the ordinary way" (*The Way of Life* [London, 1641], p. 166).

13. Bernard, *Faithful Shepherd*, pp. 65–66.

14. This is the first of a pair of doctrines. The second, mentioned just before the selection and developed just after it, reads: "That God's Spirit gives special notice of God's acceptance to an enlightened soul, and that is the first voice of the Spirit to the understanding."

15. A writing taken in a bare literal sense without reference to its spirit.

16. Supernaturally.

17. The first point actually begins with the next paragraph. Headings for point 2 and point 3 are our additions.

18. Num. 21:8.
19. stung now *1638*.
20. Cited earlier: 1 Cor. 1:21.
21. Church practice such as prayer, preaching, baptism, and communion.
22. 2 Cor. 2:16.
23. Because may *1638*.
24. to *1638*.
25. "Eatonists" refers to the followers of John Eaton (born ca. 1575), an
    English minister active in Suffolk, whom Anthony à Wood called "a
    grand Antinomian" (*Dictionary of National Biography*). "Familists"
    refers to that group of the Anabaptist sect called the "Family of
    Love." Both were terms of abuse among the Puritans.
26. Craft.
27. we *1638*.
28. Rom. 6:16.
29. 7.5 *1638*.
30. Liquid essence.
31. Medicines to invigorate the heart.
32. upon them *1638*.
33. 1 *1638*.
34. Compassion.

SELECTION V. THE SOUL'S VOCATION, DOCTRINE 7

Copytext: 1638. The Soules Vocation or Effectual Calling to Christ. By
T[homas] H[ooker]. London, Printed by Iohn Haviland, for Andrew Crooke,
and are to be sold at the Black Beare in S. Pauls Church-yard. 1638. [Har-
vard]

1684. The Poor Doubting Christian Drawn to Christ. Wherein the main
Lets and Hinderances, which keep Men from coming to Christ, are discov-
ered. With special Helps to recover God's Favour. By Thomas Hooker . . .
London; Printed by J. D. for Nath. Ranew at the King's Arms, and Jonath.
Robinson at the Golden Lion in St. Paul's Church-yard, M.DC.LXXXIV.
[Harvard]

Part of the text of this second Hooker selection, the similitude of the soul
and the political criminal, is found almost verbatim as an interruption of
the text of his popular tract, *The Poor Doubting Christian* (1684, sigs.
B5^r–B7^r). Other editions of this often-reprinted work have not been collated. Variants in the 1684 edition have been noted, excepting the uniform
change of third-person singular verbs ending in "th" (1638) to the corresponding verbs ending in "s" (1684).

1. Hooker, *Soul's Vocation*, sig. D1^v.
2. Ibid., pp. 109–110, 283–284.
3. Ibid., pp. 335, 202–204, 199.
4. Thomas Shepard, *The Parable of the Ten Virgins*, 2 vols. (London,
   1660), 1:68.
5. The images of wandering and love making derive, like most of the

preachers' imagery, ultimately from the Bible—in this instance, from the Song of Solomon.

6. Hooker, *Soul's Vocation*, pp. 284, 237.

7. This is the seventh doctrine of eight in the volume; this selection includes about one-sixth of the sermonic treatment of that doctrine.

8. Phrases, expressions.

9. be *1638*.

10. Margin: "Romans 8:8."

11. Margin: *"Simile."*

12. Matt. 26:49, Matt. 21:9.

13. Matt. 8:19.

14. Margin: "Matthew 13."

15. he] *omit 1638*.

16. Underhand purposes.

17. Matt. 10:37.

18. grounds what *1638*.

19. *Beginning of corresponding passage in 1684.*

20. you must know] *omit 1684*.

21. the second affection] *omit 1684*.

22. meet that Goodness *1684*.

23. and] *omit 1684*.

24. Jesus] *omit 1684*.

25. the] *omit 1684* / Song of Sol. 3:1.

26. of] *omit 1684*.

27. him whom her Soul loved *1684*.

28. desire] *omit 1684*.

29. thing] *omit 1684*.

30. she *1684*.

31. reveal a Christ *1684*.

32. A gathering for discussion of Scripture and of preaching.

33. a] *omit 1684*.

34. Jesus] *omit 1684*.

35. and] *omit 1684* / *new paragraph 1684*.

36. Jesus] *omit 1684*.

37. hath thus hungered *1684*.

38. Lord Christ is *1684*.

39. the *1684*.

40. John 1:29.

41. thirsteth after *1684*.

42. Christ, here he is *1684*.

43. *New paragraph 1684*.

44. there are two . . . gracious work.] *omit 1684*.

45. Margin: *"Simile."*

46. Warrant officer.

47. as it is with a Traitor who is pursued, and takes a stronghold, and is *1684*.

48. there is] *omit 1684*.

49. even] *omit 1684*.

50. to submit and lay his Head on the block *1684*.

51. Messenger *1684*.

52. hope he may *1684.*
53. Tower of London?
54. pardoned; The poor Traitor in the prison with that is stirred *1684.*
55. hears by another *1684.*
56. say] *omit 1684.*
57. to *1684.*
58. it's *1684.*
59. this is . . . shalt be pardoned.] *omit 1684.*
60. continually there] *omit 1684.*
61. there *1684.*
62. I] *omit 1684.*
63. tell *1684.*
64. *1684* / and you sorry *1638.*
65. for what you have done *1684.*
66. you are like . . . hereafter] *omit 1684.*
67. traitor? One says yes, if it please your Highness *1684.*
68. pleads *1684.*
69. Hereupon, the King being full of mercy, tells *1684.*
70. a-drawing *1684.*
71. towards *1684.*
72. to so poor a traitor *1684.*
73. for *1684.*
74. all done *1684.*
75. and that . . . faith] *omit 1684.*
76. the *1684.*
77. haply God lets *1684.*
78. a *1684.*
79. with a heavy stroke and indignation *1684.*
80. conscience at work *1684.*
81. as a Pursevant *1684.*
82. sent *1684.*
83. can no way escape *1684.*
84. is] *omit 1684.*
85. and hope. *1684* / *end of corresponding passage in 1684.*
86. Margin: "Isaiah 40:2 opened."
87. Margin: "Isaiah 66:2 opened."
88. Margin: "Jeremiah 31:18,19,20."
89. Emotions of pity and compassion.
90. Yearn.
91. Behavior, conduct.

SELECTION VI. THE SOUL'S EXALTATION

Copytext: 1638. The Soules Exaltation. A Treatise containing The Soules Union with Christ, on 1 Cor. 6.17. The Soules Benefit from Union with Christ, on 1 Cor. 1.30. The Soules Justification, on 2 Cor. 5.21. By T[homas] H[ooker]. London, Printed by John Haviland, for Andrew Crooke and are to bee sold at the black Beare in S. Pauls Church-yard, 1638. [Harvard]

Apparently the only edition of this work was published in 1638. A copy (listed in the *National Union Catalogue*) dated 1639, in the library of Brown University, has not been consulted.

1. Hooker, *Soul's Vocation*, p. 668.
2. Thomas Hooker, *The Soul's Exaltation* (London, 1638), pp. 25, 29, 35, 43.
3. Ibid., p. 25.
4. This drifting indicates that for Hooker no stage of salvation was ever finalized: "When Christians grow cold in prayer and careless in holy duties, the Lord taketh away the light of His favor . . . so that now they begin to think they never had grace" (*The Soul's Implantation* [London, 1637], p. 130).
5. This preface begins the sermon-series by recapitulating the material of earlier sermons on preparation and vocation.
6. rases *1638*.
7. Commensurate.
8. I.e., in writing about.
9. Otherwise.
10. Collection of scriptural texts to explain an obscure passage.
11. The rest of this selection constitutes a full sermonic unit on this doctrine.
12. Hooker follows the Aristotelian and Thomistic theory that the soul diffuses itself through all parts of the body and interacts with them by means of the "spirits" of the blood.
13. Through.
14. Digest.
15. I.e., unites with.
16. 1 Coloss. 23 *1638*.
17. Hindered.
18. Held in contempt.
19. 1.17 *1638*.
20. Savior that *1638*.
21. Deut. 33:29.
22. Luke 3:19 / margin: "Luke 13."
23. 82.5 *1638*.
24. Manner?
25. Compass.
26. Wart.
27. Invigorating medicine.
28. Rom. 8:38,39.
29. 2 Pet. 2:22.
30. Behavior.

SELECTION VII. THE WAY OF LIFE

Copytext: 1641. The way of Life. Or, Gods Way And Course, In Bringing The Soule Into, keeping it in, and carrying it on, in the wayes of life and peace. Laid downe in foure severall Treatises on foure Texts of Scripture. Viz. The pouring out of the Spirit, on Zach. 12.10,11,&c. Sins deadly wound, on Acts 2.37. The Christians Charge, on Prov. 4.23. The Life of Faith, on

Gal. 2.19,20. By that learned and judicious Divine, and faithfull Minister of Jesus Christ, John Cotton . . . London, Printed by M. F. For L. Fawne, and S. Gellibrand, at the Brasen Serpent in Pauls Church-yard. 1641. [Harvard]

The only authoritative edition is that of 1641. A German translation (*Weg des Lebens*, trans. Peter Streithagen, Heidelberg, 1662) has not been consulted.

1. Perry Miller and Thomas H. Johnson, eds., *The Puritans*, 1:314; Everett Emerson, in *John Cotton*, p. 41, cites a passage on baptism from *The Way of Life* which appears to address an English audience (he dates *The Way of Life* from between 1624 and 1632 [p. 163]); Cotton's reference to charitable coexistence on p. 82 of *The Way of Life* also seems to reflect the English rather than the American environment. Jesper Rosenmeier, in his unpublished Harvard dissertation of 1965, "The Image of Christ: The Typology of John Cotton," p. 227, establishes 1627 as the earliest date, by Cotton's reference on p. 87 of *The Way of Life* to John Davenant's commentary on Colossians, published in 1627. The latest date is surely 1630, when Cotton's severe malaria followed by increased Laudian persecution halted his active ministry in Boston, England (Ziff, *Career of John Cotton*, p. 64).

2. Ziff, *Career of John Cotton*, pp. 58–59. The sermons were apparently published without Cotton's knowledge, implying that the author's own text was not available to the printer. William Morton, the editor of *The Way of Life*, speaks in his preface of having intervened to edit the sermons when he discovered that they were "designed for the Press." Morton acted without Cotton's knowledge: "How grateful it may be to this Reverend Author, that this work of his should come abroad into the public view and censure, I know not, but that it will be very welcome to the Church of God (whose he himself is) I doubt not" (Cotton, *The Way of Life* [London, 1641], sigs. A4^r–A4^v).

3. Emerson, *John Cotton*, p. 41.

4. In America, Cotton's audience would necessarily be more homogeneous. Even American listeners, however, were by no means uniformly sanctified.

5. Cotton, *Way of Life*, p. 132.

6. Ibid., p. 28.

7. Ibid., p. 4. This doctrine—the sufficiency of the Spirit in conversion—led Anne Hutchinson, Cotton's ardent disciple, to condemn the preparationists in the great New England controversy of 1636 to 1638.

8. Ibid., sig. A2^r, pp. 12, 109, 119.

9. Ibid., pp. 305, 270, 421. Emerson points out that Cotton's preaching in *The Way of Life* makes him seem "no Antinomian": "Diligence in one's vocation is so supremely important for Cotton that he conceives of it as the outward parallel to the inward life of faith" (*John Cotton*, p. 45).

10. Cotton, *Way of Life*, p. 127. In the faculty psychology underlying this preaching, the understanding or reasoning faculty would ideally

operate before the will. That the preachers did not ignore that prior stage is borne out by the selection from Davenport's *The Saint's Anchor-Hold*. Norman Pettit (*Heart Prepared*), both in the language of the title of his study of preparation in this sermon literature and especially in the first pages of that study, explores the "biblical metonym" of the heart.

11. Cotton, *Way of Life*, pp. 224, 125, 218, 214.

12. The text is here reproduced as it appears in the copytext, with Cotton's interpolation.

13. Cotton refers to the first and second parts of *The Way of Life*—"The Pouring Out of the Spirit" and "Sin's Deadly Wound." This selection begins pt. 3, "The Christian's Charge."

14. Prov. 4.

15. Doctrines.

16. 2 Kings 10:29, Acts 24:25, Mark 6:20.

17. *Ultimo versu* (?), "in the last verse": Ps. 111:10.

18. Constraint, imprisonment.

19. heart, A *1641*.

20. Gatherings for discussion of Scripture and of preaching.

21. Merchant, peddler.

22. The unregenerate state, participation in original sin.

23. 32.9 *1641*.

24. Josh. 7:16.

25. A church practice such as prayer, preaching, baptism, and communion.

26. Translated in the following clause.

27. Laces for attaching hose to doublet.

28. 2 Sam. 12.

29. I.e., to mend it.

30. undefiled, an *1641*.

31. 1.2 *1641*.

32. 4.7 *1641*.

33. Isa. 40:2,31.

SELECTION VIII. THE PARABLE OF THE TEN VIRGINS

Copytext: 1660. The Parable Of The Ten Virgins Opened & Applied: Being the Substance of divers Sermons on Matth. 25.1,–13. Wherein, the Difference between the Sincere Christian and the most Refined Hypocrite, the Nature and Character of Saving and of Common Grace, the Dangers and Diseases incident to most flourishing Churches or Christians, and other Spiritual Truths Of greatest importance, are clearly discovered, and practically Improved, By Thomas Shepard late Worthy and Faithfull Pastor of the Church of Christ at Cambridge in New-England. Now Published from the Authors own Notes, at the desires of many, for the common Benefit of the Lords people,

By { Jonathan Mitchell Minister at Cambridge, Tho. Shepard, Son to the Reverend Author, now Minister at Charles-Town } in New-England . . .

London, Printed by J. H. for John Rothwell, at the Fountain in Gold-
smiths-Row in Cheap-side, and Samuel Thomson at the Bishops Head in
Pauls Church-yard. 1660. [Harvard]

1695. Re-printed, and carefully Corrected in the Year, 1695. [Harvard]

1797. Falkirk [Scotland]: Printed and sold by T. Johnston. 1797. [BPL]

1853. The Works of Thomas Shepard, First Pastor of the First Church,
Cambridge, Mass. [Ed. John A. Albro;] With a Memoir of his Life and
Character. Vol. II. Boston: Doctrinal Tract and Book Society. 1853.
[Harvard]

The following cataloged texts have not been consulted: a probable variant
of the 1660 edition ("By J. Hayes, for John Rothwell, 1660"), Huntington
Library; a two-volume edition by J. M'Auley, Glasgow, 1796; and an edition "with a biographical preface by . . . J. Foote . . . Aberdeen, 1853."

1. Thomas Shepard, *The Parable of the Ten Virgins,* 2 vols. (London,
     1660), 1:sigs. A3^v, A3^r. Another folio edition was published in
     London in 1695. Three editions appeared in Scotland, in 1796
     (Glasgow), in 1797 (Falkirk), and in 1853 (Aberdeen). In 1853
     in Boston, John A. Albro published this series in his edition of *The
     Works of Thomas Shepard.*
2. Shepard, *Parable,* 1:2–3. Shepard defines the second coming of Christ:
     "This coming is meant either of his coming to the last Judgment,
     or of his coming to particular Judgment immediately at and after
     death" (ibid., 2:47).
3. Ibid., 1:10; 2:106; 1:sig. A3^v; 2:5, 172–173, 101.
4. Ibid., 1:68.
5. Ibid., p. 37.
6. The selection comprises the whole of chap. 8 (misnumbered "7" in
     early editions). The text is drawn into doctrine, reasons, and two
     uses. The third use, "A Fourfold Exhortation to Believers," makes
     up the next chapter.
7. Concerning] *omit 1853.*
8. Thus Shepard designates a particular phrase of the text as the concern
     of this sermon. "2" indicates that this is the second such phrase
     examined in the sermon-series.
9. See the full text, especially verses 3 and 4.
10. Conception, theory.
11. From the opposite.
12. eternal *1695.*
13. Shepard probably refers to the Roman Catholic translators and inter-
     preters of the Vulgate New Testament (the Rheims-Douay version).
14. Thomas Cartwright (1535?–1603), Puritan leader and author.
15. Shepard refers here to verse 13 of his text.
16. From] *omit 1853.*
17. travel *1797.*
18. Again, Shepard refers to Matt. 25.
19. Betrothed, engaged to be married.

20. I.e., this eschatological interpretation is found in Scripture (Rom. 9:22).
21. a] *omit 1797.*
22. a] *omit 1797.*
23. Numbing, depressing.
24. happily *1695.*
25. And has Christ writ *1853.*
26. hands? but *1853.*
27. he fears and sees this *1797.*
28. had] *omit 1853.*
29. I.e., throughout chap. 38 of Isaiah.
30. is ready and prepared for *1797.*
31. *1853* / too? And *1660.*
32. and that while *1797* / and him while *1853.*
33. armor of proof on *1797* / of proof: impenetrable.
34. Heb. 11:35.
35. Luke 24:25.
36. I.e., when she has no.
37. love it is not *1797.*
38. he is no *1797.*
39. Ps. 39:13.
40. to *1797.*
41. *1797* / Sun *1660.*
42. the fit and set time *1797.*
43. Church practices such as prayer, preaching, baptism, and communion.
44. when once that is come *1797.*
45. *1853* / that. *1660.*
46. accounts *1660* / account is *1797.*
47. *1853* / seen; So *1660.*
48. *1695* / by, you *1660.*
49. *1695* / neglected. Oh *1660.*
50. alarms *1695.*
51. *1797* / lives, work *1660.*
52. *1853* / lives *1660.*
53. Professed believers.
54. Heaped up without order.
55. *1853* / find it's *1660.*
56. Shepard refers to the night before John Knox's death: "Satan, he declared, had tried him with a new form of temptation—the plea that his own merits were sufficient in the sight of God" (P. Hume Brown, *John Knox* [London, 1895], 2:287).
57. 2 Chron. 32:24.
58. *1853* / love much *1660.*
59. Of the text, Matt. 25.
60. Qualities.
61. *Ultimo versu* (?), "in the last verse": 1 Cor. 3:23.
62. I.e., counting the hours.
63. Song of Sol. 6:3.
64. as it is in Psalm *1853.*
65. very] *omit 1797.*

66. Instrument of torture.
67. Searches, as in hunting?
68. Name's sake.
69. taken *1797*.
70. of] *omit 1797*.
71. whether *1797*.

SELECTION IX. THE SAINT'S ANCHOR-HOLD

Copytext: 1661. The Saints Anchor-Hold, In All Storms and Tempests, Preached in Sundry Sermons. And Published for the Support and Comfort of Gods People, in all times of Tryal. By John Davenport, B.D. sometime Minister of Stephens Coleman-street; London; and now Pastor of the Church of Christ in New-Haven, in New-England . . . London. Printed by W. L. for Geo. Hurlock, and are to be sold at his shop at Magnus Church corner, in Thames-street, 1661. [BPL]

1682. London, Printed for Tho. Guy, at the Oxford Arms, on the West side of the Royal Exchange, 1682. [Harvard]

1701. London, Printed and Sold by Benj. Harris, at the Golden-Boar's-Head, against the Cross-Keys-Inn, in Grace church-street, 1701. [Yale]

The editions of 1682 and 1701 are nonauthoritative reprintings of the first edition. The third edition adds some allegorical engravings of minor interest.

1. The evidence is by no means conclusive, but it hints of a text in Davenport's hand: "As touching the *Author* of this *Treatise* (in whose heart the *Text* was written by the finger of God, before the Discourse was penned by his own hand)" (John Davenport, *The Saint's Anchor-Hold* [London, 1661], sig. a3ʳ). Babette Levy, in *Preaching*, p. 82, states that "Davenport was known for this habit of writing out his sermons more largely than many of his peers." These data are corroborated by Davenport's letter about the texts of *The Knowledge of Christ* (see "The Texts of the Sermons").
2. ". . . lastly let it please you to accept a book newly Come forth which I make bold to Present unto you for a *Vade mecum*, in your voyage at sea, and for an help to Fix your Anchor aright when you come to land" (Calder, ed., *Letters of John Davenport*, p. 193 [Aug. 19, 1661]).
3. London, 1682 and 1701. The third edition boasts an engraved frontispiece and emblems with explanatory verses on the theme of hope.
4. Davenport, *Saint's Anchor-Hold*, sig. a3ʳ, p. 193; Calder, ed., *Letters of John Davenport*, p. 138 (July 28, 1659). It is possible that the predicament of the English church influenced even more directly the preaching of these sermons. Franklin B. Dexter, in "Sketch of the Life and Writings of John Davenport," in *Papers of the New Haven Colony Historical Society*, vol. 2 (New Haven, 1877), pp. 205–238, writes: "In 1661, New Haven (and especially Mr. Davenport) sheltered the two Regicides, Whalley and Goffe [two judges at the trial

of Charles I, now fleeing England]; and some time before their
coming he preached to his people a series of sermons [*The Saint's
Anchor-Hold*] preparatory to such questions about harboring trai-
tors as their presence might excite" (pp. 231–232). Dexter's link of
the fugitive judges with Davenport's preaching probably depends
on such internal evidence as this passage: "Withhold not countenance, entertainment, protection, from such, if they come to us,
from other Countries, as from *France* or *England*, or any other
place" (Davenport, *Saint's Anchor-Hold*, p. 198).

5. Calder, ed., *Letters of John Davenport*, p. 125 (Aug. 8, 1658); p. 140
   (Aug. 8, 1659); p. 178 (Oct. 17, 1660): "We, at Newhaven, are still
   under God's afflicting hand"; p. 184 (Dec. 17, 1660): "vehement
   coughs and colds, from which but few persons, no families, are
   free, in one degree or other."

6. Davenport, *Saint's Anchor-Hold*, p. 147. The similitude that follows
   ("God dealeth with his people, as Physicians are wont to do with
   their patients" [pp. 147–148]) incorporates a significant number of
   details from Davenport's letters about the sickness of his son and
   the effects of Winthrop's medicines (Calder, ed., *Letters of John
   Davenport*, pp. 184–189 [Dec. 17 and 23, 1660]).

7. Davenport, *Saint's Anchor-Hold*, pp. 3, 31, 64.

8. This selection constitutes one complete sermonic unit, the third of five
   in the volume.

9. Inferential.

10. *1682* / him, He *1661*.

11. soul *1701*.

12. and and *1701*.

13. thousand *1701*.

14. *1682* / they they *1661*.

15. *1682* / good, reason *1661*.

16. from] *omit 1701*.

17. Translated in the following clause.

18. In Aristotelian logic, topics are the sources from which arguments may
    be derived or to which they may be referred.

19. dialogismoi *1682* / translated in the following phrase.

20. *1701* / in, 1 *1661*.

21. make *1701*.

22. is they that shall *1701*.

23. Esther 5:4.

24. Translated in the following phrase.

25. Translated in the preceding phrase.

26. 77.23 *1661*.

27. dianoia *1682* / translated in the context.

28. such spiritual conclusions] *omit 1701*.

29. apt] *omit 1701*.

30. temptation. 1. *1661*.

31. and *1701*.

32. Job 14,15 *1682*.

33. Jacob.

34. consisted *1701*.

35. of] *1682* / *omit 1661*.